Lawrence Durrell

Between Love and Death, East and West

Jeremy Mark Robinson

CRESCENT MOON

CRESCENT MOON PUBLISHING
P.O. Box 393
Maidstone
Kent, ME14 5XU
United Kingdom

First published 1995. Second edition 2008.
© Jeremy Mark Robinson 1995, 2008.

Printed and bound in Great Britain.
Set in Garamond 9 on 13pt.
Designed by Radiance Graphics.

British Library Cataloguing in Publication data

Robinson, Jeremy Mark
Lawrence Durrell: Between Love and Death, East and West
I. Title

828.912

ISBN 1-86171-066-6
ISBN-13 9781861710666

Contents

Acknowledgements

I would like to thank Lawrence Durrell above all, and also Ian MacNiven and Susan MacNiven, Frank Kersnowski; Paul Lorenz, Peter Christensen and Edmund Keeley for sending me essays; Richard Pine, Robin Rook, Peter Baldwin, Simon Miles, David Gascoyne and Karl Orend; staff at Southern Illinois University, Carbondale; François Kestelman and the Centre d'Études et de Recherches Lawrence Durrell at Sommières; Rupert Pole; Anne Lilios and others at the Lawrence Durrell Society, including the *Lawrence Durrell Newsletter* and *Deus Loci* and *On Miracle Ground*; *Twentieth Century Literature*.

Photos: Jill Krementz. Durrell collection. Jeremy Robinson.

Abbreviations

Lawrence Durrell

J	*Justine*
B	*Balthazar*
M	*Mountolive*
Cl	*Clea*
DL	*The Dark Labyrinth*
BB	*The Black Book*
M	*Monsieur*
L	*Livia, or Buried Alive*
C	*Constance, or Solitary Practices*
S	*Sebastian, or Ruling Passions*
Q	*Quinx, or The Ripper's Tale*
T	*Tunc*
N	*Nunquam*
SME	*A Smile in the Mind's Eye*
SP	*Spirit of Place*
BT	*Blue Thirst*
CP	*Collected Poems 1931-1974*
Cell	*Prospero's Cell*
RMV	*Reflections on a Marine Venus*
BL	*Bitter Lemons*
GI	*The Greek Islands*
SC	*Sicilian Carousel*
CVG	*Caesar's Vast Ghost: Aspects of Provence*
PJ	*Pope Joan*
AC	*Antrobus Complete*
K	*Key to Modern Poetry*
BS	*The Big Supposer*
FMJ	"From a Writer's Journal"
FEB	"From the Elephant's Back"

TC	"Lawrence Durrell Answers a Few Questions"
KT	"The Kneller Tape"
Mon	interview, in Huw Wheldon
Med	Paul Hogarth: *The Mediterranean Shore: Travels in Lawrence Durrell Country*
Ald	*Literary Lifelines: The Richard Aldington-Lawrence Durrell Correspondence*
LJF	*Letters to Jean Fanchette, 1958-1963*
Ill	Durrell archive at Southern Illinois University, Carbondale
Som	Durrell archive at the Centre d'Etudes et de Recherches Lawrence Durrell at Sommières

with Henry Miller

PC	*Lawrence Durrell and Henry Miller: A Private Correspondence*
DML	*The Durrell-Miller Letters 1935-80*
AO	*Art and Outrage: A Correspondence About Henry Miller, Perlès and Durrell*

Henry Miller

HMR	*A Henry Miller Reader*
TA	*The Time of the Assassins: A Study of Rimbaud*
LT	*My Life and Times*
PHM	*Paint As You Like and Die Happy: The Paintings of Henry Miller*

Other abbreviations

W	*The World of Lawrence Durrell*
Lab	*Labrys: Lawrence Durrell*
Ker	*Into the Labyrinth: Essays on the Art of Lawrence Durrell*
Mac	*Twentieth Century Literature: Lawrence Durrell Issue, I & II*
OMG II	*On Miracle Ground II: Second International Lawrence Durrell Conference Proceedings*
OMG I	*On Miracle Ground: Proceedings From the First National*

For Tony Maestri

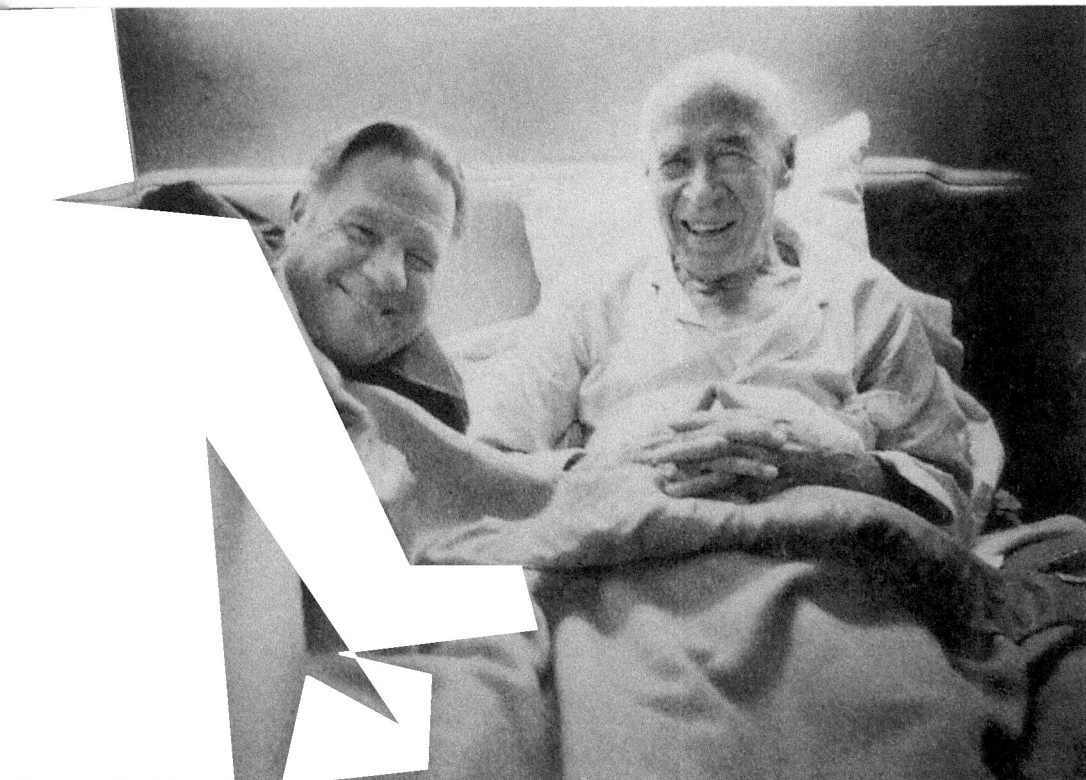

Lawrence Durrell with Henry Miller, in 1973, above (Jill Krementz). And when Miller visited Sommières, France, where Durrell spent the latter part of his life. (Durrell Collection)

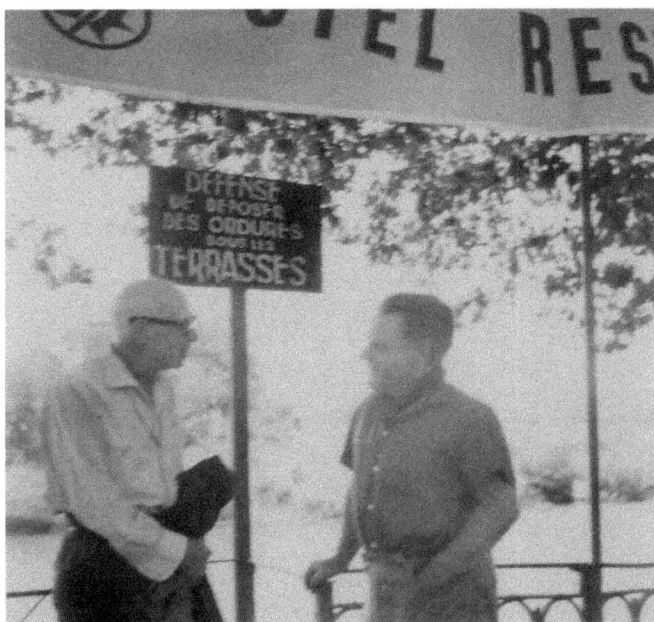

1

Introduction
A Character-Squeeze
of Lawrence Durrell

I have a confession to make. I am Lawrence Durrell, the writer, who wrote until one day the world came into terrible focus.

Lawrence Durrell, *Asylum in the Snow* (SP, 263)

Reality has become provisional and tentative. There is no such thing as a stable fact in all nature. Everything is subject to qualification.

Lawrence Durrell, *Caesar's Vast Ghost* (200)

This book studies some of the works of Lawrence George Durrell (February 27, 1912 - November 7, 1990). There is nothing final and fixed about the discussions that follow: there is still much more to say about Durrell and his works, which will have to wait for another book (probably an artistic biography). These discussions, then, are preliminary critical appraisals.

For this second edition, I have opted not to rewrite the whole book; instead, I have made minor revisions to the text, and added some new material. Most of the views put forward here have remained unchanged since this book was published in 1995. There are some aspects I would want to alter – the views on feminism, for instance, but I have decided to leave them in the book.

The response that Lawrence Durrell so often generates is negative: critics call him pretentious, baroque, overblown, high-flown, too intellectual, too metaphysical, overwritten, too rich, etc. The *Quintet* was received as 'lush', with 'fantastic characters, opulent landscapes', 'flamboyant asides... rich, easy style', prose that was 'ringingly evocative', 'an elaborate tapestry'.[1] Yet they acknowledge his attempts at 'great art'.

For some critics, Durrell's books are 'accurate, moving and intensely readable' as a critic wrote of *Bitter Lemons*,[2] while another critic sees Durrell's novels as 'so beautiful in surface and so uncertain below it';[3] Alessandro Serpieri reckoned that Durrell's 'prose is so exquisitely romantic that it has no equal in recent English literature'.[4] *Balthazar*, said a critic, has 'an annoying fancy and phony ring',[5] while Frank Kermode said *Justine* failed as great art.[6]

Jacques Howlett put *Justine* on the same level as Malcolm Lowry's *Under the Volcano,* Henry Miller's *Plexus*, John Cowper Powys' *Wolf Solent*, and D.H. Lawrence's *The Plumed Serpent.*[7] R.W. Flint compared Durrell with Thackeray, Stendhal and Turgenev.[8] Baumgart reckoned that Durrell's sensationalism tended ultimately towards 'sheer brutality' and even fascism (see H. Isernhagen, 4). Anthony Burgess was another critic who regarded Durrell's ornate prose sceptically. For Burgess, a grand old denizen of British letters in the old tradition, the *Quartet*'s prose tends to flaccidity, and melts at times into a 'romantic wash a little too close to the

---

1 James Meehan: review of *Monsieur, Library Journal*, 99, 1 Dec 1974, 3145; Julian Barnes: "Trick or Treat", *New Statesman*, 96, 22 Sept 1978, 378; Anne Tyler: "Avignon at War", *New Republic*, 187, 22, 6 Dec 1982, 37; Samuel Coale: review of *Constance, America*, 148, 3, 22 Jan 1983, 60
2 Joseph G. Harrison: "Fond Visitor, Sad Land", *Christian Science Monitor*, 6 March 1957
3 Pamela Hansford Johnson: "New Novels", *New Statesmen*, 56, 25 Oct 1958
4 Serpieri: "*Il Quartett di Alessandria* di Lawrence Durrell", *Ponte*, 18, 1962
5 Charles Rolo: *Atlantic Monthly*, 202, Sept 1957, 80-81
6 Kermode: "The New Novelists: An Enquiry", *London Magazine*, 5, no. 11, 1958, 21-25
7 Howlett: "Roman étragers: *Justine*", *Les Lettres Nouvelles*
8 R.W. Flint: "A Major Novelist", *Commentary*, 27, 1959

old lending-library sadistic-sentimental exotic escapism beloved of the dreaming shop-girl.' (1971, 98) Burgess's view, disregarding its facile sexism, is odd coming from an ardent disciple of James Joyce.

Durrell knew that his restlessness creative personality was partly responsible for his flitting excitably from one form to another (BS, 67). Karl Miller found that the *Quartet* ran down 'into a series of annotations'.[9] For Walter Allen, the over-rich writing is again a problem, those lapses into 'an easy, florid romanticism, the exotic in Technicolour' (W. Allen, 286). William Boyd found the *Quintet* 'clever, glittering, intricate, but without any real strength', 'and was suspicious of Durrell's dandyism, 'paraded symbols', and philosophical dallying.[10] No amount of criticism mattered, though, when one had old Henry to bolster one's shaky writer's ego: Miller wrote to Durrell on 17 January 1958, exclaiming: '[w]hat a huge arc you describe in literature – a cathedral, a forest of statues, Angkor!' (PC, 326)

Durrell's art has been the subject of not a little critical inquiry. There have been useful collections of essays (Moore, Friedman, Kersnowski, Begnal), the Durrell conference books and Durrell Society Newsletter (including the *Deus Loci* series). Durrell has been the subject of some critical monographs (Fraser, Friedman, Unterecker, Pinchin, Pine, Weigel). However, the number of individual, book-length studies of Durrell's writing is very small compared to the welter of critical data that surrounds, say, James Joyce, T.S. Eliot or Samuel Beckett. There have been many articles, essays, theses and papers on Lawrence Durrell.[11] Students have been

---

9 Karl Miller: "Poet's Novels", *The Listener*, 61, 1959
10 Boyd: "Strung Quintet", *New Republic*, 1984, CE, 56
11 Apart from the articles noted in the bibliography, here are some others: A.K. Weatherhead: "Romantic Anachronism in *The Alexandria Quartet*, L. Fraiberg: "Durrell's Dissonant *Quartet*", A. Bosquet: "Lawrence Durrell ou l'azur ironique", John Carey: "Durrell's Drift", J. Kruppa: "Durrell's *Alexandria Quartet* and the 'Implosion of Modern Consciousness", C. Burns: "Durrell's Heraldic Universe", Ann Gossman: "Love's Alchemy in the *Alexandria Quartet*", G. Lebas: "The Fabric of Durrell's *Alexandria Quartet*", M.T. Chapman: "Dead or Just Pretending? Reality in *The Alexandria Quartet*", Carl Dawson: "From Einstein to Keats: A New Look at the *Alexandria Quartet*", Suzanne Henig: "Lawrence Durrell: The Greatest of Them All", J.V.D. Card: "Tell Me, Tell Me!: The Writer as Spellbinder in Lawrence Durrell's *Alexandria Quartet*", Roderik Nordell: "Durrell in Sciliy: Rich Prose From a Bus", Leo Lerman: "Shifting Prht of in a Durrell Scape", Naomi Bliven: "Alexandria in Tetrameter", Nigel Dennis: "New Four-Star King of Novelists", John Arthos: "Lawrence Durrell's Gnosticism", W.F. Smyth: "Lawrence Durrell: Modern Love in Chamber Poets"

particularly vigorous in tackling a wide variety of Durrellian subjects in their papers and theses. I have noted some of them in the bibliography.[12]

Lawrence Durrell did not win the Nobel Prize for Literature (he was nominated in 1988) – but then, he joined a long list of writers who also did not win the most prestigious literary accolade: Hardy, Freud, Joyce, Lawrence, Brecht, Nabokov, Tolstoy, Calvino, Lowell, Conrad, Lorca, Rilke, Zola, Strindberg, Ibsen, Tolstoy, Borges, Mandelstham, Akhmatova and Gorky.

Early on in his career, in the *Black Book* days, Durrell planned '3 *real* novels: youth, maturity and old age'.[13] In a 1945 letter to T.S. Eliot,[14] Durrell outlined his project of three sets of works, which he kept to:

agon	pathos	anagnorsisis
The Black Book	*The Book of*	*The Book*

12 In addition to those listed in the bibliography, here are some examples from the University of Baltimore seminar papers: "The Grail Quest in *Clea*", "From Universe to Multiverse: Durrell and Pynchon", "Existentialism in Durrell", "The Significance of Doors as Symbols of Relativity in Durrell's Novels, *Justine* and *Clea*", "Love Goddesses of the Mediterranean", "Eyes and Their Relation to Vision in *The Alexandria Quartet*", "Patterns of Music in *The Alexandria Quartet*" and "The Cabbala and the Occult in *The Alexandria Quartet*" (OMG, 142-4). Other theses include Sharon Lee Brown: "Lawrence Durrell and Relativity", Joanna L. Hawkins: "A Study of the Relationship of Point of View to the Structure of *The Alexandria Quartet*", Joan S. Goulianos: "Lawrence Durrell's Greek Landscape", Walter G. Creed: "Contemporary Scientific Concepts and the Structure of Lawrence Durrell *Alexandria Quartet*", Michael Cartwright: "*The Alexandria Quartet*: A Comedy for the 20th or Lawrence Durrell, the Pardoner and His Miraculous Pig's Knuckle", Dion W. Nittis: "The Heraldic Universe of Lawrence Durrell", W. Weide: "The Unity of a Continuum: Relativity and *The Alexandria Quartet*", James R. Morrison: "Time Structure in the Novels of Lawrence Durrell", T.B. Young: "Thematic Emphasis and Psychological Realism in Lawrence Durrell's *Alexandria Quartet*", F. Goldberg: "The Movement Towards Survival: Remystification in the Works of Lawrence Durrell", C.M. Mablekos: "The Artist as Hero in the Novels of Joyce Cary, Lawrence Durrell and Anthony Burgess", R.K. Anderson: "*À la Recherche du temps perdu* and *The Alexandria Quartet*", Carolyn L. Leithman: "Romantic Self-Consiousness in Certain Novels of Hawthorne, Conrad and Durrell", John W. Barrett: "Lawrence Durrell's *The Black Book* and *The Alexandria Quartet*: Some Existential and Jungian Correspondences", Glenda L. Chaffin: "Musical Structure in Lawrence Durrell's *The Alexandria Quartet*"
13 letter to Miller, 1958, PC, 302
14 5 May 1945, in MacNiven 1987, 354

	the Dead	of Time
the dislocation	the uniting	the acceptance and death

Durrell kept to this scheme of things very closely, although it was planned in his youth. Each of the three stages is expressed in a major work. Apart from *The Black Book* itself, for years Durrell referred to *The Alexandria Quartet* as his 'Book of the Dead'. Finally, *The Avignon Quintet*, his last major fiction, became 'the Book of Time' (or 'Book of Miracles', the *Quintet* is also a 'Tibetan' or 'Indian' novel, also a 'Book of the Dead'). The work that does not fit into this artistic scheme is also the work that many critics find difficult, *The Revolt of Aphrodite*, which is not really a 'Book of the Dead', or a 'Book of Time', but covers the territory of psychic decay (the 'English Death') of *The Black Book* (Durrell said that the *The Revolt* represented the 4th component of Greek theatre, the *sparagmos* or hero's dissolution (Pine, 1994, 34)). Anaïs Nin did not rate Durrell's later work very highly. Durrell's *Tunc* and *Nunquam* certainly foxed some critics. They do seem to be about 'ideas' or 'dry' abstractions. Describing a visit to Durrell in 1973, Anaïs Nin said that he had 'gone into sterile abstractions (*Tunc*). His work is sterile.'[15] Nin's books, though, are just as much about 'ideas' or life-philosophies', as Durrell's books.

Tunc is a depressing book because, Durrell said in an interview, '[r]eality is depressing'. *Tunc* was intended to be something of a poetic study of contemporary culture, a dive into the sorrow of culture in order to find out how to get the joy out of it.[16] Alexandria is the abyss through which characters must pass to achieve transcendence and wholeness. (C.P. Cavafy knew that one had to experience 'both the high and low of life').[17] Affad's problem in *The Avignon Quintet* is that his Gnosticism is not the whole picture.[18]

In *The Avignon Quintet*, Durrell goes over all his old obsessions (these include illness, redemption, repetition, imagination, islands, Eastern philosophy, the heraldic world, morality, Gnosticism, narcissism, sexuality,

---

15 Nin, *Journals*, vol. 7, 309
16 Margaret McCall: "*The Lonely Roads*: Notes for an Unwritten Book", in MacNiven, 1987, 383
17 Douglas Robillard, Jr.: "In the Capital of Memory: The Alexandria of Durrell and Cavafy", OMG I, 85
18 Durrell commented: 'Sebastian's gnosticism might be described as Jungian, a philosophy of archetypes; it attempts to make the inexplicable too explicit and is the cause of his undoing. It lacks the totality psyche found in Buddhism.' (*The Mediterranean Shore*, 110)

spirituality). He replays them, parodies them, improvizes on them. In *The Avignon Quintet* we find the familiar Durrellian obsessions – sex, death, art, the relation of art to life, war, 'high culture', such as psychoanalysis, painting and literature, exotic landscapes, and so on. In *The Mediterranean Shore*, Durrell writes:

> The concept behind the *Quintet* is derived from the thinking of Einstein and Freud: the Five Power Principle, Unified Field Theory and Relativity of Einstein; impulse and inhibition from Freud. It is essentially what makes the *Quintet* a modern novel and separates it from the classical tradition. (Med, 110)

Lawrence Durrell long dreamt of writing a truly comic book, something irreverent and 'totally unpredictable – a sort of *Ship of Fools*' (R. Pine, 1994, 48-49). The themes of a 'ship of fools', of a pantomime or circus of clowns and lovers occurs towards the end of the *Quintet* (particularly in the 'Minisatyrikon' chapter in *Quinx*) and in the last part of *Caesar's Vast Ghost*. Parody is uppermost in *The Avignon Quintet*. Always in Durrell's fiction we are aware of parody, and the narrators make us aware of it too. In *The Avignon Quintet*, though, humour and parody are very prominent.

This is indeed the major theme of the book, the relation of art to life, which is expressed in the multiple futures and lives of each character.[19] The novels are, in a sense, 'stereophonic and stereoscopic.' (Med, 110)[20] Durrell had already attempted this multi-dimensionality in the *Quartet*, which has a 'multiplicity of mutually qualifying voices' (CE, 64), or as Balthazar puts it, 'at every moment in Time the possibilities are endless in their multiplicity' (B, 193). The notion that all characters are fragments or aspects of one character is central to *The Avignon Quintet*. So, to explore this idea, Durrell uses parody and humour. In *The Avignon Quintet* Durrell parodies his own fiction as well as those of others. There are key cultural reference points in the *Quincunx*. Perhaps the main one is psychoanalysis. No previous Durrell fiction has been so full of one 'movement' or worldview. Psychoanalysis is cited through the *Quintet*. In *The Alex-*

---

19 'the three big words of Durrell's poetic vocabulary are art, love, and death.' Ian MacNiven: "Mirror of Crises: The Poetry of Lawrence Durrell", in CE, 101; Lionel Trilling speaks of love and art in the *Quartet* being 'beyond the reach of the moral will' ("*The Quartet*: Two Reviews", W, 62)
20 Durrell says in *From the Elephant's Back* that he is using the 'same old stuff of fiction and Christmas pantomime, the same archetypal cast of characters: 'two women blonde and dark, two clowns, lovers, poets, warriors, monks, villains and seers.' (8)

andria Quartet Freud was also cited, as was Spengler and Bergson, with their views of history and time.

Indeed, Freud has been crucial to Durrell's fiction since the beginning. His *The Black Book*, written in the 1930s, when psychoanalysis was fashionable in Paris and London,[21] is a Freudian (Rankian, Adlerian and also Jungian) take on sexual neuroses. *The Black Book* is an extended improvization on Freudian themes, but given that idiosyncratic post-*Tropic of Cancer* slant that Durrell has made his own. In the letters of the *Black Book* days Durrell is always talking about 'purity', about how important it is for the artist to be pure, to her/ himself, in her/ his art, about how 'pure' *Tropic of Cancer* is (Durrell's idea, at the time, of the book to aim for, if not emulate). It is also an attempt to stir up some trouble, to rage against England and the 'English death'; it's an effort to 'change England, to create her'. [22]

The Black Book is a sub-standard *Tropic of Cancer*: this is not a particularly 'cruel' thing to state: Durrell was well aware of the merits and failures of *The Black Book*.[23] He knew it was a 'birth book',[24] in which the writing itself, as literature, is as 'nothing compared to the grind of the personality against its own sicknesses', as Durrell wrote to T.S. Eliot in 1937.[25] Themes appear in *The Black Book* which would become Durrell perennials: 'heraldic' prose; multiple narrators/ narration; diarists; letters; pathology; retrospection; 'purple prose'; psychoanalysis. In *The Black Book* we see Durrell struggling to assert himself, to climb out from under the pressure of his literary and psychological influences, to break free of all the people who impressed him. The stamp of Henry Valentine Miller is all

---

21 With the knowledge of psychoanalysis the artist, Durrell said in *Key to Modern Poetry*, became aware that 'the symbols he had been using were far richer than he had known', and these symbols started to have a 'multiple impact' (63).

22 Herbert Howarth: "Lawrence Durrell and Some Early Masters", *Books Abroad*, vol. XXXVII, no. 1, Winter 1963, 5-6

23 Dylan Thomas was 'sickened and excited' by the book (cited in Harry T. Moore: "Durrell's *Black Book*", W, 100) In January 1937 Durrell said he was rewriting *The Black Book*, going through it with a blue pencil and excising all the Milleresque bits. The book, he told Miller, had '[a] Henry Valentine [Miller] hangover which disgusts my admirers' (letter, January 1937, PC, 49)

24 'In *The Black Book* there was nothing for me to be, really. I'm still nobody. But I think I will be', Durrell wrote in May 1937 (PC, 94) 'I really believe *The Black Book* was my first essay: and I was defeated and thrown back on myself. Couldn't advance from there.' (Durrell, 1959, Ald, 111)

25 Durrell to Eliot, July 1937, in MacNiven, 1987, 348

over *The Black Book*, however. Listen:

> When I go mad, and rip the clothe off your trembling body, when I bite your nipples and groan, it is this expiatory half-death I am consummating. It is not necessary and so poignant to fuck you like that, when you are like a tumbled feather-bed, when your mouth is clammy with stars, and your soft cunt breathing its velvet musky pollen over the earth. (160)

Miller praised *The Black Book*, as he often did with Durrell's work: 'I read goggle-eyed, with terror, admiration and amazement... You are *the* master of the English language – stupendous reaches, too grand almost for any book. Breaks the boundaries of books' (DML, 55). Miller and Anaïs Nin helped Durrell push out his *Black Book* into the world: they spent hours typing up extra copies of the book, which appeared in 1938 as part of the 'Villa Seurat series', published by Kahane's Obelisk Press. Durrell gobbled many dictionaries and tried to dazzle with his word games.26 But Henry Miller had already done all that *The Black Book* was trying to do in *Tropic of Cancer*. Indeed, Miller's *Tropic* series are archetypal 'outsider' novels, prefiguring Albert Camus' *L'Etranger* and Sartre's *Nausea*. In *Quinx*, Durrell's last novel, he parodies the earlier self of his first real novel:

> When he was young he headed for Paris, capital of synthetic loves. Tall beauties like well-trained rocking-horses. Love was a jubilant relation, placental in rhythm; we danced the foetal swirl, the omni-amni blues. (Q, 139)

This is Durrell in Henry Miller mode, one he assumes more often than one would think. In *Constance*, for example, Blanford conjures up Milleresque sentences, such as this one which occurs during Blanford's reverie while Cade reads from the *Bible*: '[s]he was beautiful with her swarthy rose-black skin and the apricot-fashioned mouth sticky as a fresh hymen – the silkworm's tacky passage across a mulberry leaf.' (C, 360)

When Miller wrote *Sexus*, Durrell reacted badly. In a famous letter, Durrell wrote to Miller, exhorting him to take out the sex scenes, which were bad writing, Durrell reckoned ('the moral vulgarity of so much of it is *artistically* painful. These silly scenes which have no *raison d'etre*, no humour, just childish explosions of obscenity' [DML, 232]).

---

26 'I am trying to eat the whole pantheon of spirits, with a dictionary', said the narrator in *Asylum in the Snow* (SP, 272) 'I have great reverence for the word because behind it lies what I call magic', said Miller (LT, 54)

Then there's Durrell's telegram of 10 September 1949: 'SEXUS DISGRACEFULLY BAD WILL COMPLETELY RUIN REPUTATION UNLESS WITHDRAWN REVISED' (DML, 233) Later, however, Durrell changed his view of *Sexus* and *The Rosy Crucifixion* (another telegram to Miller, of 29 September 1949, said: 'DEEPEST APOLOGIES UNJUST CRITICISM WRITING NOTHING SAID QUALIFIES ADMIRATION YOUR GENIUS HOPING FRIENDSHIP UNAFFECTED' [DML, 237]) and in *The Avignon Quintet,* Durrell wrote his own version of sexual experience. The *Quintet*, though, is never as 'explicit' or detailed in its portrayal of sexual experience as, say, Miller or Norman Mailer, Charles Bukowski, William Burroughs, J.G. Ballard, Kingsley Amis, or Durrell's hero, D.H. Lawrence.

Durrell, though, is not averse to a good bout of bawdiness. His word games include turning the title of his novel *Tunc* into, inevitably, *cunt.*[27] He also places a crude drawing of a vagina in *The Revolt of Aphrodite*. And the 'quincunx' form of the *Quintet* becomes, inevitably, a play on 'cunx'/ 'cunt'.[28] As with Shakespeare, if there's a pun in there somewhere, Durrell will tease it out.[29] Durrell may not be able to out-pun master punner Shagspeer, but he has a good try. The further along his career he went, the more punning, one of the major literary devices of his beloved Elizabethan writers,[30] he employed. So, while deploring Miller's exuberant (and sexist) sex in *Sexus*, Durrell also plays around with bawdy games in a trite and superficial manner. Towards the end of *Justine,* for instance, there is another of Pursewarden's idiot sayings: 'Food is for eating/ Art is for arting/ Women for ———/ Finish/ RIP' (J, 183). Knowing Pursewarden's way of thinking, and Durrell's persistent sexism, there is only one thing that women 'are for': fucking.

Another of Pursewarden's limp squibs, addressed to the England he loathes: 'Abhorring cant, adoring ****'. I wonder what juicy noun Purse-

---

27 In *Tunc* and *Numquam*, Durrell plays his usual numerological games. For example, there are forty four section and fourteen chapters (44 divided by 14 equals π).
28 "Your quinx, rather. My cunx… Quinx to Cunx, eh?" (C, 351)
29 "Ban! Ban! Caliban!" "That's the spirit!" exclaim Sutcliffe and Blanford, in another pun to make you groan (C, 352)
30 'Are you heartwhole – lovely Elizabethan word? [Durrell wrote to Jean Fanchette] Or still heartsick – a lovelier Elizabethan word? What the fucking hell has happened to the British since 1615? It's a mystery to me. Just reading some letters of the Elizabethans – what punch and nuance.' (August 1960, LJF, 80) 'I admit to having 'Elizabethanized'' (W, 67) His favourites of the Elizabethan and Jacobean eras included Campion, Marlowe, Middleton, John Marston and Thomas Nash.

warden has in mind here. *Cunt*, perhaps? Why yes, *cunt*, of course: nothing else fits the rhyme scheme (rhymes with 'front') and fits in to four asterisks, plus has the necessary bawdy Pursewarden overtones.31 'Cunt' is indeed Pursewarden's project in *The Alexandria Quartet*. Except he gives his quest a different name, using the highest name for it in the English language, 'love':

> 'Our topic, Brother Ass,' Pursewarden tells Darley, 'is the same, always and irremediably the same – I spell the word for you: l-o-v-e. Four letters, each a volume!' (echoing the construction of the *Quartet* (Cl,113).

Durrell's *The Black Book* is really a birth book, a novel in which the young writer gives birth to himself, comes awake and alive, learns how to write, etc. The birth needs a midwife, hence the craving in poets for a Muse, a woman to help with the delivery. The Muse arrives fully fledged later on, in the figures of Justine and Clea. In *The Black Book* we see Durrell testing himself and the limits of the writing game. How far can one go in writing? *The Black Book* is the answer to that question.32 As it's a book of birth, it's messy, for birth is a messy event. *The Black Book*, then, is dissatisfying. *Prospero's Cell* was more successful, though some might find the poetic 'impressions' of that Corfu book a little insubstantial. *The Dark Labyrinth* is also mediocre, really.

It was *Justine* that really launched Durrell's career,33 for *Justine* was a large, complex work that promised much for the following instalments in the *Quartet*. Durrell's reputation rests largely on the achievement of *The Alexandria Quartet*, and it is to the *Quartet* that critics generally refer when they discuss Durrell. When debates about Durrell appear in books on that curious animal, 'the English novel', or about 'British novelists', *The*

---

31 In Belgrade Durrell toyed with an epitaph which ran:
Hated Cant
Revered Cunt.
32 Even though, as Durrell notes matter of factly in *Key to Modern Poetry*, '[t]o speak of reality at all is to limit and debase it' (84). In the poem 'In the Garden: Villa Cleobolus', the narrator wonders 'how to capture... or measure/ The full round of this simple garden...?' (Med, 32) In 1962 Durrell wrote that '[f]or the poet less and less can be spoken about – for the novelist more and more *must*' (Ill, 42, 19, 10).
33 Richard Aldington's judgment – 'a wonderful book... a great achievement' – was echoed by many readers (Ald, 47). Durrell, Aldington reckoned, was not only a 'damned good writer', and the only one in his class, he had also 'hit the lit'ry public's taste' (22 November 1958, 65)

Alexandria Quartet is usually the centrepiece of the critique. When Durrell's name appears in the index of a book of literary criticism, *The Alexandria Quartet* is usually being considered. In the *Rough Guide to Egypt*, Durrell's *The Alexandria Quartet* is summarized amongst other 'foreign novelists' who have set fictions in Egypt thus: '[e]ndless sexual and metaphysical ramblings, occasionally relieved by a dollop of Alex atmosphere, from one of the century's most overrated writers.'[34] This is a typical view of Durrell's art: good on 'atmosphere' and description, but let down by 'metaphysical ramblings'.

Randall Stevenson's *The British Novel Since the Thirties* is typical of humanist literary criticism: '[s]uch 'multidimensional' interests make *The Alexandria Quartet* – despite its occasional melodrama, 'baroque' prose and deliberate complication – one of the most ambitious and exciting of mid-century novels.' (207)[35] Here Stevenson grudgingly admits that *The Alexandria Quartet* is a powerful piece of experimental fiction. And this is generally how Durrell is summed up in critical circles. Despite its flamboyant prose style, critics reluctantly acknowledge that *The Alexandria Quartet* is a worthy addition to exploratory European novels, such as James Joyce's *Ulysses,* Marcel Proust's *À la Recherche du Temps Perdu,* Aldous Huxley's *Eyeless in Gaza,* Samuel Beckett's *The Unnameable,* Joyce Cary's triptych (*Herself Surprised, The Horse's Month, To Be a Pilgrim*), Virginia Woolf's *To the Lighthouse,* Italo Svevo's *Confessions of Zeno,* André Gide's *The Counterfeiters* and Thomas Mann's *The Magic Mountain.* More recent novels in *The Alexandria Quartet* mode include Anthony Powell's *A Dance to the Music of Time,* Thomas Pynchon's *Gravity's Rainbow,* Doris Lessing's *The Golden Notebook* and William Golding's *Rites of Passage.*

Critics still, though, are not sure whether Durrell is first or second rate. That is, whether or not to place him critically in the front rank of modernists:[36] Woolf, Lawrence, Greene, Beckett, Joyce, Proust and Mann (one critic calls Durrell 'the post-Hiroshima Proust', and another sees that

---

34 Dan Richardson and Karen O'Brien, 626
35 Cecily Mackworth calls the *Quartet* 'a sort of multi-rectangular girl-meets-boy story' ("Lawrence Durrell and the New Romanticism", W, 25)
36 F.R. Leavis apparently said that Durrell 'is not one of us'. Quoted in Reed Way Dasenbrock: "Centrifugality: An Approach to Lawrence Durrell", OMG II, 199. Alberto Manguel said Durrell was a 'novelist of genius' ("The Novelist as Poet", *Books in Canada*, 12, March 1983, 12)

Proust, not Joyce or Miller, is the spirit that presides over the *Quartet*).[37]

For many critics, Durrell remains a second rank novelist,[38] but one of the good ones, alongside, say, Huxley, Joyce Cary and William Golding. For one critic the *Quintet* was 'puerile to adolescent'.[39] Again and again, two aspects of Durrell seem to annoy critics; first is his lush prose style,[40] which critics dislike partly because it seems out of synch with postwar 'realism', with 'kitchen sink' 1960s drama, with pseudo-socialist notions of art. The rich prose is too obviously Romantic, for some tastes, too 'indulgent', whatever that means. Although British art has always had a Romantic element, which is revived from time to time (as each generation has its 'New Romantics', or its 'Last of the Romantics'), Durrell's Romanticism is not balanced, for some critics, by a healthy dose of 'reality' and 'realism'.

Secondly, Durrell's art is concerned with 'big ideas', which some critics cannot help but interpret as 'pretentious'. Durrell is 'pretending', they say, his 'big ideas' are tacked on to his books, is one critical reading of his art. The *Quartet* grapples with 'essentially unimportant ideas', it was 'no more than an overlong prelude to a rather uninspiring discovery', a journey which involves 'the absurd cancelling confrontation with previous knowledge', where the 'reader cannot find a stable foothold'.[41] It's interesting to see how writers like Proust or Mann or Shakespeare, who also use 'big ideas' in their works become exalted, while Durrell is denigrated. Is Durrell 'pretending'? Not really, he loves ideas. Like Aldous Huxley and Julian Barnes, Durrell is a novelist very much of ideas, so much so that critics see

---

37 Martin Green: "Lawrence Durrell: A Minority Report", W, 132; Scholes, in Hazell, 131. Mahmoud Manzaloui reckoned that while Proust added to the complexity of his characters by successive revelations, Durrell cancelled them out with each volume of the *Quartet* ("Curate's Egg: An Alexandrian Opinion of Durrell's *Quartet*, *Études Angltionals*, 15, 3, July 1962)

38 Durrell accepted that he was 'not of sufficient size' in poetry, that he was not in the front rank of poets (Mon, 120).

39 Harriett Gilbert: "Under the Skin", *New Statesman*, 104, 15 Oct 1982, 28

40 Here's an example of Durrell's rich prose style, some colour poetry from *Reflections on a Marine Venus*: 'Westwards along the shingle beaches around Trianale the sea was laying down its successive washes of prussian blue and violet, and thinning them out as they touched sand to green and citrons and the innocent yellows you can see on the ripening skins of tangerines.' (108)

41 John Mortimer, 1958, 84; Walter Creed, 1975, 173; John Coleman, 1960, 256; R.T. Chapman, 1972, 411

his characters as 'puppets',[42] not 'flesh-and-blood' characters (although a character can never be 'flesh-and-blood', for a character is a figment, as Samuel Beckett knew, existing somewhere between texts and readers). Durrell admitted his characters were something like puppets,[43] which he wielded in abstract explorations of notions such as culture, time, death, love and freedom.[44] Anaïs Nin wrote: 'Durrell does not have a deep knowledge of character... Like Henry [Miller] he invents. He does not *see*.'[45]

Cultural curator George Steiner sees the *Quartet* as a series of brilliant miniatures rather than a unified and broad canvas. Instead of the central figures (Justine, Nessim, Darley) Steiner reckons the marginal characters are more successful and memorable (Scobie, Narouz, Pombal).[46]

It is Durrell's melding of fantasy and realism, of opulent settings and hi-falutin' ideas, of fashionable appearances and stereotypical Third World squalor, that annoys some critics. His novels are not obviously fantasy genre material, like Michael Moorcock's *Jerry Cornelius* books, or Mervyn Peake's *Gormenghast* trilogy. They are not coruscating socio-political satire, like George Orwell's *Animal Farm* or *1984* (although *Tunc* aims to be social commentary and satire, and fails. Durrell does not have much to say, really, about politics). Durrell's novels are not thriller, spy or detective novels, like Ken Follett, Agatha Christie or Dan Brown (though there are elements of 'intrigue' in *The Alexandria Quartet* and *The Revolt of Aphrodite*).[47] Durrell's novels are not science or 'speculative' fiction, like Brian Aldiss, Thomas Disch and J.G. Ballard (they are, though, heavily freighted with metaphysical speculations, the blurred area where science meets religion, the zone where mathematics and poetry co-exist, Q, 141).

---

42 'the characters exist on the surface only', writes Walter Allen (287)
43 In a notebook for the *Tunc-Nunquam* novels, Durrell noted that there ought to be only '[o]ne thing per person to define his bent of mind. Chess king, scholar, butcher, poet.' (Ill, 42, 19, 8) This compares with the 'character-squeezes' in the *Quartet*, where just one phrase defines a character.
44 Margaret McCall: "*The Lonely Roads*: Notes for an Unwritten Book", in MacNiven, 1987, 384; contravening this view, Durrell also said: 'I invent my characters. I detest photography in literature.'
45 Nin, *Journals*, vol. 7, 297
46 George Steiner: "Lawrence Durrell: The Baroque Novel", *Yale Review* 1960, W, 22
47 One critic called *Mountolive* 'a spy tale with operatic interludes' (Benjamin DeMott: "Grading the Emanglons", *Hudson Review*, 13, 3, Fall 1960)

Durrell's novels, are not 'blockbuster', in the epic style of Olivia Manning's *Levant Trilogy*. Manning's novels are set very much in Durrell territory (British intellectuals in Mediterranean exile). But rather, Durrell employs elements of genres such as Gothic fantasy, horror, science fiction, thriller, romance, etc, and creates something unclassifiable. (Other writers who made the trip South included Norman Douglas, Aldous Huxley, Graham Greene, T.E. Lawrence, Compton Mackenzie, Eric Linklater, Francis Brett Young, Forster, H.G. Wells – and earlier wanderers, such as Sir Richard Burton, Shelley, Keats, Byron.) In *Livia*, Blanford is consumed by the South: 'the whole harmony of the Mediterranean south swept over him' (L, 106.)

Durrell is firmly weighted towards the South, as against the North: he speaks of the North as Gothic, the South as Romance; for one beer, the other wine; for one butter and cream, for the other, the olive; the North is Puritan, the South is pagan.)[48] On the one hand his novels are, like V.S. Naipaul's *The Enigma of Arrival*, novels of 'residence', of being in one exotic place for a certain amount of time. At the same time, like Jeanette Winterson's *Sexing the Cherry*, Peter Redgrove's *The Sleep of the Great Hypnotist* or Emma Tennant's *Sisters and Strangers*, Durrell's novels are fantastical, other-worldly, and 'magical', in the sense of South American 'magic realism' (Jorge Luis Borges, Carlos Fuentes, Gabriel Garcia Marquez). Durrell's novels have much in common with complex self-reflexive literary edifices, such as those architectonic structures built by André Gide, Borges and Proust. The use of North Africa in Durrell is mirrored by Paul Bowles in novels such as *The Sheltering Sky, Let It Come Down* and *The Spider's House*. Both Durrell and Paul Bowles are partial to the portrayal of sudden, meaningless North African violence, sudden bursts of senseless pain (as also in Camus' *The Happy Death* and *The Outsider*).

The *Quartet* has its fair share of deaths, some comic, many violent: six murders, a faked murder, a suicide, and deaths by 'heartsickness'. Both Durrell and Bowles employ the image of the labyrinth: Bowles' Fez, in *The Spider's House*, is a warren of streets desires and politics, as is Durrell's Alexandria. Both Durrell and Bowles write evocatively of the desert, the over-arching (sheltering) sky and the void and vacuity behind modern life.

There is more than a little existentialism in Durrell's novels, which is practically inescapable for a male European writer in the mid-century era. One can see the links between the discourses of subjectivity, spirituality,

48 Durrell: "Women of the Mediterranean", SP, 372

meaninglessness and social order in Jean-Paul Sartre's *Nausea,* Hermann Hesse's *Steppenwolf,* Samuel Beckett's *Malone Dies* and Albert Camus' *The Outsider.* In Durrell's novels, as in those of Hesse, Camus, Sartre, Lawrence and Huxley, we find bourgeois male individuals and anti-heroes struggling to 'come into being', as Lawrence put it. On one level, Durrell's *The Black Book, The Alexandria Quartet* and *The Avignon Quintet* are about 'coming into being', about maturing, about the second, spiritual birth, the ontological rebirth,[49] just as in Goethe's *The Sorrows of Young Werther,* Gide's *The Immoralist* and J.-K. Huysmans' *À Rebours* (Clea is reading a copy when Darley visits her studio).

In Durrell's fiction too we detect the stylish, liberal traveller, the spirit of wanderlust as displayed in Bruce Chatwin's books (in *The Songlines* and *What Am I Doing Here*) and in other travel writers such as Paul Theroux, Patrick Leigh Fermour, Rose Macaulay, etc. Durrell's novels have the free and easy atmosphere of travel writing, the sort of writing that appears in glossy magazines and the Sunday newspapers, where one can be on a plane to Hong Kong one week and stuck in a dire Tashkent hotel the next. Indeed, Durrell began writing travel books early on in his career, but around 1958 he started writing travel pieces for magazines such as *Holiday* and *Elle,* on the back of the success of *The Alexandria Quartet* (he also contributed to film screenplays, most famously Elizabeth Taylor's 1963 blockbuster movie, *Cleopatra*).

Durrell's novels are also part of that (usually masculinist) love of diving into degradation, into the depths of human experience, characterized by slime, poverty, extremity, despair and madness. Thus, Durrell is a part of a tradition which goes to sensory extremes: Georges Bataille exploring the links between sex and death and eggs, eyes and anuses in *The Story of the Eye*; Samuel Beckett's derelicts and tramps crawling through forests on crutches or fucking whores on junk heaps; William Burroughs' junkies combining heroin, ejaculation and death in hanging rituals ('light the ovens!'); Patrick Süskind's misogynist social outcast in *Perfume* exploring scent and death; Charles Baudelaire in *Intimate Journals,* Arthur Rimbaud in *A Season in Hell* and J.K. Huysmans in *Against Nature* navigating the boundaries of sensuality, and so on.

On film the rendition of a world closest to Durrell's was Bernardo Bertolucci's 1990 version of Paul Bowles' *The Sheltering Sky.* Bertolucci is

---

49 Durrell wrote to Alfred Perlès: '[b]ut the key to everything seems to me to be self-liberation and self-discovery.' (AO, 24)

the director who could bring the necessary opulence and cinematic flamboyance to Durrell's *The Alexandria Quartet*. The late 1960s film version of *Justine* was bound to be awful, with Michael York as Darley and Dirk Bogarde as Pursewarden. Two 1960s stars of European cinema played Justine and Melissa – Anouk Aimée and Anna Karina – which might have augured well for the film. But no. Durrell wrote: 'from friends I gather it's the worst film ever made of a decent book' (DML, 435). The Hollywood *Justine* could never have worked: Durrell's work requires a European art cinema approach. Bertolucci in *The Sheltering Sky* got close to a Durrellian sense of the Maghreb, the strangeness of Arabic towns, a sexual relationship in decay, the nothingness behind life (love in Durrell's art is 'the flirtation of minds prematurely exhausted by experience' [J, 23]). Perhaps another Italian director, Pier Paolo Pasolini, could have made *The Alexandria Quartet* into something interesting. Pasolini had a perceptive grasp of Classical mythology (in his *Medea* and *Oedipus Rex*), and produced the most lyrical evocations of the dust-blown Mediterranean landscape in cinema. Pasolini's deep understanding of the poetics of Greek mythology and the Mediterranean world is eminently suitable for a transcription of Durrell's novels into films.

Durrell's art would also require the touch of Federico Fellini, who would have been able to capture the carnival, circus side of Durrell. Richard Pine wonders what Fellini might have done with Durrell's clowns and his brothel scenes, if they had been filmed in the style of Fellini's *City of Women* and *Satyricon* (Durrell was a fan of Petronius' *Satyricon*, calling it the 'first European novel', and siting it in the background texture of *The Alexandria Quartet* and *The Revolt of Aphrodite*).

A pity, then, that Durrell did not get the European art film treatment of the late 1960s/ early 1970s era of Fellini, Antonioni, Pasolini, Truffaut, Bertolucci, Godard, Fassbinder, Bergman and Visconti. Some directors came close to Durrell in other ways: some critics have noted the similarities between Alan Resnais' art movie classic *Last Year in Marienbad* and *The Alexandria Quartet*, in particular the explorations of space and time. But, apart from the disastrous Hollywood version of *Justine,* it is best perhaps that Durrell's books are not made into films, for the process always involves massive disappointment and compromises. Some books are simply too visual anyway: they do everything with words; they describe things in such detail, and so vividly, that the film version can only reproduce the visuals, or set off in a completely different direction.

Films from books such as *Tess of the d'Urbervilles, Women in Love* and *The Rainbow* prove this point. The books are so full and rich, the films can only disappoint. Like Thomas Hardy and D.H. Lawrence, Durrell's novels are visually rich, and no film, perhaps, could match such visions. When films try to deal with the emotional relationships in books, too, much is lost. Sexual encounters, for instance, are practically impossible to convey in cinema. Film versions of *Lady Chatterley's Lover* show how difficult it is to portray the subtle, spiritual, intimate, orgasmic and multi-sensory experience of lovemaking. Lawrence's fiction is unfilmable, for he describes the invisible economics of feelings and desires. Durrell, too, because so much of his fiction relies on sexual relationships, is essentially unfilmable. Pornography has grappled with ways of making desire manifest and visual – by getting closer and closer to genitals, by showing ejaculation, the 'come shot', by showing female ejaculation, a visual sign of orgasmic pleasure in women. Ejaculation is 'visible evidence' of orgasm.[50] Orgasms, though, cannot be filmed, and, as Lawrence showed in his 'rippling, rippling, rippling' descriptions of Connie's orgasms in *Lady Chatterley's Lover*, they can't be depicted in prose.

Film and television offer a limited range of desires and responses, and although they thrive on 'excess', Durrell's fictions conjure up more excesses of desire and sensuality than film or television could portray. Every *James Bond* film, it seems, has a carnival or festival scene in which Bond is chased by villains through chaotic noise and light and colour. No filmed masquerade, though, could approach the strangeness of Durrell's carnivals in *The Alexandria Quartet*. And Durrell's carnivals, though, like the exotica in *The Arabian Nights* or *The Perfumed Garden,* are far less strange or exhilarating than real life in Egypt or India.

Of the many would-be projects of Lawrence Durrell, one of the more intriguing is his 'Piero della Francesca book', hinted at in a letter of 1962 (SP, 153). Now this would be something rich to contemplate. Then there was the book on the tramps of South France. It would have been wonderful too to see a film script or play turned into a feature film (but not in the manner of the disastrous *Justine*). The play *Sappho* started life as a

---

50 see Shannon Bell: "Feminist Ejaculations", in Arthur and Marilouise Kroker, eds: *The Hysterical Male: New Feminist Theory*, St Martin's Press, New York, 155-169; also Chris Straayer: "The Seduction of Boundaries: Feminist Fluidity in Annie Sprinkle's Art/ Education/ Sex", in Gibson, ed, 168f

novel (1961), of which twelve chapters remain. The original title was *The Dark Peninsula*, as unsatisfactory a title as *The Dark Labyrinth*. The novel *Sappho* depicts the enigmatic poet as a fluctuating personality, whose poetry is more real, in some ways, than the person herself, in the typical Durrellian manner (Ill, 42, 10, 8f).

At one time, Durrell planned and researched a book on his beloved Elizabethan writers: "The Writer in the Elizabethan Age" or the anthology "An Elizabethan Bedside Book", as edited by Durrell, would have been something to treasure. Alongside the well-known poets of the time (Marlowe, Spenser, Sidney, Shakespeare) Durrell had prepared biographies and data on lesser-known writers, such as Thomas Nash, John Marston and Parr. He had read widely in the Elizabethans, and had a large library about the Elizabethan era.

The film of *The Tempest* which Lawrence Durrell contemplated with Mai Zetterling, which would have been made in Corfu (Durrell reckoned Corfu was Prospero's island retreat) sounded promising, but never came to anything, like the film versions of *The Dark Labyrinth*, which Durrell thought of scripting in 1958. There were also movie treatments Durrell started of *Oedipus*.

On the internet, useful Durrell websites include the International Lawrence Durrell Society at lawrencedurrell.org, the Durrell School in Corfu, at durrell-school-corfu.org, and the Lawrence Durrell Archive, at idir.net/~nedblake/lgd_biography. For Henry Miller, have a look at: henrymiller.org and henrymiller.info.

Images of Lawrence Durrell

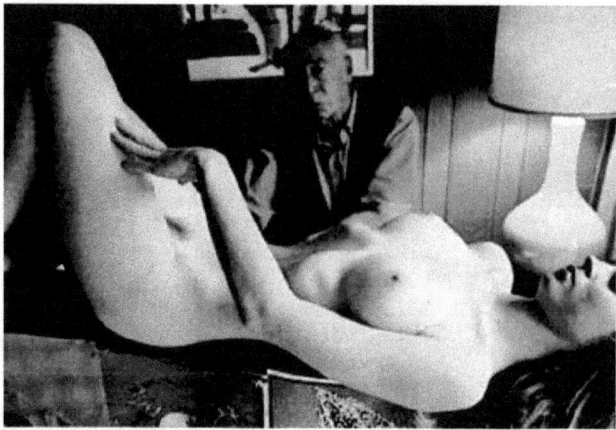

Photos of Henry Miller

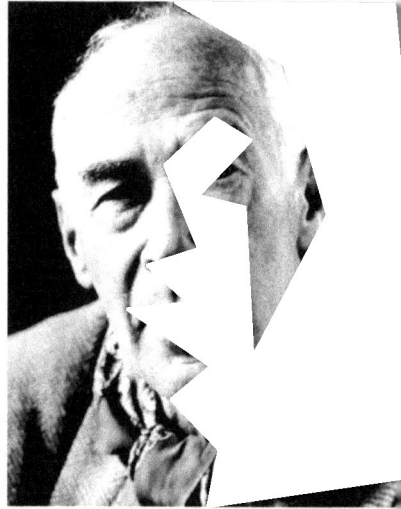

2

Lawrence Durrell and Henry Miller

It's worth reminding ourselves of the nature of Henry Miller's writing. Miller (1891-1980) was absolutely crucial in Lawrence Durrell's development as a writer. Time after time Durrell paid tribute to Miller, often claiming that Miller had written some of the best prose of the century. In 1936 Durrell wrote from Corfu that 'TROPIC OF CANCER IS THE PUREST BOOK WRITTEN IN OUR TIME... this is at once the greatest piece of writing in our time, and also the most religious book' (SP, 49-50). Durrell said (in 1958) that his debt to Miller 'isn't yet repaid nor will ever be' (PC, 343). Durrell said that Miller:

> has affected an imaginative junction between the obscene and the holy – not exactly a new thing to the East but new and rather off-putting to the prurient West. (AO, 23)

Miller burst into life as a writer with *Tropic of Cancer*. Of course he had been writing before *Tropic of Cancer*, but it was with *Tropic of Cancer* that Miller blossomed artistically. It is a book which goes for its target with complete savagery and lyricism. In its semi-autobiographical pages, Miller portrays himself as a bohemian down-and-out, a literary tramp, who doesn't care a damn for convention, the establishment, the status quo. T.S. Eliot called it 'remarkable', Ezra Pound said *Tropic* 'out-Ulysessed Joyce', and George Orwell rated Miller highly, calling him 'the only imaginative prose-writer of the slightest value' to appear in years (Brown, 2). When, in 1946, the two *Tropic* books were banned in France, the big guns of the French literary scene came to Miller's defence: Jean-Paul Sartre, Andrés Gide and Breton, Albert Camus and Paul Éluard.

Tropic of Cancer famously opens with the archetypal Miller persona rejoicing in his utter destitution: 'I have no money, no resources, no hopes. I am the happiest man alive' (HMR, 169). Miller writes from the standpoint of someone who has nothing, yet who is permeated with a spiritual richness. It's about being at the bottom of the pile, and learning to live with it, to accept it: *acceptance* is one of the great Millerian words (LT, 165). 'I am the hero and the book is me', Miller stated.[1] Miller lashes out at those who seem to have everything. His targets include God, art, religion, sex, cities, morality and friends. *Tropic of Cancer*, like the rest of the *Tropic* trilogy and *The Rosy Crucifixion* trilogy, is about being liberated, about having one's soul dragged in the mire yet surviving, about going through hell and back again. *Tropic of Cancer* shows Miller when he's 'cooking', as he calls it, which means writing stretched to the limit and flowing, as in *Sexus*, where the writing and the subjects are given the same vivacious treatment.[2]

At his best, Miller goes for it with a vengeance, he writes with every stop pulled out, at top speed, in the highest gear. His prose is like a runaway train, wild, wild, but never completely out of control. In his most lucid moments, Miller creates passages of extraordinary splendour, of religious intensity, of existential agony and unbridled lust.

If one had to pick just one passage from the whole of Henry Miller's *œuvre*, it would probably be something from *Tropic of Cancer, Tropic of Capricorn* o r *Sexus*. The following is an extract from *Sexus*. It shows Miller at his wildest, chewing up words like a leviathan, and conjuring up bizarre images of the inhabitants of a rundown hotel. The protagonist is with Mara (later called Mona). They've spent the night feverishly trying to achieve orgasm in a sweaty iron bed. Miller frequently lopes along to the lavatory, to wash his dick. He meets an old man with crinkled skin like an

1 Miller, letter, 18 May 1938, *New Republic*, in Wickes 1963, 29
2 In a letter to Durrell of 6 July 1944, Miller wrote of *The Rosy Crucifixion* thus: '[t]his revives the mantic and the obscene, and how! And will be devilishly long. But readable.' (PC, 194-5) Miller was ever the optimist.

elephant's hide who snorts like a walrus. After sex, Miller describes their surroundings:

From the ocean front came the boom of surf followed by a frying pan symphony of exasperated sheet metal cooling off in a drizzle at a hundred and thirty-nine degrees centigrade. The hotel was droning and purring like a fat and moribund swamp fly in the solitude of a pine forest... Here and there an open door revealed the presence of grotesquely plastic water nymphs who had managed to squeeze their mammiferous trundles of avoirdupois into sylphlike fish nets made of spun ribbons of wet clay... We stretched ourselves out in the hollow of a suppurating sand dune next to a bed of waving stinkweed on the lee side of a macadamized road over which the emissaries of progress and enlightenment were rolling along with that familiar and soothing clatter which accompanies the smooth locomotion of spitting and farting contraptions of tin woven together by steel knitting needles. The sun was setting in the West, as usual, not in splendour and radiance however but in disgust, like a gorgeous omelette engulfed by clouds of snot and phlegm. It was the ideal setting for love, such as the drugstores sell or rent between the covers of a handy pocket situation. I took off my shoes and leisurely deposited my big toe in the first notch of Mara's crotch. Her head was pointed South, mine North; we pillowed them on folded hands, our bodies relaxed and floating effortlessly in the magnetic drift, like two enormous twigs suspended on the surface of a gasoline lake. (HMR, 135-6)

Easy to see how some of Durrell's writing is inspired by Miller's *Tropic* and *Rosy Crucifixion* trilogies. When Durrell's narrators turn brash and bombastic, or dictionary-chewing and hyper-articulate, one can't help thinking of Henry Miller. The tone of Pursewarden's and Sutcliffe's pronouncements, two key writer figures of Durrell's fiction, chimes with Miller's authorial voice. In Miller's evocation of the rundown hotel in *Sexus* one can see not only Durrell, but also writers such as William Burroughs and the Beat generation poets with their Bohemian sojourns. Also, the hotel in *Last Tango in Paris* is Milleresque, with its alcoholic, alienated residents. In Bernardo Bertolucci's 1972 art movie two strangers meet in a deserted flat to fuck: Bertolucci consciously evoked Henry Miller in Paris.

Keeping in mind the passage from *Sexus* quoted above, compare it with this Milleresque moment from *The Black Book*: it is a sexual moment,[3] and it is often in Durrell's erotic evocations that we see Miller's influence at its greatest (think of Durrell's brothel scenes, which come straight out of lighter, more carefree Miller – such as *Quiet Days in Clichy,* for example):

An instant's vision of the underwater girl, thighs drawn back in an arch to admit rape, tangled in the flowing weeds and fucus. I am with you to the hilt now, Excalibur bedded in the warm stone flesh, pushing open new continents, new vistas of emotion. The inexecrable reaping penis stiffened in a field of parched corn. The trees are dragging their heads, caught in the wind. The river is glacial. The kingcups shine and shine, and scent of the crushed marshflower enters us... The womb emptied like a bucket of musk into silence.' (197-8)[4]

There is nothing that distinctive about this passage from *The Black Book*. We have read paragraphs like it many times. It seems no male writer of the 20th century could avoid creating similar mega-phallic flights. We find them in the work of James Joyce, D.H. Lawrence, William Burroughs, J.G. Ballard, Ted Hughes, Philip Roth, Martin Amis, Norman Mailer, Joseph Heller, J.P. Donleavy, even in the more 'restrained' writers, such as Aldous Huxley or Rainer Maria Rilke (his 'Seven Phallic Poems', for example).

The Nin-Miller-Durrell Paris years have been romanticized, not least by the authors themselves. They called themselves the Three Musketeers, haunted Paris's cafés (the Dôme, the Flore, the Coupole), produced special issues of *The Booster* ("Special Peace and Dismemberment Number with Jitterbug-Shag Requiem", 1937-8), and put out the Villa Seurat trilogy, *Tropic of Cancer, House of Incest* and *The Black Book* (the 'Villa Seurat Library', published by Jack Kahane of the Obelisk Press, was *The Black Book,* Nin's *Winter of Artifice* and Miller's *Max and the White*

---

3 'Though he tried [to depict sex] in his early novel *The Black Book,* he was no D.H. Lawrence' (Carl Bode: "A Guide to Alexandria", W, 209). James R. Nichols notes that though critics see Durrell as 'without the English prudery', it does not really describe Durrell's complex view of the body and sex ("Sunshine Dialogues: Christianity and Paganism in the Works of Lawrence Durrell", OMG II, 129)
4 Other Milleresque sentences in Durrell's *œuvre* include these from *Zero* (which was dedicated to Miller): 'I am teaching everyone how to experience phenomena... The teacups will be brimming with polarized light, the parasols hectic with dinosaurs... The limbo of egoists... Twenty spines curved over a ravenous dinner-table in a dance of food... You have nothing to lose, because all is lost' (SP, 248, 251, 256).

Phagocytes).[5] The Miller-Nin-Durrell trio were for revolt – against the (literary) establishment – for an art which drew on psychoanalysis, mysticism, Surrealism, and a Rimbaudian passion (Durrell was not convinced by Surrealism – it did not touch his 'deeper preoccupation with form, and the rupture of form by science' FEB, 5).

D.H. Lawrence was a common love among the three. Miller was bound for his mythic realm of 'China', Nin for Jungian/ Rankian self-realization, and Durrell for the 'Heraldic Universe'. It was only in their fictions (fantasies) that these goals were realized. It was not until some twenty years later, in *The Alexandria Quartet*, that Durrell put the ideas of the Three Musketeers Paris years fully into prose. Most of the notions of the *Quartet*, from Justine's concept of multiple selves and Arnauti's Freudian analyst lingo to Pursewarden's concept of the heraldic artist and Clea's near-death baptism in order to become an artist, have their roots in the Miller-Nin-Durrell 1930s era.

In a late interview Durrell said that Nin and Miller helped him enormously in the 1930s Paris years. 'They gave birth to me', he said. 'I was really invented by them in some way because I was so young' (in Fitch, 211). This is a typical Durrellian statement, but was he really so young, at twenty-five? After all, by the time Shelley and Keats were 25, they had written some extraordinary and lasting work. Perhaps Durrell overplayed his naïvety of this time: he had lived in India, London, the provinces and Corfu, had moved in some of London's Bohemian circles, ran a photographic studio, been a railway porter and a rent-collector, had played jazz in a nightclub, had written and sold jazz songs (using his mother's surname as a *nom-de-plume*), and so on.

Henry Miller overwrites, sometimes drastically. There are as many passages of flat writing or chugging along, as there are of radiance and violence. *Nexus* and *Plexus*, for instance, are far too long. But it is Miller's penchant to keep writing until exhaustion; he simply *has* to circumvent the topic, and doesn't stop until he has it all written down. He is encyclopædical, cosmological, and aims to incorporate great slabs of the universe in his novels. Hence the massive overwriting, the bizarre word choices, the lengthy paragraphs.

When he writes dialogue it can be trenchant and hilarious, but his preference is for long, sometimes rambling paragraphs. His prose style is

---

5 The Villa Seurat crew included Alfred Perles, Lowenfels, Rattner and the painter Hans Reichel, as well as Nin, Durrell and Miller

casual, worldly, knowing, but can also be deliberately cryptic and difficult.[6] He is seldom secretive, though. His æsthetic sensibility is such that the reader always knows what he's doing. He does not hide in his prose behind walls of vagueness. His narrators are upfront about their desires and goals.

His books are journeys, and read like journeys. They are the records of Miller's travels through life. They move from scene to scene like a high-speed biography. At the same time as the narrative drives along at a breakneck pace, large chunks of prose could be shifted to the beginning or end of the novels without altering the book much. Though the 'auto-biograhical' novels are chronologically sequential, charting the protagon-ist's life (the *Tropic* and *Rosy Crucifixion* trilogies), episodes could be changed around, particular diatribes could be inserted elsewhere, and so on. Miller goes on about the same themes, the same situations, the same people, time after time. All writers do, but Miller doesn't bother to pretend. He doesn't hide his intentions from the reader.

Henry Miller wrote to Alfred Perlès, offering his opinion of writing as an initiation or prelude to living: 'the highest art is the art of living, that writing is but a prelude or form of initiation for this purpose.' (AO, 40) Here Miller is distinctly Taoist: for the true Taoist, one must go beyond art, as well as all other systems. Miller became something of a guru for the young from the 1960s onwards. He was seen as one of the godfathers of the Beat poets. People used to come out to Big Sur in California to visit the writer of *Tropic of Cancer*. Women supposedly expressed a desire to sleep with the author of the infamous books of sexual antics. Two o'clock in the morning one night in February 1958 two people burst into Miller's room in Big Sur: '[t]he woman, who was drunk, had come to bawl me out for something I had written', Miller told Durrell (PC, 330).

There is tons of humour in Miller's work, and most of his books contain many laughs and smiles. He is not a dour, sombre, bashful figure, and neither is his writing. Miller is an earthy, bold, idealistic, optimistic, crazed writer, someone who believes in the ability of art to nourish the spirit but who remains also sceptical and cynical about the world of people and morality. His writing bombards readers with imagery and ideas. Everything is taken to extremes, everything is passion, veering from nothingness to

---

6 Durrell was very complimentary about *Nexus*, saying that Miller had attained 'fountain-like effortless rhythms' and a 'fine rare harmony'. While *Nexus* performed 'giant trapeze acts', Durrell said, other writers were still gingerly climbing up ladders on the side of the cliff. (letter, 25 November 1958, PC, 353)

abundance, from boredom to ecstasy.

Much of the humour in Miller's fiction is brazen, childish, scatological, blasphemous. Miller loves to upset people. He loves to be antagonistic, difficult, obscure, weird. He gets bored easily, and so buries some explosives under 'normal life'. The ordinary, domestic life bores him to death, but he can be in a state of bliss wandering around the backstreets of a city. There are many passages of walks in Miller's books, accounts of his meetings with strangers and unexpected corners of the world. Much of the humour stems from satirical, savage character portraits. Miller's friends form the source of much of his writing, not only in *The Book of Friends,* the letters, *The Colossus of Marousi,* but throughout the fiction.

Miller's ideal world is one of great fucks, great meals, and great talk. The three things he cherishes are great talk, food and sex. A good day is one in which one has had a good meal, a good long talk, and a juicy fuck. Miller's after-dinner talks were famous - he could go on for hours, it seemed. When Durrell first met Miller (in Paris in August, 1937) there was much wine and talk - of Madame Blavatsky, Jiddu Krishnamurti, Knut Hamsun, Vaslav Nijinsky, Lao tzu and Corfu (R. Ferguson, 252). Similarly, Miller wrote thus of the Durrell of the *Black Book* era: '[h]e was an exceedingly well read man even then. I could sit back and listen to him by the hour.'[7] When they got together, Miller said he and Durrell 'could spend days on end getting drunk on Spengler' (ib.). All the protagonist of *Sexus* cares about, he tells Mara, is fucking and eating (HMR, 162). The reality of Miller's fiction is that these seemingly simple goals are constantly subverted by all manner of problems. Miller, the romantic, the idealist and optimist, knows that life can be fantastic, but most of the time it can be awful. For Miller, the causes of the suffering among humans are other humans.

One of the most often discussed aspects of Miller's writing is the sexual content. Miller has a lot to say about fucking - in *Tropic of Cancer, Black Spring, Quiet Days in Clichy, The World of Sex,* and throughout *Sexus.* There is a lot of talk of genitals in Miller's work, particularly penises and vaginas, which are always called pricks and cunts. Miller on porn movies: '[i]t's a cock and a cunt and they're fucking and it's exciting!' (LT, 70) Those photographs of Miller (in *My Life and Times*), late in life, writing at his desk with a nude woman (Candice Thayer) in the background, or playing ping pong with her, are stereotypical portrayals of Miller as the great sex guru.

---

7 Miller: "The Durrell of the *Black Book* Days", W, 98

We read of women as 'cunts': there are big cunts, such as Llona in *Tropic of Cancer*, who was '[o]ne cunt out of a million... Cunt international.' (HMR, 173) There are cunts who sit on Miller's knee, let him slide a hand up their skirts. There are cunts who nearly work his prick off as they fuck. There are men (Wambly Bald, for instance) who dream of cunt endlessly. There are references galore to cunts, crotches, cocks and asses in Miller's writing. Miller evokes a 'Land of Fuck', a 'Cosmcoccic' universe; Miller intended *Tropic of Capricorn* to be his 'last fuck': 'fuck everybody and everything!'[8] Oddly, 'Tropic of Cancer' and 'Tropic of Capricorn' were Miller's names for his wife's June's breasts.

Women are either great fucks – or bitches if they don't want to fuck. Miller's view of the transcendent power of sex can sometimes result in banality, which often seems dangerously close to fervent religiosity. All the talk of sex and cunts and fucking seems wildly sexist, and it is. Miller, though, just like Durrell, is mad about women, which can seem to be misogynism, but is really enthusiasm allowed to soar in overblown prose. Miller's protagonists do seem to fuck like machine guns, going blam-blam-blam, but really this is part of Miller's natural exuberance. It's true, Miller's world is thoroughly masculinized, thoroughly a boys' zone. Miller is distinctly 'one of the lads', bragging, joking, yelling, acting like a kid.

But in Miller's fictional world of Paris and New York, the women also take advantage of the men. There are women portrayed as dolts or dollies in Miller's work, but there are also clever women, powerful women. The bravado and machismo, though, can smother any inkling of the protagonists of the novels being sympathetic to women. They might be 'feminized' men, in touch with the 'feminine' values and energies inside them, but they still act like women-haters some of the time. This figure of American fiction is not confined to Miller – ErneHogarth Pressst Hemingway, Charles Bukowski, Raymond Carver, Philip Roth, and others have written in a similar way about women. Writers such as Bukowski seem to be wholly in the Henry Miller tradition.

Miller loves books. He has the delight in books of a collector, an amateur, a passionate admirer. In Miller's works we find many moments where he exalts certain authors and certain books. Like Durrell, Miller has a cherished view of the artist. Both Durrell and Miller regard the artist as crucial, as an explorer of the key realms of experience. This love of the artist is sometimes expressed in ironic, satirical outbursts, but the irony

---

8 Miller, letter to Hiller, April 1936, R. Ferguson, 261

masks the intense love of artists, of the artistic life. Pursewarden lambasts the English for not celebrating the artist, as when he dances with Liza when it's William Blake's birthday. Pursewarden weeps when he thinks of James Joyce's encroaching blindness. Blanford thinks of Joyce's 18 year long struggle to get published (S, 132). Miller wrote at his most lyrical and fanciful when he spoke of the artist. His identification with Rimbaud was total: '[i]n Rimbaud I see myself as in a mirror. Nothing he says is alien to me' (108).

And with D.H. Lawrence, Miller recognized a spiritual forefather. The affinities between Miller and Lawrence are many, though they diverge at key points too (in their politics, for instance). Interesting to note that five years separate *Tropic of Cancer* from *Lady Chatterley's Lover*: there is an æsthetic, moral and spiritual continuity between the two works, between Lawrence's last fiction (with *The Escaped Cock*) and Miller's triumphant entry into the world of fiction.

In his books on Arthur Rimbaud (*The Time of the Assassins*) and D.H. Lawrence (*The World of Lawrence*), Miller sees the artist as an outsider, someone who fits in nowhere, who is despised, who is a mystic and martyr in the cultural wilderness, who has immense potential, someone who can really make things *happen*, who goes beyond Hamlet and Faust, whose plight is both tragic and farcical, who is both reckless and conservative, who is a rebel, child-like, difficult, uncompromising, highly sensitive yet insensitive, subtle but brutal, deeply in the world but aching for transcendence, who restlessly travels and quests, who is never satisfied, who is obsessive, who is full of contradictions and tensions, who is energetic yet lazy, who is mad yet sane.

This resumé of Miller's view of the artist chimes withLawrence Durrell's at most points. Durrell does not put his thoughts on the artist in such excessive, apocalyptic language, as Miller employs in his books on Rimbaud and D.H. Lawrence. Through mouthpieces such as Pursewarden (in the "Brother Ass" sequence) and Sutcliffe (throughout the *Quintet*), Durrell states that all is not lost if the birth pangs of the artist can still be heard. Pursewarden's pontifications in "My Conversations with Brother Ass" are pure Durrell of the *The Black Book*/ Villa Seurat/ Miller-Nin era:

> Whoever makes this enigmatic leap into the heraldic reality of the poetic life discovers that truth has its own built-in morality! (again the Pursewarden exclamation mark, Cl, 132)

Henry Miller is at his most annoying and far-fetched and silly when he's in preaching mode and goes too far. It's the same with D.H. Lawrence, and with Durrell. Most of what Miller says when he's fired up with some subject or other is true, but not often right. The way Miller writes is to find a subject that excites him. If it's an artist – Uccello, Picasso, Dostoievsky, Hamsun – he's off and away. No trouble. If the subject is something he loathes, he wades in firing off his guns in all directions.

Soaring over the planet in a jet Miller gets to musing on the state of the world and technology in *Stand Still Like the Hummingbird*. Miller has always been wary of technology and machines, and in *Stand Still Like the Hummingbird* he wonders just how far things will go. We don't need more technology, Miller muses, it won't make them any happier. 'Just to breathe, to know that you are alive, isn't it marvellous?' (HMR, 300) He looks down and sees the marks of humanity as a few scratches on the surface of the planet. Look at the bird, riding the wind, Miller says, it's happy enough without machines and cities. No machine or device can emulate the flights of the imagination, Miller reckons. People are already astonishing. 'Are we not miraculous in our very being? Why not think miraculously, act miraculously, live miraculously?' (ib., 301).

Miller's philosophic stance chimes with Durrell's at many points: they are both advocates of Chinese repose, the Tao and the Zen Buddhist ways of aligning oneself with the cosmos ('[t]he fulcrum is repose', Durrell wrote to Miller [PC, 288]). In *From the Elephant's Back* he speaks of 'a fulcrum of repose at the heart of reality' (2).

In both Miller's and Durrell's late works we find an emphasis on the miraculous, as with Prospero in *The Tempest*. The key is to realize that life itself is magical, without the additions of technology, machines, art, talk, books, cities, etc. 'The greatest miracle', writes Miller, 'is the discovery that all is miraculous' (ib., 301). Both Durrell and Miller ended up evoking old Chinese sages such as Lao Tzu and Chuang-tzu. There is an acquiescence and tranquillity in Durrell's and Miller's late works that is distinctly Oriental: one does not see this repose in the last works of Lawrence, Rimbaud, Dostoievsky, Kafka, Woolf, and Brontë. Durrell acknowledged Buddhism as his favourite religion – if he had to choose one. Of Western philosophies, he was most drawn to Epicureanism, a philosophy 'based on sincerity, honesty, engagement'.9

---

9 Durrell, in MacNiven 1987, 375

ff

LAWRENCE
DURRELL
Justine

ff

LAWRENCE
DURRELL
Constance

'SUPERBLY ACCOMPLISHED'
London Review of Books

ff

LAWRENCE
DURRELL
Balthazar

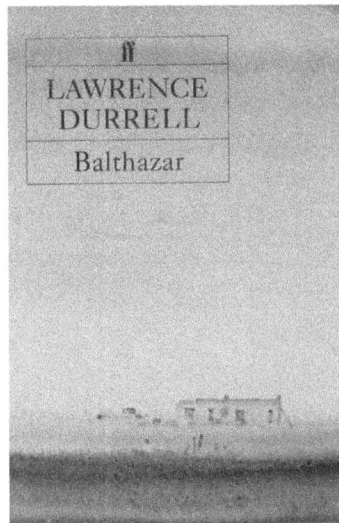

Some book covers from British editions
of Lawrence Durrell's books

One of the great images of Henry Miller
(New Directions)

3

The Art of Art

I always feel about art that it must rape me, as it were, squeeze me dry.

Lawrence Durrell, letter to T.S. Eliot[1]

Is art always outrage – must it by its very nature be an outrage?

Lawrence Durrell (AO, 9)

Like many writers, Lorenzo Durrell has a special affection for the artist. Like Proust, Stendhal, Rimbaud, Gide, Miller, Huxley, Novalis, Petrarch, Dante and Shakespeare, Durrell regards the writer/ poet very highly. For him, as for Rimbaud, Graves and Sappho, the poet is a 'seer', a shaman, a magical worker with words, someone who can really change things. The artist, Durrell says, is asked to be 'more than human', or more fully human than others. Only artists can make things really *happen* claims Pursewarden (M, 193-4). Artists, Durrell states, are shamans or witch doctors: they are necessary for a nation's psychic health. Art, says Durrell, 'is a direct contribution to the health of the human psyche'.[2] This nourishing, altruistic aspect of art is only a sideline, though. It is not,

1 Durrell, in MacNiven, 1987, 350
2 Durrell: "No Clue to Living", 1960, 339

Durrell says, the artist's main intention, her/ his chief concern. 'It is a by-product of the work. The artist is only concerned with the pure act of self-penetration, of self-disentanglement, when he addresses his paper or canvas.' (ib.) The artist's primary concern is with her/ his own work, with her/ his own calling.

Lawrence Durrell has an exalted view of language and poetry (poetry as *poiesis,* the act of creation). For him, language needs to be replenished by 'great language', otherwise it withers. 'Great language' (he is thinking of his beloved Elizabethan writers) 'makes the sober drunk and stretches the sinews of the psyche, flooding it with new self-comprehension'.[3] Durrell said: 'I don't want to stir up contention; I want to excite understanding, to kindle.' (Ald, 148) Durrell has an erotic view of art. For him, the art object is a 'highly erotic and irreverent thing' (Pine, 1994, 56). Durrell spoke of wanting to 'create a throb' in prose; urging writers to put 'some cock' into their work, to 'put your sperm to work! So long as the reader gets the pelvic thrust'; one has to open one's legs to a book, metaphorically, to enjoy it fully Durrell said in his Pursewarden mode.[4]

Pursewarden's dictum is that one should not get stuck on the metaphor or the mask, but look to what it hides or suggests, to what is behind it.[5] 'Good art points', Pursewarden says (Cl, 122), but one should not be concerned with the pointing finger (the artwork) but with the target (not the thing in itself, but what lies beyond). 'It points towards a Something which itself subsists without distinction', Durrell writes (K, 90). In his 'Asides of Demonax', Durrell writes that 'the poetic flashpoint comes where the meaningless meets the sublime' (Som, 52).

Lawrence Durrell is a disciple of the Decadent and Symbolist poets[6] (Baudelaire, Rimbaud, Mallarmé, Wilde, Laforgue) in this respect: the work of the second type of (French) Symbolist poet (Rimbaud, Ducasse, Laforgue) was 'semantically disturbed', that is, it 'jumps the points at every curve' (K, 100). The Symbolist fragmentation and derangement is found in Durrell's notebook prose style in the *Quartet,* and also in Darley's project: to get the important facts down first, rather than establish a neat chrono-logical order. In "The Kneller Tape" Durrell says that '[i]f art preaches, it isn't in terms of ethics or tabus or behaviors. It inspirits and urges people

3 Durrell: "Sappho and After", [1961] Lab, 33
4 Durrell, Ill, II, 1, 5; 42, 19, 10
5 Because language is not 'fine enough to capture the æsthetic experi-ence', Durrell said, 'Hints must do' (Ill, box 1)
6 Durrell said 'we were brought up as Pre-Raphaelites' (FEB)

to wake up by giving them the vicarious feel of the poetic illumination' (W, 165). Durrell's view was fine for modernism, but cultural theory criticism, from deconstruction onwards, has shown that every artwork carries masses of social, economic, political, ideological, symbolic and other elements with it, which are built into it, even if the author is not aware of them.

In the *Quartet* self-realization is the goal: '[t]he struggle is always for greater consciousness', says arch-mage Pursewarden (Cl, 123). The Grail-goal is defined by Pursewarden as turning art into living, as becoming the artwork itself, instead of maintaining one's distance. Instead of being 'about' we must be 'for' ourselves (Cl, 115). As long as the artist still lives, as long as the sad cry of the birth-pangs of the artist are still heard, all is not lost, Pursewarden says (Cl, 101).

In *The Black Book,* Lawrence Durrell wrote as richly as he could, yet in *The Alexandria Quartet* he created his most baroque prose, far more delicate and dense than *The Black Book*'s flights of fancy. One of his most stylized excursions was the early pair of pieces *Zero* and *Asylum in the Snow* (dedicated to Henry Miller and Anaïs Nin). These two texts are written in the very self-conscious, abstruse style of *The Black Book*, where prose style is everything, and what is said not nearly as important. This extract demonstrates the primacy of style over content:

> The snow is growing upward from the earth. There is a quiet light in the passage. Life is passing into us like the light through a filter. I make my feet like compasses and draw Ptolemaic universes on the floor, skating to make him envious or angry. (SP, 260)

The Black Book is where Durrell goes wild with words, as wild as he can. It's interesting to quote his denunciation of the Beat poets – Kerouac, Ginsberg *et al.*[7] Miller of course loved Kerouac ('surpassingly good' [DML, 332]), but Durrell, ever the English puritan, reacted negatively to them. Despite doing similar things in *The Black Book* (existentialism, disaffected anti-hero, jazzy/ 'free-form' prose, etc), Durrell was not impressed with the Beats:

> I found it really corny, and deeply embarrassing... and worst of all

---

7 In his introduction to Jacques Lacarrière's book on Gnosticism, Durrell compared 'the grand poetic Gnostics' with the 'shallow hippy defeatism' of the 'pathetic cockroach world of the anti-hero with his anti-memoirs, not to mention his anti-poetry.' (7)

pretentious. All these nincompoops crawling up hills with their food in polythene bags and attitudinising about religion like Oxford Groupers... this really seems campus stuff. And all those cute little fucks in the name of Zen (just substitute the word Jesus and see what you make of the *content*). It is hick stuff. (DML, 332)

Durrell is not averse to using words like *subfusc, purblind, propinquity, quiddity, suasion, daimon* (not *demon*), *mnemonic, thaumaturgic, egopetal, mordant, ideate, roseate, eschatology, noetic, mœurs, ratiocination, potations, haptic, inchoate, desultory,* and *mica*. The rejoicing in words is apparent in everything Durrell writes.[8] Critics reacted negatively to Durrell's ornate prose, skilled as it is.[9] In a letter of the time of the creation of the tetralogy (February, 1958) Durrell wrote to Miller:

> I work hot to cold like a painter. Hot noun, cold adjective ("mathematical cherry" rather than "sweet cherry"). Or on a sour abstract word like "armature" a warm and sweetish one like "melodious" (DML, 308)

In another letter, Durrell again speaks of approaching prose style as a scientific, philosophic activity: '[e]ven the prose of the *Quartet* was intended to have the intermittency of quanta movements, non-deterministic that is – NONASSOCIATIVE in the joyce [*sic*] sense which is a dead end' (DML, 447). In *The Avignon Quintet*, Durrell moved further into pure lyricism, using a fluid style that recalled his early pieces *Asylum in the Snow* and *Zero*. 'I am developing a new kind of gnomic prose which now resembles jump cutting' (DML, 474).[10] Earlier (in 1946) Durrell had described to Miller his 'newish kind of prose – not surrealistic but gnomic. It is lucid and yet enigmatic' (PC, 224).

By the time of *Quinx*, the narrator/ Blanford was musing upon the adjective, an important tool in prose, but 'the perverter of poetry'. Blanford wondered whether there could be a prose which could not be weighed down and sidetracked by adjectives and 'memory's slow ooze'. A prose that would be interspersed with moments of silence, pauses in prose

---

8 Henry Miller wrote that 'like Flaubert, [Durrell was] a stickler for the right word, the precise image' ("The Durrell of the *Black Book* Days", W, 95
9 Durrell aimed, with *Acte*, to write poetry, that would lift the 'effective charge of words by an octave or so without imposing rhetoric upon the ear'(Ill, 42, 18, 8)
10 Middleton called Durrell's prose 'emblematic' (CE, 18)

in which 'packets of silence drift about like mist' (Q, 178).[11] The endpoint of art in Durrell's æsthetics is silence ('genius is silence' he says in the *Quincunx*). A 'pleasant silence', he writes in an article in *Holiday* (1962) is 'the only sort of tribute one can pay to artistic experience.' (SP, 318)

Durrell's work is theatrical, cinematic, painterly, and self-consciously so.[12] It always draws attention to its manufacture, like the Post-Painterly Abstract artists who left the canvas showing in their 1960s paintings. Durrell loves baroque/ Mannerist effects. For instance, when Darley meets Justine for the first time after years apart at the beginning of *Clea*, she appears in the darkness at the top of the staircase at Karm El Girg, holding a candle (C, 42). The image suggests a stern Bette Davis or Barbara Stanwyck in a Hollywood movie of the 1940s. One recalls, too, that Angel, another ineffectual Englishman, returned from overseas to find his former lover a changed woman, standing on the stairs in the guest house in Thomas Hardy's *Tess of the d'Urbervilles*. Justine's *fin-de-siècle* appearance (dark taffeta dress, perfume, candlelight) contrasts clearly with Darley's reunion with Clea, his new lover: it is afternoon, a café in a quiet square in the centre of Alexandria (C, 67).

Another set-piece is the 'spree' at the end of *Livia*, which has, of course, fireworks, which are described in Durrell's landscape/ 'residence book' mode ('a succession of bangs and strings of coloured snakes hissed up into the air around them, only to spit out their hot coloured stars and plumes and subside groundward again', L, 260). These descriptions reprise the passages from the island books. In another place in *Livia*, a sunset is likened to 'a stained-glass window being slowly shattered' (L, 229). This description recalls Durrell's description of Venice in *Reflections on a Marine Venus.*

Durrell's writing in his poetry is also ornate, but he pulls back and prunes his poems, often using short lines or half lines. The punctuation is sparse. This last stanza is from one of Durrell's more well-known poems, 'Deus Loci':

So today, after many years, we meet
at this high window overlooking
the best of Italy, smiling under rain,

11 In *Monsieur* Sutcliffe contests that language 'corrupts silence', it 'tears petals off the whole mind' (M, 89)
12 '...the insistent meaningless dramatization of everything – theatricliz-ation' in the *Quartet* (Martin Green: "Lawrence Durrell: A Minority Report", W, 135)

that rattles down the leaves like sparrow-shot,
scatters the reapers, the sunburnt girls,
rises in the sour dust of this table,
these books, unfinished letters – all
refreshed again in you O spirit of place,
Presence long since divined, delayed, and waited for,
And here met face to face. (CP, 217)

Here is Durrell's dry, succinct poetic tone, set in a loose pentameter. It is world weary ('after many years'), and cosmopolitan ('the best of Italy'). The metaphors of hunting and shooting are familiar Durrell trademarks ('sparrow-shot'). The narrator is, like Prospero, 'at his books', and, like Prospero, wishes to have the whole enterprise (life itself) rounded out and completed. Sun and the Mediterranean world is here, and eroticism ('sunburnt girls'). Durrell's poetry, unlike his prose, is heavily condensed. While he might 'overwrite' in his novels, he always holds back in his poems. They are never wild, as some of the scenes in his books are.

Durrell treasures poetry, and, like Thomas Hardy, would wish to be remembered as much for his poetry as for his novels,[13] although, in this day and age, it is the novels which have made him famous, if one can call Durrell 'famous'. Poetry, though poets cherish it and hold it highly, is nevertheless secondary to fiction in the eye of the public, and many critics. Novels are consumed in vast quantities, but not, alas, poetry.

Durrell's poetry is a distillation of all that he puts into his novels. Or, rather, the novels are the watered-down versions of what concerns him in his poetry. Durrell's poetry is central, as with other poets who also write novels. Hardy regarded his poetry as dearer to him than his novels. In his poems Hardy exalted Emma and other past loves, like C.P. Cavafy; Hardy's novels, however, deal with many other matters. Hardy's poems remained very personal, close to his heart, so to speak. It's the same with Durrell. Robert Graves called his poetry a 'spiritual autobiography'. And, typically, there is more autobiography in Durrell's poems than in the novels. There are poems, for instance, that are distinctly autobiographical ('Cities, Plains and People' being the most obvious one). The poems are Durrell's 'inner', 'poetic' voice. In the poems, Durrell unleashes his personal concerns, without needing to integrate them into the narrative of a novel. *The*

13 Derek Stanford reckons Durrell has 'written lines more charged with magic and music than any poet I know of since Rimbaud and Verlaine' ("Lawrence Durrell: An Early View of His Poetry" [W, 43]). Hayden Carruth is impressed by Durrell's learning, multi-lingual skill, craftsmanship, esoteric reading, avant nature' ("Nougat For the Old Bitch", W, 125)

Avignon Quintet veers more towards poetry. The narrative thrust is increasingly replaced by the Blanford-Sutcliffe conversations and other commentaries, which slow up the storylines and allow lateral digressions.

Looking at the *Collected Poems*, we see that Durrell wrote the bulk of his poetry in the 1940s and 1950s: the quantity tails off a little in the 1960s, and there is not much from the 1970s. The tone of Durrell's poetry doesn't change that much, so that early poems such as 'Themes Heraldic' (1938) can read in a similar way to late pieces, such as 'A Farewell' (1973). The tone is questing, metaphysical, speculative; the style is architectural, designed, condense, 'classical'.[14]

The Durrell voice stems partly from T.S. Eliot: a modernist voice; cultured; well-mannered; precise; ironic; dry; seldom declamatory, though often prone to metaphysical speculations, a voice both private and public. This sequence from 'The Anecdotes' displays Durrell's poetic voice well: you see the control here, the choice vocabulary, the sensuality, decadence, unassuaged lust and irony:[15]

> Wind among prisms all tonight again:
> Alone again, awake again in the Sufi's house,
> Cumbered by this unexpiring love,
> Jammed like a cartridge in the breech
> Leaving the bed with its dented pillow,
> The married shoes alert upon the floor.
>
> Is life more than the sum of its errors?
> Tubs of clear flesh, Egyptian women:
> Favours, kohl, nigger's taste of seeds,
> Pepper or lemon, breaking from one's teeth
> Bifurcated as the groaning stalks of celery.
>
> Much later comes the tapping on the panel.
> The raven in the grounds:
> At four thirty the smell of satin, leather:
> Rain falling the mirror above the mad
> Jumbled pots of expensive scent and fard,
> And the sense of some great impending scandal. (CP, 206)

When you hear Durrell reading this poem on one of the poet's

---

14 Derek Stanford: "Lawrence Durrell: An Early View of His Poetry", W, 39f
15 Kenneth Rexroth spoke of Durrell's 'great poems, lovely, temperate, with every subtle cadence so carefully controlled, so excruciatingly civilized.' (In CE, 26)

recordings, you hear the clipped, suave English tones. It's a voice which, once you've heard it, is as unmistakably English as Dirk Bogarde or Laurence Olivier (Bogarde appeared in the film of *Justine*, while Miller thought Durrell looked like Olivier, although Durrell was more often compared to W.C. Fields).

The act of writing the *Quartet*, for both Durrell as author and Darley as author's stand-in or narrator, becomes continually foregrounded. We see how Darley resuscitates his project of reinventing Alexandria from time to time. Each new section of the *Quartet*, for instance, typically begins with a piece of descriptive writing evoking the landscape of Egypt and Alexandria. By such means, the writer journeys back into the past, back into her/himself. In evoking the visual and sensual aspects of the city of Alexandria, the narrator helps his shamanic (poetic) journeying back to the site of his most poignant life-experiences.

Just as the typical film opens with establishing shots, long shots and descriptive shots, so Durrell's texts open with landscapes. The *Quartet* books begin with 'landscape-tones', which are actually *notes* for descript- ions of landscapes, as well descriptions of landscapes in themselves.16 In the *Quartet*, Durrell foregrounds the notion of notes, of notes for notes: each of the books ends with various forms of notes: the 'workpoints', Scobie's sayings, Pursewarden's marginalia, notes in the text, 'consequential data', and so on. We see Durrell's narrator reprising certain sections or passages of the *Quartet* as he goes along, just as artists look back over their work and rework earlier items. The painter J.M.W. Turner would rework early works: he took up the painting *Regulus*, for example, and added masses of white paint to the sky, transforming it from a historic description of a classical harbour to a depiction of a mythic, visionary moment. Similarly, Durrell rehashes sequences from the *Quartet* from time to time. The list of names of society glitterati, for instance ('Count Banubula, Jacques de Guéry, Athena Trasha' etc) which appears on pages 37 and 38 of *Balthazar* reappear towards the end of the novel as a list of people invited to the domino carnival (B,185).

Like *The Wasteland* and William Burroughs' *The Naked Lunch*, *The Alexandria Quartet* is a cut-up novel. The models suggested for the æsthetic architectonics of the *Quartet* are a palimpsest, with one layer on

16 Hayden Carruth has re-arranged a paragraph from *Justine* so it reads as poetry (Carruth: "And I shall clynken yow so merry a belle that I shal wakyn all this company", *Poetry*, 93, no. 5, Feb 1958)

top of another, a basket of crabs, crawling over each other, or a movie film, randomly edited. The disjointed structure echoes the fragmentary nature of memory: what makes the *Quartet* work, and what makes movies work, is the imaginative ability of the viewer/ reader to put together and make sense of all the pieces ('what I call life', Durrell said around 1958, 'I see as an act of the imagination, a poem'.[17] And Akkad tells Sutcliffe in *Monsieur*: 'what is imagined with enough intensity has a claim to be real enough' (M, 218).

Durrell often employs deft tense changes, as in *The Alexandria Quartet*, most obviously at the start of *Justine*, where the narrator tracks back and forth between the present and the past, between reality and memory.[18] The tense changes unite past and present, as at the beginning of *Balthazar*, where the narrator evokes his life with Pombal (22-23). For Durrell's narrator, the writing of the *Quartet* recreates the past, so that he turns from writing 'was' to 'is'. This is the Cavafian condition of the *Quartet*.[19] For Cavafy, the 2,000 year-old historic past was as alive as the everyday present of Alexandria. ('The past is always magical', says Durrell in *The Black Book*, 169). The unification of past and present was made possible by the art of invention, that is, poetry. The poem is like an alchemical vessel, and allows the Faustian artist to mix memory and desire, past and present, dream and reality, in the same space. The poem (or painting/ play/ performance, etc) enables the artist to place all manner of feelings and things side by side.

This is precisely Durrell's ambition with *The Alexandria Quartet*, which is a basket of psycho-social crabs crawling over each other, layers of data in the palimpsest of life. The model is the novel as a post-Rimbaudian prose-poem, a gigantic journal in which hallowed memories are mixed in with cheap banalities, spiritual yearnings are jumbled up with talk of

---

17 Durrell, Ill, Accession II, box 1, Provence notebook, 17
18 In *Monsieur*, Bruce notes how his verb tenses shift as his memories move in and out of focus, likening the movement to the time-shifts of dreams (M, 50)
19 Poet Kenneth Rexroth called *Justine* 'almost a novelification (like a versification but backwards) of Cavafis' poetry' ("Lawrence Durrell", CE, 23). On Cavafy and Durrell see: C.G. Katope: "Cavafy and Durrell's *The Alexandria Quartet*", *Comparative Literature*, 21, 1969; Jane A.L. Pinchin: "It Goes on Being Alexandria Still: C.P. Cavafy and the English Alexandrians", Ph.D thesis, Columbia University 1974; Peter Bien: *Constantine Cavafy*, Columbia University Press, New York 1964

finance.[20] The *Quartet* is a novel which should be printed just as the 'interlinear' itself is: 'cross-hatched, crabbed, starred with questions and answers in different-coloured inks' (B, 18). Ideally, Durrell's novel should be, physically, a huge notebook or journal, printed with Balthazar's ironic annotations in his spidery handwriting, Leila's letters with her 'tall thoughtful handwriting' (B, 65), Pursewarden's scribblings, and so on. During the 1950s, when Durrell was writing the *Quartet*, artists such as Robert Rauschenberg and Jasper Johns started sticking anything they could find onto their 'combine' paintings (forks, beds, sheep, tyres, birds, planks). Before Johns' and Rauschenberg's mixed media extravaganzas, artists such as Kurt Schwitters and Marcel Duchamp stuck objects onto their paintings. Kurt Schwitters is often cited as a major exponent of multi-media formalism. Schwitters explained how he came to do it:

> I simply could not see any reason why old streetcar tickets, driftwood, coat checks, wire and wheel parts, buttons, junk from the attic and heaps of refuse should not be used as material for paintings, any less than colours made in a factory.[21]

Durrell, like D.H. Lawrence, believed that the novel could be the 'big book of life', an artwork so expansive, it could, theoretically, include 'anything'. It could incorporate letters, diary entries, mathematical formulas, mini-essays, historical conjectures, all of which Durrell puts into his fiction. For painters such as Kurt Schwitters, Robert Rauschenberg and Jasper Johns, using 'real' objects stuck onto a painting sets alight the surface of the work. Jasper Johns explained why he uses 'real objects' stuck onto his paintings:

> I like what I see to be real, or to be my idea of what is real... I find it more interesting to use a real fork as painting than it is to use painting as a real fork.[22]

In the mixed media world of postwar art, anything can be incorporated into a work of art. Durrell's artistic persona wonders, why can't a novel fold in chunks of a philosophical treatise or an alchemical essay? The

---

20 For Alfred Kazin, the *Quintet* contained 'no sharp edges, no painful passions, no real losses, no hurts', CE, 31
21 Schwitters, quoted in James Pearson, *Frank Stella*, Crescent Moon 1995, 18
22 Johns, quoted in David Sylvester: "Interview", *Jasper Johns Drawings*, Museum of Modern Art, Oxford 1974, 14 15-16

problem, for (pre) modernist critics and readers, is that this fragmentary notebook method of writing destroys the digetic effect, the veracity of art, that flow of information which constitutes 'realism'. The paragraphs and sections are organized at times like poems, and Durrell's fiction always moves toward the condition of the lyrical, with its open, associative, metaphoric modes.[23] Durrell's fiction moves beyond modernism, becoming, like T.S. Eliot's *The Wasteland* or André Gide's *The Counterfeiters*, a self-reflexive work.[24]

The sense of play, parody, fragmentation and self-reflexivity makes *The Alexandria Quartet* a postmodernist text, a text that reveals its creation, a text that reveals its constructedness.[25] It is this playfulness that seems to unnerve some critics, demonstrating that Durrell is perhaps not to be regarded as a 'serious' author. Durrell loves to play, as when he has D.H. Lawrence writing to Pursewarden 'In you I feel a sort of profanity' and Pursewarden replying 'watch your step' (B, 94-95).

Typical Durrellian word play occurs in *The Red Limbo Lingo* (the title itself a word game), one of Durrell's poems in French:

PO—E—SIE
Manque de Peau
Pot de fleurs
A fleur de peau
Manque de pot
Pot de chambre
Pot de rouge
Coup de Vampire... (16)

More word games, from Durrell's last novel:

Tomboy with a clitoris like an ice-skate seeks rational employ [...]
Mud...Merde...Mutt... love-bewitched in old Bombay – my think is
spunk when thunk... chunks of thought thunk spill spunk. (Q, 137-8)

Durrell's texts are full of the startlingly obvious, the heavily stylized

---

23 Hayden Carruth: "Nougat For the Old Bitch", W, 120
24 Campion's notion of the artist, in *The Dark Labyrinth*, is like Stendhal's idea of 'crystallization': 'the artist gets fixed in his destiny and irresistibly begins to manufacture his own personal myth, his reality" says Campion (113).
25 It is a 'portrait of the artist, a *Künstlerroman,* about a character in a book who is writing a book in which he is a character.' (Robert Scholes, in Hazell, 125)

gestures of someone who knows exactly what he's doing. Occasionally, this baroque stylization is disappointing: we expect more. Durrell is not always subtle. For instance, at the Cervoni ball, in *Balthazar*, the revellers see an image of Pan raping a goat as they approach the house (170). Earlier, Balthazar is compared to the phallic Pan, in an evocation straight out of late D.H. Lawrence (B, 15) The atmosphere of sexual and moral decadence is spelt out playfully and blatantly by Durrell's narrator.[26] Before they go to the ball, Pursewarden relates a tale out of Byron or Baudelaire in ironic fashion (166f). At the ball, Darley escapes the throng to look up the latest Cavafy manuscripts in the Cervoni's library. There he finds the pornographer, Capodistra, dressed in, would you believe it, a Mephistopheles costume. References are hardly necessary to the Devil and Beelzebub, and the descriptions of Da Capo as a ravenous, bird-like creature (176-7). At Narouz' death, Durrell goes mythic: for instance, the dying man is wrapped, like a Roman Emperor, in an 'enormous purple curtain' (Mt, 275). In the same paragraph, Narouz is compared to a 'wounded stag', which is one of the names for Christ crucified.

One of Durrell's faults is his inattentiveness when writing in the baroque mode, as used in *The Alexandria Quartet*. You have to be on your toes to keep up a heightened sense of decadence and world-weariness coupled with incisive, ironic, and lush prose. In the set-piece at the end of *Balthazar*, for instance, Durrell over-uses the word 'great', which he often does when he's in a melancholy but ornate mode: we hear of the 'great' ball at the 'great' Cervoni house with its 'great' gates (B, 163). There is the 'great car', the 'great desk', the 'great lounge'.[27]

The themes that Durrell pursues are the time-worn ones of Western culture (in *Key* he defines the major themes as 'time and the ego', 83).[28] Having nothing strikingly new to say about sex, death, morality, art or

---

26 Mandel compares the 'refined sensualism' in the *Quartet* to that of Baudelaire, Huysmans and Rimbaud (39-40); Christopher Middleton says that 'sex opens the Pandora's Box of the lover's whole being' ("The Heraldic Universe" (in CE, 16)

27 Mahmoud Manzaloui is one of the very few critics to pick up on Durrell's comic, tired over-use of the word 'great' ("Curate's Egg: An Alexandrian Opinion of Durrell's *Quartet*", *Études Angltionals*, 15, 3, July 1962)

28 The last poem of his last book, *Caesar's Vast Ghost*, states that '[m]ere time is winding down at last' (204). Again, there is the curious use of the word 'mere', as in *The Revolt of Aphrodite*.

religion, Durrell merely puts his own twist on the themes.[29] How tired and overdone, for instance, are the constant evocations of sex mingled with death, as when Justine and Darley make love just after Pursewarden's suicide: 'in a queer sort of way his death actually enriched our own love-making', says Darley (B, 191), or when Athena has sex with Jacques on top of the dying Toto de Brunel (B, 179).

Durrell and Gide, Schopenhauer, Wordsworth, Hopkins, Rilke, Jung, Lawrence, Eliot, and Nietzsche

Henry Miller did not invent the alienated outsider genre. Thomas Hardy's *Jude the Obscure*, Fyodor Dostoievsky's *The Brothers Karamazov*, the Marquis de Sade's *Justine* and J.-K. Huysmans' *À Rebours* can all be seen as stories of alienated white males.[30] André Gide wrote the marvellous *The Immoralist* in 1902, one of the great works of modern literature. The correspondences between Gide and Durrell are many. Both became enamoured in their youth of North Africa: Algeria was the setting for Gide's *Fruits of the Earth* and *The Immoralist*, while Egypt was for Durrell a major component of *The Alexandria Quartet* and *The Avignon Quintet*. Both Gide and Durrell are part of the modern European tradition, of Rilke, Mallarmé, Valéry, Beckett, Flaubert, Nietzsche and Rimbaud. Durrell cites Stendhal as an influence – *Mountolive*, Durrell reckoned, with its 'mildly gorgeous' prose,[31] was a Stendhalian novel (DML, 307), something in the style of *Scarlet and Black*,[32] perhaps – as well as Italo Svevo, Denis de Rougemont, Lord Byron, George Seferis, Gustave Flaubert

29 'Four volumes of mystery ending up with what happens in the country every wet Sunday afternoon', wrote Francis Hope: "Strange Enough: *Nunquam* by Lawrence Durrell", *New Statesman*, 27 March 1970, 451
30 In *Livia* Durrell parodies the alienated bourgeois outsider (whom Blanford is in the process of becoming) thus: '[h]e would write poems in invisible ink, then, and post them to himself.' (185)
31 George P. Elliott: "The Other Side of the Story", *The Griffin*, 1960; W, 94
32 'Stendhal bewitches me with his curious shyness and tenderness and the sudden flashes of mordant humour and irony', Durrell wrote to Miller (Oct 1958, PC, 342)

(in an interview, Durrell cites Henry de Montherlant, Marcel Proust, Henry Miller, Jorge Luis Borges, Nikos Kazanzakis and Italo Svevo [Lab, 42]).

In *Pope Joan*, Durrell's translation of and adaption of Emmanuel Royidis's novel, 'Byron is repeatedly quoted, alluded to, parallelled'.[33] Like Byron, Durrell is interested in studying sexual repression in Christianity (*Pope Joan*, 7). But just as important are the literary heroes of 'Pudding Island', Durrell's term for England: you can see in Durrell's work writers such as Norman Douglas (the travel writer of *South Wind* and *Siren Land*), Somerset Maugham, Roy Campbell, John Gawsworth, Rudyard Kipling (*Kim*, India and British colonialism), P.G. Wodehouse (most obviously in the Wodehousean humour of the Antrobus diplomatic stories, gentle humour aimed at a newspaper-reading audience, which mocks Englishness),[34] Aldous Huxley (the social satirist of *Chrome Yellow* and *Antic Hay*, the 'ideas' novelist of *Eyeless in Gaza* and the syncretic guru of *The Perennial Philosophy*),[35] Oscar Wilde (Irish wit), T.S. Eliot (precision in poetry, dry irony and cynicism), Wyndham Lewis (critical bombast)[36] and Dylan Thomas (dictionary-chewing word-mongering). And, of course, D.H. Lawrence. Durrell's description of his first book, *The Black Book*, neatly summarizes his 'influences': 'I think it's a book Huxley could have written if he were a mixture of Lawrence and Shakespeare.' (DML, 55) (Durrell is something of a *poseur*. He claimed that the first book he bought in French was *Les Chants de Maldoror*,[37] a story to be taken with a pinch of salt, like Durrell's anecdote about finding *Tropic of Cancer* in a lavatory.)

---

33 Gordon K. Thomas: "Joan and Juan: Christ and Eros", in Ker, 43
34 Typical of Durrell's Wodehousian style and humour in the Antrobus stories is this passage from "Stiff Upper Lip" (the title itself is archetypally 'English'): 'What wines! Wines to set dimples in the cheeks of the soul. Some were little demure white wines, skirts lifted just above the knee, as it were. Others just showed an elbow or an ankle. Others were as the flash of a nymph's thigh in the bracken. Wines in sable, wines in mink!' (AC, 109)
35 Aldous Huxley was reappraised during his centenary year, 1994, with the publication of articles and books by and about Huxley (*The Hidden Huxley*, ed. David Bradshaw, Faber 1994; Erica Wagner: "Brave new Huxley", *The Times*, 2 July 1994; Andrew Motion: "Whoosh of a nose in air", *The Observer*, 17 July 1994, 22). Durrell has to wait until 2012 for his centenary celebrations.
36 Durrell's ideas on art and culture chime with those of Wyndham Lewis at many points (in *Time and Western Man*, especially, but also in Lewis's *Tarr*, *The Apes of God*, and his writings on art, as critics have noted. (Reed Dasenbrock: "Death and the Counterlife of Heresy in Wyndham Lewis and Lawrence Durrell", in OMG I, 306-327)
37 "Entretien avec Lawrence Durrell", in MacNiven 1987, 373

Lawrence Durrell   62

Pursewarden writes on a postcard to one of his long-cherished literary heroes, D.H. Lawrence, that he thinks *Lady Chatterley's Lover* is a 'Taj Mahal' built on a fuck:

> My dear DHL. This side idolatry - I am simply trying not to copy your habit of building a Taj Mahal around anything as simple as a good f—k.'
> (B, 94)

In other words, Lawrence, Pursewarden reckons, founded an elaborate but ultimately artificial and synthetic philosophy on something as ordinary as sex. For Durrell, Lawrence was a bad artist but a great philosopher or mystic, because of what he was trying to achieve.

> I love him [Durrell wrote to T.S. Eliot] because he is a rotten artist at bottom! He is concerned with something that is beyond either his art or himself. I like the struggle in him - the heroic struggle.[38]

For Durrell, Lawrence's 'discovery of sex and eros was a breakthrough for us Anglo-Saxons' (Sanavio, 54).

> ...everything Lawrence touches, even a postcard, curls up at the edges with fire and liveliness. What a pity the methodist thing drove him to prophecy; and his thinking box is often in a bloody muddle. But he's the darling of eng. lit. despite every reservation. Currents run though him.
> (1959, Ald, 98)

In *Key to Modern Poetry* Durrell namechecks among his contemporaries poets such as Anne Ridler, Dylan Thomas, Robert Graves, William Empsom, W.H. Auden, T.S. Eliot, Kathleen Raine, George Barker, Edith Sitwell, Stephen Spender, C. Day-Lewis, Christopher Isherwood, Roy Campbell. Among these contemporaries, Durrell expressed his particular affection (in *Key to Modern Poetry* and other places) for Campbell, Barker, Eliot and Thomas. In *Key to Modern Poetry,* Eliot gets a chapter to himself, as one might expect, for Eliot's influence, particularly on British poets, has been huge (Auden and Yeats are far over-shadowed by Eliot in terms of

---

38 Durrell, letter, November 1938, in MacNiven 1987, 351. Richard Aldington also loved, even revered D.H. Lawrence. In a letter to Durrell (Christmas Eve, 1959) Aldington wrote about the way other writers were exalted by the literati but not Lawrence: 'Sickening the way the swine sentimentalise about RLS [Robert Louis Stevenson] and his TB, and never once give a much greater man the slightest mercy. I do more and more loathe the British - what fearful shits.' (Ald, 118)

influence. The influence of Auden on Durrell is just as strong as Lawrence, as Durrell acknowledged).

In his chapter on Eliot, Durrell discusses the relation between the cut-up style of cinema and *The Waste Land*, which is a common treatment of that poem (later on in his Eliot chapter, Durrell rejigs *The Waste Land* as if it were a radio play). Baudelaire and Laforgue, as well as Freud and J.G. Frazer, are referred to; again, time-honoured ways of approaching Eliot's poem. *The Four Quartets* is clearly more to Durrell's taste: while Durrell's approach to *The Waste Land* (and 'The Hollow Men' and 'Gerontion') allows for much pontification on societal decline, the discussion of *The Four Quartets* allows Durrell to return to the main critical theme of *Key to Modern Poetry* (and the *Quartet*): the merging of science and religion, East and West, where, as Werner Heisenberg noted, modern physics chimes with Heraclitus's fire and strife philosophy (71). *The Four Quartets*, Durrell notes, refer to mystics, some of whom are Durrell's favourites (such as Buddha and Lao tzu). In *The Four Quartets* Durrell sees a new affirmation of Oriental precepts, which he also endorses: non-attachment, non-action, going with the flow, unification of opposites, transcendence of the ego and so on (K, 160-2).

There is nothing exceptional in Durrell's appraisal of T.S. Eliot. More surprising, perhaps, is Durrell giving a whole chapter to Gerald Manley Hopkins (the only other poet to have a chapter to themselves in *Key to Modern Poetry*). Durrell makes the usual critical points about Hopkins' intense spiritual sense, and his 'strict discipline over form and emotion' (K, 165). It is as a stylist and craftsman that Durrell admires Hopkins. Durrell is impressed, for example, by Hopkins' invention of phrases such as 'thunder-purple' and 'very violet-sweet', the kind of hyphenations which poets employ when no other words seem to do the trick (Rilke was fond of such word-coining). One can see the influence of Hopkins' compact word magic in Durrell's own poetry, and prose (most notably in *The Alexandria Quartet*).

In much of *Key to Modern Poetry*, where Durrell is discussing other poets, he is coasting, simply relaying the basic information about each poet for the benefit of a student audience. He has his favourite poets, though, and his descriptions of them stand out from the ones he feels obliged to discuss, simply because they are part of the curriculum. Edward Thomas, for example, is a poet Durrell feels affection for: Thomas is a 'quietist', a 'pure contemplative', with a poetry of 'still piety', unsentimentality, 'delicacy of observation' and 'an extraordinary and felicitous gift of ear and feeling for emotional line' (K, 135-6).

Durrell is not convinced about Thomas Hardy. In the letters he speaks about the tiresome whingeing nature of Hardy's characters. In *Key to Modern Poetry* he allocates only four or five paragraphs to Hardy, whereas, for poets such as Ted Hughes, John Cowper Powys and Philip Larkin, Hardy is one of the modern masters. Durrell calls Hardy's poetry 'not formally graceful' (K, 111), although other critics have seen an astonishing range of different poetic forms in Hardy's poems, and an amazing command of style. Durrell found Hardy's poetry 'at its best... cold and exact and moving' (ib.). Durrell simply could not quite understand the attraction of Hardy: there was, perhaps, not enough affirmation of life in it for his tastes. Yet Durrell's own poetry is often 'cold and exact', detached and sceptical, ironic and dry. And at times Durrell's poems seem more despairing, in their own quiet way, than Hardy's.

Another 'influence' or parallel with Durrell, is William Wordsworth. Durrell edited a selection of Wordsworth's poetry for a Penguin book. Durrell used a saying of Wordsworth's ('...must itself create the taste by which it is to be judged') as an epigraph for his last work of fiction (*Quinx*). Durrell was fond of saying the same thing himself: '[e]very question *contains* the answer – it is built in'.[39]

Another parallel is Rainer Maria Rilke, not only because of the Lou Andreas-Salomé connection (though that was sufficiently intoxicating for Durrell), but because of Rilke's metaphysics of poetry, which chimes so often with Durrell's own æsthetics. Rilke's views on the relation between life and death and art, for example, as expressed in his letters and *Duino Elegies*, are Durrellian. Both poets had a complex view of death-consciousness, and how it related to time, life and art. In *Key* Durrell quotes from Rilke's letters which are so lyrical and full of insight into the 'Open', that 'open' world that surrounds initiates (usually lovers or artists) when they become acutely conscious of death (K, 36-7), thus enabling them to experience a spiritual continuity with (people in) the past, and maybe the future.

Other parallels are Lewis Carroll, whose dream worlds have their own inexplicable but persuasive logic. And Giordano Bruno, the Renaissance philosopher whose restless investigative mind resembles Sir Thomas Browne's (another star in the firmament of Durrell's influences and

---

39 Gordon K. Thomas: "Durrell and Wordsworth" (OMG II, 194)

favourites).

More influences included: Homer, Francois Rabelais, René Descartes, Maurice Maeterlinck, Henri Bergson, Dante Alighieri, William Blake and Paul Valéry. Alexandra David-Neels' book on Tibet and its customs and mysticism inspired him.[40] Many of these writers and influences Durrell devoured in the Reading Room of the British Museum (Freud, Jung and Groddeck, for instance). Reading Freud, Jung, Darwin and Groddeck, he said, led him towards Schopenhauer and Spengler.[41]

Durrell, like Gide, acknowledges the influence of Friedrich Nietzsche. In the book which might be regarded as the non-fiction companion to *The Avignon Quintet*, *The Smile in the Mind's Eye*, Durrell explores Nietzsche, and the relationship that Nietzsche had with Lou Andreas-Salomé. C.G. Jung's description of Nietzsche in *Memories, Dreams, Reflections* has affinities with the stereotypical images of many artists' mental state:

> Nietzsche had lost the ground under his feet because he possessed nothing more than the inner world of his thoughts – which incidentally possessed him more than he it. He was uprooted and hovered above the earth, and therefore he succumbed to exaggeration and irreality. For me, such irreality was the quintessence of horror, for I aimed, after, at *this* world and *this* life. (214)

Jung seems to be describing the typical state of the creative genius as a psychotic, a state of madness sometimes evoked in descriptions of Vincent van Gogh, Leonardo da Vinci and Beethoven, as well as Nietzsche.

The Nietzschean influence also comes through D.H. Lawrence, one of Durrell's heroes. Keith M. May is one of a few critics who have discussed the links between Lawrence and Nietzsche. Durrell regards Europe (*pace* Schopenhauer and Nietzsche) as a 'civilization based on the principle of the Will' (FMJ, 54). Ruth Adams, in *The Dark Labyrinth*, says (*pace* Oswald Spengler) that all of the West is 'based on the Will' (and the goal is to move into 'repose', into a participation '*with* everything' (DL, 244).

Matthew: Excellent, for when nothing begins to happen
   at long last Everything
Begins to cohere, the dance of the
   pure form begins. (*Faust*, 85)

40 Alexandra David-Neel: *My Journey to Lhasa*, Heinemann 1927; *With Magicians and Mystics in Tibet*, John Lane 1931
41 Durrell in *Construire*, 1985

The goal, Durrell said in an interview, is 'to win over the will to produce that inner order called love-in-time' (FWJ, 54).

Another cultural reference point for Durrell and *The Avignon Quintet* is Arthur Schopenhauer. *The Avignon Quintet* is loaded with cultural references, but they are mentioned in passing, as if casually. Yet they make up a precise cultural space firmly founded on the modern European tradition. So, when Constance questions Blanford about 'S', a product of Blanford's habit of scribbling in notebooks, he replies that 'S' stands for Schopenhauer. Sutcliffe, born in notebooks, starts out under the disguise of Schopenhauer, but soon emerges as a personality in his own right: a flippant, desperate, splintered, marginal, lonely and hunted intellectual (L, 115), whose method of setting himself to work on his novel is to recite the 'Lord's Prayer' putting a 'damn' between each word (L, 71). The choice of Schopenhauer is another indicator of the highly sophisticated cultural space of *The Avignon Quintet.* For Schopenhauer of course influenced the Germanic tradition which forms a subtext of *The Avignon Quintet,* and who influenced Nietzsche, and Freud. Schopenhauer, too, is one of the most gnostic of modern philosophers, his views according with Gnosticism and Buddhism, which are two of the more important strands of *The Avignon Quintet.*

Both Gide and Durrell absorbed the ascetic Gnosticism of the Middle East and the sensual paganism of Greece. Both writers play off rainy, dark, Puritan/ Protestant Northern Europe against the sunny, pagan Mediterranean world. Paganism, presided over by Pan and Aphrodite and other ancient gods, is Durrell's basic philosophy from the heraldic universe onwards. Like Gide, Lawrence, Miller and Rilke, Durrell was a prolific letter writer, and scribbles, letters, telegrams, notes and codes are found throughout his fiction.[42] Gide in *The Counterfeiters* created a novelist very much the ancestor of Durrell's Pursewarden, Blanford and Sutcliffe. For Gide's Edouard the writing of his novel, also called *The Counterfeiters,* is more interesting than the novel itself. Similarly, both Blanford and Sutcliffe are writing books called *Monsieur* and *The Prince of Darkness* in Durrell's *Monsieur.* For Gide's Edouard and Durrell's Blanford, the diary/ journal becomes more important than the artwork itself; and the act of *writing*

---

42 Durrell cited Gide's novel in *Key* (26)

about the art becomes more important than *making* the artwork itself.[43] As Gide's novelist says: 'the history of the book will have interested me more than the book itself'.[44] Indeed, so crucial was the 'Making of the book *The Counterfeiters*' to Gide that he published a book after *The Counterfeiters*, called precisely that, *The Journal of The Counterfeiters*, although he swore he'd never do that, despising artists 'explaining' their works.

Durrell, meanwhile, has not written many essays about literature. He does not write reviews, as other writers often do, but short travel pieces (collected in *Spirit of Place*, the title echoing D.H. Lawrence). Durrell's non-fiction consists of the six travel books: the short, poetic *Prospero's Cell, Reflections on a Marine Venus, Bitter Lemons,* widely regarded as his best travel book*, Sicilian Carousel,* the disappointing *The Greek Islands,* in which he seemed to be rushing through Greece,[45] and his last book, which was also disappointing, *Caesar's Vast Ghost.* This is the one 'major' work after *The Avignon Quintet*; it was a travel book which he paced wrongly, he reckoned. Indeed, *Caesar's Vast Ghost* reads as a footnote to *The Avignon Quintet.* For Durrell had done everything with Provence he wanted to do in the *Quintet.* All *Caesar's Vast Ghost* did was to add more of the same material. There is nothing new in *Caesar's Vast Ghost*, only some details that Durrell did not squeeze into *The Avignon Quintet.*

---

43 Art is also founded on essentially mysterious experiences and notions. In *Quinx*, Sut and Blan discuss the relation between art and life, recognizing that the root-source of life remains mysterious, it's a 'dark river flowing from nowhere to nowhere. The pen touching paper marks the point of intersection merely.' (Q, 52-3) The mistakes arise when critics mistake the point of intersection with the whole of life.
44 André Gide: *The Counterfeiters*, tr. Dorothy Bussy, Penguin, 1966, 170
45 Gregory Dickson: "Lawrence Durrell and the Traditional of Travel Literature", OMG II, 46

Durrell and Shakespeare

William Shakespeare, now called 'Shakespeare' in quotation marks, because 'he' is now a cultural edifice, a social phenomena, a socio-political entity, is the one writer with whom all British writers seem to have to grapple. One of the figures from literature who features in Lawrence Durrell's art in one form or another is Prospero. Durrell reckoned that Corfu was Prospero's island, and discussed the possibility in *Prospero's Cell*. In 'Cities, Plains and People', Durrell wrote:

> Prospero upon his island
> Cast in a romantic form,
> When his love was fully grown
> He laid his magic down. (CP, 161)

The figure of the magus is central to Durrell's version of the Faust myth, in his play *Faustus*. Faust appears in *The Revolt of Aphrodite*, this time in the characters of Julian, and Felix, though it is the English Faust that is cited - Merlin. Julian is Durrell's most ruthlessly Faustian figure, pursuing his alchemical quest, a Prince of Darkness with his cosmic *hubris*.[46] Julian is literally a demiurge who 'falls', like Lucifer, to his death, in St Paul's Cathedral. This scene is a comic parody of the Gnostic fall into matter. Fearmax, in *The Dark Labyrinth*, is another would-be magician, a provincial dilettante who obsessively consumes any occult book he can get his hands on (DL, 115f). Fearmax becomes 'a remarkable type of the provincial derailed by wide reading' (115).

The real reason for Durrell's fascination with Prospero is that Prospero, like Faust, is one of the great depictions of an artist, and *The Tempest* is one of the great works of literature about art, about the problems of making art, and, ultimately, about the redeeming magic of art. In a letter of July 1940, to Henry Miller, part of the 'famous correspondence', Durrell outlines his interpretation of Prospero and *The Tempest*:

> Here is this outcast holy man in his cell on Corcyra; his retreat is really voluntary, because he is dealing with reality, his many inner selves... in the epilogue you have the clue to the whole artistic stance. The gesture of renunciation is pure wizardry; artist laying down his medicine, releasing his spirits, and putting himself AS A HUMAN BEING at their mercy.... It was the artist who came away to the island: it was Shake-

46 J.R. Morrison: "Memory and Light in Lawrence Durrell's *The Revolt of Aphrodite*", Lab, 142

speare who came home as a man. (DML, 140)

The Avignon Quintet, then, is Durrell's version of *The Tempest*. The Prospero figure in *The Avignon Quintet* is partly Blanford, partly Sutcliffe, partly Affad, partly Constance, but mostly Durrell himself. For *The Avignon Quintet* is the work in which Durrell takes leave of his craft. In *The Avignon Quintet*, Durrell breaks his staff and ends his 'rough magic'; 'he falls upon his sword, blessing; not cringing like Hamlet or Macbeth', Durrell writes (DML, 140), and this is the aim of *The Avignon Quintet*, to produce the sweetness and roundedness of dying. As Durrell puts it in 'The Anecdotes':

Sometime we shall all come together
And it will be time to put a stop
To this little rubbing together of minimal words... (CP, 206)

The sense of an ending pervades the *Quintet*, and Blanford's and Sutcliffe's struggles with their books echoes Prospero's struggle to free himself of his art and magic. The farewells to magic of Prospero are echoed especially in *Quinx*, not least in that ending, where all the characters enter the caves, so like the final scene of a play, or like curtain calls. The ending of *Quinx* recalls Prosper's leavetaking speeches in *The Tempest*:

Our revels now are ended. These our actors,
As I foretold you, were all spirits, and
Are melted into air, into thin air;
And, like the baseless fabric of this vision,
The cloud-capp'd towers, the gorgeous palaces,
The solemn temples, the great globe itself,
Yea, all which it inherit, shall dissolve,
And, like this insubstantial pageant faded,
Leave not a rack behind. We are such stuff
As dreams are made on; and our little life
Is rounded with a sleep. (4.1.148-158)

Charles Arrowby, protagonist of Iris Murdoch's 1978 novel *The Sea, the Sea*, is also a Prospero figure, retiring to a house encircled by the sea. The affinities between Murdoch's novel and *The Avignon Quintet* are obvious: Charles Arrowby, for instance, is interested in 'writing my life... as a novel',[47] just like Blanford and Sutcliffe (and Darley, Pursewarden, etc). Charles muses on the prospects of self-fictionalization: 'if one had time to

47 Iris Murdoch: *The Sea, The Sea*, Granada, 1978, 153

write the whole of one's life... as a novel how rewarding this would be' (in ib., 99).

The atmosphere of *The Tempest* is very much in tune with the temperament of Durrell's fictions. The combination of warmth and melancholy, of despair set against idealism, of sensuality mixed with asceticism, which marks *The Tempest*, is an important ingredient in Durrell's art. The atmosphere of resignation and acquiescence of *King Lear*, where 'ripeness is all', is also apparent in *The Avignon Quintet. The Tempest* counters *King Lear*'s resignation and pain with a new warmth, vision and hope. *The Avignon Quintet* veers between the despair of *King Lear* and the affirmation of *The Tempest,* ending up, significantly, at a new affirmation of life, which is firmly embedded in the stance of Oriental philosophy. *The Tempest* is the closest Shakespeare gets to Taoism, to the acquiescence and balance of *yin* and *yang* working together, the mythic 'harmony of opposites'. Durrell notes the Taoist slant of *The Tempest*:

> This last poignant verse [the Epilogue] is really a pure statement of the Hamlet-Prince theme: but with the problem resolved in Tao. (DML, 140)

But Shakespeare only gets to the relative calm and repose of *The Tempest* after the trials and agonies of *Hamlet, King Lear* and *A Winter's Tale.* Durrell writes:

> You can look at the whole of Shakespeare's work through this final lens of the telescope, and you see the diminished figures of Hamlet and Lear and Macbeth, like in the wrong end of the telescope. In the new dimension which he found beside the Avon at Stratford the emphasis on the struggle was no longer important; it was better to smile and bless and enfold. So that the epilogue is a little benediction on a world which he at last allowed to *wound him to the quick*; in *Hamlet* and *Lear* he had been fighting against the death, like the neurotic fighting, with the cold wheels of his will-power. (DML, 140)

The Tempest is the end of the fight. Durrell naturally finds so many resonances with *The Tempest* because, as he writes to Henry Miller, '*The Tempest* is like one long quiet smile' (DML, 141). This quiet smile is precisely the effect Durrell would like his work to have, and *The Avignon Quintet* strives for this Taoist smile, 'the smile in the mind's eye', as Durrell says in his book of the same title. Hamlet and Faust, like *Crime and Punishment* and *The Wasteland*, were part 'of the Western world's guilt cycle', as Durrell put it, the struggle of the opposites which's resolved in the figure of Lao tzu.[48]

'Now I want/ Spirits to enforce, art to enchant', says Prospero (*The Tempest*, Epilogue), sentiments which Durrell would endorse wholeheartedly. The parallels between himself and Shakespeare would not be lost on Durrell. After all, he remains very much a British writer, and Shakespeare is the God of British literature. In reaching his final major work, *The Avignon Quintet*, Durrell must have been conscious (for he is a very self-conscious writer) of the Shakespearean parallels. He had already used Shakespeare before, most notably *Antony and Cleopatra* in *The Alexandria Quartet* (Shakespeare via Plutarch and Cavafy),[49] as well debating *Hamlet* with Henry Miller. There are many points in which the *Quartet* chimes with Shakespeare's *Antony and Cleopatra*. Justine, for example, is compared to a mindless, primeval Aphrodite or Venus, a holy whore, just like Shakespeare's Cleopatra.[50]

48 Notebook, late 1930s, quoted In R. Pine, 1994, 75.
49 Carol Peirce: ""One other gaudy night": Lawrence Durrell's Elizabethan *Quartet*", in Ker, 112.
50 J, 77, B, 115, M, 205, Moore, 158. Carol Peirce: ""A Lass Unparallel'd": The Memory of Shakespeare's Cleopatra in *The Alexandria Quartet*", OMG II, 177.

4

The Book of Miracles: Artistic Parallels, Theories and People in *The Avignon Quintet* and Other Works

What Lawrence Durrell does in *The Avignon Quintet* is to include the metafiction within the fiction. He includes the discussions about the writing of the book within the book itself. Instead of an essay about the manufacture of *The Avignon Quintet,* it is woven into the novels. Sutcliffe and Blanford are writing different versions of the same book. In a similar way, Henry Miller and Anaïs Nin enjoyed a symbiotic creative relationship, where they discussed their books and exchanged ideas. (When Miller met Nin, he reckoned she was a formidable woman who made D.H. Lawrence seem 'small by comparison'.[1]) Nin writes in a letter to Miller:

> *Your* book swells up inside of me like my very *own* – more joyously even than my own, for *your* book is for me a fecundation, while mine is an act of narcissism… I'm *glorying* in your immense plans, in your ideas

1 Miller, letter to Emil Schnellock, October 1932, Henry Miller Collection, UCLA

Lawrence Durrell   73

- those talks of ours, Henry, how they *rebound,* they are so firm – Henry there will never be drabness because in both of us there is always movement, renewal, surprises.[2]

Blanford and Sutcliffe do not speak of each other's work in the same warm way, but then, they are not lovers. Even so, the Sut-Blan relation is at times like a noisy marriage, with arguments over trivialities followed by affectionate reunions. Durrell too must have enjoyed this kind of artistic symbiosis – he speaks lovingly of the Paris years with Nin and Miller, and of writing *Justine* on a typewriter with his wife Claude working at the other end of the table (DML, 279). Towards the end of *Constance* Sutcliffe tries to negotiate with Blanford about his own future. As Caliban to Blanford's (and Durrell's) Prospero, Sutcliffe has to do pretty much what Blanford wishes. Sut and Blan exchange their views on the way the novel – the *Quintet* itself – will proceed. But Sutcliffe is no Ariel, and goes along doggedly.

The Avignon Quintet is a postmodern work in this sense, then, in this self-reflexivity. *The Alexandria Quartet* is founded on modernist tenets – the post-Bergsonian exploration of space and time, something found in the work of Marcel Proust, Jim Joyce and Sam Beckett (from Proustian-Bergsonian *durée* to Einsteinian space-time). 'The ground plan, if I can do it', wrote Durrell, in the midst of writing the tetralogy, 'is four books of which the first two fit into each other – different but the same book – Giordano Bruno!' (DML, 287) Durrell was careful to keep his form (in the *Quartet*) under control: in *Key to Modern Poetry,* Durrell discussed modernists such as Henry James, joseph Conrad, Bertie Lawrence, Virginia Woolf and James Joyce in the light of William James's notion of 'stream of consciousness' and Henri Bergson's 'duration'. What the ideas of James and Bergson did, Durrell reckoned, was to destroy the sense of form, which ruined Lawrence's novels, and made Woolf tiring to read (K, 116-7).

The Avignon Quintet is halfway between modernism and post-modernism, perhaps, a wannabe postmodern text, recalling Thomas Pynchon, V.S. Naipaul, J.G. Ballard, Paul Auster and late Samuel Beckett. The self-reflexivity in *The Avignon Quintet* is relentless. It is a self-portrait of a novel, a series of novels which mirror each other. As Constance so accurately cries: '[l]ove! It's all done by mirrors!' (C, 30) This describes neatly the Freudian view of love as narcissism, the Lacanian 'mirror stage' taken to extremes. The narcissism of love which is found through Durrell's

---

2 Anaïs Nin: *A Literate Passion,* 99

fiction is echoed in the mirror-imaging, the *mise-en-âbyme*, the self-reflexivity of his fictions.3 His novelist characters are incessant scribblers, they have 'amazing eloquence', and Darley, Justine, Felix, Arnauti, Balthazar, Purse-warden, Leila, Liza, Keats, Clea, Mountolive, Blanford, Sutcliffe, Constance, the Prince and Benedicta are all writers, in one way or another. They are like Anaïs Nin, who produced hundreds of pages of her journal.

André Gide too produced huge amounts of diary material. With Gide, and perhaps Nin, one gets the impression that as they are living they are wondering how their experiences will be later written up in some journal or novel. Life becomes fused with art in a new, prescient way: even as Gide experiences something, he's wondering how to present it in literature. This is Blanford's problem, and Durrell's problem as a narrator in his novels, and as a writer in the midst of real life. Even as Pursewarden is fucking Melissa, he is also writing, far below the realms of self-disgust and humiliation (M, 155). For Pursewarden, life and art are interchangeable and simultaneous. Even as it's lived, experiences are turned into art.

Which is the more 'real', life or art? This is one key question all Durrell's fiction poses, and *The Avignon Quintet* in particular explores. Gide was shocked and saddened when he found his letters to his wife had been destroyed. 'My entire work is inclined towards her', Gide wrote, 'I wrote everything to convince her, to win her esteem. It's all but one long plea'.4 Similarly, Pursewarden's main love (perhaps only love) was his sister and his prized piece of writing was not his novels but his love letters to her, which she burnt (maybe this was inspired by Gide). For Gide and Durrell, personal truths come out not in art but in letters, which are part of everyday life, existing in an in-between zone, halfway between art and life. There is an *art* to letter-writing, but letters concern life not art. It is in these places, in the 'margins' of life as Durrell puts it often, that true life is lived. Often his characters scribble in the margins of some book or other, or on a napkin in a café, or an envelope, on in lipstick on the dressing table mirror.

Darley raves madly about Pursewarden's letters, which're '[f]erocious, sulky, brilliant, profuse'. They are literature, nay, life itself, illusion and

---

3 There are more than 120 mirrors in *The Alexandria Quartet*, not counting synonyms and cognate forms. (Ray Morrison: "Mirrors and the Heraldic Universe in Lawrence Durrell's *The Alexandria Quartet*", in MacNiven 1987, 500)
4 Gide: *Et nunc manet in te*, 77

reality in one, a 'single blinding vision', full of 'tremendous sorrow and beauty', '[t]he cruelty and the richness!' (152) Wow. So incredible are Pursewarden's letters, they are burning to be quoted and analyzed at length. But no. Darley (Durrell) does not quote even a single line to demonstrate how amazing they are. We have only had snippets of Pursewarden's novels quoted to us, so we are very unsure about their 'greatness', for Pursewarden's other portentous sayings make us doubt his talent. There are quotes from other letters by Pursewarden, and also the long "My Conversations with Brother Ass". But, of course, the deeply ironic thing is that, though Pursewarden is regarded by Darley (and Durrell) as a great writer, greater than Durrell himself, Durrell cannot write better than Pursewarden. Pursewarden's greatness in literature can only be as great as Durrell's: because the extracts from Pursewarden's books and letters must be written, finally, by Durrell. In suggesting Pursewarden's greatness, Durrell cannot actual *show it*. Pursewarden, then, is the *suggestion* of greatness, but when it comes to actually showing it, he fails, as Durrell fails. Even Keats, the journalist turned into a man of action in *Clea,* prates portentously about 'the writer's struggle' (Cl, 160).

Durrell employs many novelistic tricks to further his exploration of the interrelatedness of art and life. He has Justine seen first in a mirror, and sitting in front of an array of mirrors. *Justine* is the 'book of mirrors'.[5] Sutcliffe snaps his fingers at his reflection, or stares at it during shaving, as does Pursewarden. And of course many of his characters are writers. If one is a writer, then where does real life end and art begin? Which has more authenticity, writing or living? Is writing living in itself? Or is writing merely an escape from living? Is art a refuge, an edifice built on life, feeding off it, parasitically? Is art merely a castle in the air?

In a letter of March 1975, during the writing of *Livia*, Durrell wrote to Henry Valentine Miller: 'I have done 100 pages of the new book and have begun 'merging'. My 'real' characters are beginning to interfere in the lives of my 'imagined' ones. One should soon begin to get a marvellous sense of vertigo – stereo-scopic vertigo.' (DML, 478) And again: 'wow, it is getting delicate as the so-called 'real' characters are getting infiltrated and changed by the 'imagined' characters of their own creation' (DML, 487). Durrell refuses to distinguish between 'real' people and 'imaginary personæ'.[6]

In a speech at Pennsylvania State University, Durrell remarked that he

5 John Unterecker: "The Protean World of Lawrence Durrell", CE, 181
6 Bernard Bergonzi, in *Gemini,* 1, no 1, Spring 1957, 26-27

enjoyed finding that his characters were 'making babies everywhere, so to speak' ("Overture", OMG, 11). Durrell created many conceits, where he fuses 'real' characters and fictional ones. Blanford discusses his fictional creation Sutcliffe with no less a personage than Albert Einstein (Q, 23), which is the modern-day equivalent of having a chat with Socrates, Plato or Jesus. On the other hand, the casual conversation with Einstein is not so far-fetched, for Durrell has Sutcliffe conversing with Sigmund Freud about Pia. These two men, Freud and Einstein, form with Karl Marx the trinity of philosophers who typify Western thought for Durrell. Marx is not involved in person with the other characters, but Durrell does mention materialism a lot, often in connection with Martin Luther.

Durrell reserves a special vehemence for the propounders of various forms of Christianity, whether Catholic, Protestant, Puritan or otherwise – Luther, Calvin, St Augustine.[7] Marx might well have appeared in person in *The Avignon Quintet*. After all, communism was popular in 1930s Oxford and Cambridge, and there are references to Aubrey's time at Oxford. Durrell, though, is much further to the right, politically, than fellow Thirties writers such as Dylan Thomas, George Orwell, A.L. Rowse and Stephen Spender. With his love of royalty, cosmopolitan living and aristocrats, Durrell's politics are more those of T.S. Eliot, Durrell's mentor at Faber and Faber, who was a firm monarchist. Durrell's politics are conservative (small 'c'), liberal and humanist (Durrell acknowledged that his politics were conservative and reactionary and right-wing). And, like Eliot, Royalist, though not quite in Eliot's sense:

> ...if I am a Royalist it is in the biological sense – the only political creed possible to a poet I think, which is ultimately *only* interested in values and not politics at all.[8]

Other cultural references, which firmly site *The Avignon Quintet* within a European tradition, as well as a British tradition, include:
• Piers having a copy of *À Rebours* (M, 29), for Piers has many of the

7 Richard Aldington concurred with Durrell's loathing of Christianity: he has the same criticism as Durrell, that there is not much in the *Bible* to laugh about. 'My objection to Jesus and the other rhinos has always been that there isn't a laugh in the whole bloody bible from Gen I to Rev last.' (16 August 1960, Ald, 147)
8 Durrell, letter, September 1958, in Ald, 54. In an interview Durrell desribed himself as, unusually, a 'nothingist' (Joan S. Goulianos: "A Conversation with Lawrence Durrell", *Modern Fiction Studies*, 17, 1971, 159f)

attributes of Huysmans' decadent æsthete who takes up, dilettante-fashion, philosophical fads;

• Stendhal, where Sutcliffe says he has a case of 'the old Stendhalian crystallisation' (M, 186). Durrell mentioned the 'crystallisation' process of Stendhal (in Stendhal's *De l'Amour*) in relation to his own love affairs;

• Akkad alludes to the angels and theosophy of Emmanuel Swedenborg, William Blake and Rainer Maria Rilke (M, 218);

• Piers is suffocated by *Seraphita* by Honoré de Balzac (M, 233);

• Blanford refers to the 'double' syndrome of Arthur Rimbaud (C, 359). Durrell wrote a poem with the title taken from a famous saying of Rimbaud's: 'Je est un autre', and Durrell sent me a French magazine with articles about Rimbaud. (I'd written to about Rimbaud, among other maters);

• Van Gogh of course appears in these Provençal novels (L, 245), as also in poems such as 'A Patch of Dust' (In all this summer dust O Vincent/ You passed through my loyal mind' CP, 337);

• Aldous Huxley is revered by Blanford, and Blanford is very much a Huxleyesque novelist, a novelist who muses upon ideas ('[Livia] had left him the new Huxley, his favourite writer, with the first essay on the nature of Zen Buddhism in it, the very first mention of Suzuki, which had opened like a shaft of light in the depths of his skull.' *Constance*, 11). In a letter of November, 1955, Durrell writes in a Blanford mode: 'I'm deep into Zen Buddhist treatises these days – Suzuki! What a marvellous *speechless* religion.' (DML, 278)

One could go on listing the cultural references in *The Avignon Quintet* for ages. The ones mentioned above do not include the major influences or strands in the book: Gnosticism and the Knights Templar; Freud and psychoanalysis; and Taoist/ Oriental love-magic. Significantly, Durrell does not mention D.H. Lawrence much, if at all, for Lawrence underpins so much of the love relationships – in *Constance* especially (Durrell calls the book 'Constance in Love', echoing Lawrence with his *Women in Love* [DML, 497]). Perhaps Durrell wished to keep the D.H. Lawrence connection intact by not mentioning it very often (although a reference to *Sons and Lovers* occurs in *Constance*, 13).

The Blanford-Sutcliffe dialogues have many purposes, ranging from humour, bawdy banter, rewriting nursery rhymes, mottoes, maxims, to diatribes and mini-essays on 'serious' themes. The word-games are set side by side with the 'serious' conjectures. This is a typical selection:

Blanford to Sutcliffe: "Reading your verse is like dredging a pond without ever finding the body.' (Q, 138)

Throughout his career, Durrell has always loved inventing words and writing silly juxtapositions. Toby suggests an 'amazement' of women as a collective noun. Aubrey suggests some more: '[p]ride of lions, skirl of loafers, extravagance of poets.' (L, 205) Durrell is always shifting shapes swiftly, changing the points and zipping onto a new track. In the next sentence Sutcliffe thinks: 'he would go far away, he would eat liquid mud on toast in faraway Turkish khans.' (L, 205)

The humorous squibs and maxims blur into more serious material. The Sutcliffe-Blanford muses often have a serious, incisive edge to them. There are meditations upon Freud, psychoanalysis, the influence of Luther, the Popes, Judæo-Christianity, technology, morality, cinema, painting, etc.

A few lines after Blanford's musings in the Café Dôme in Paris, Blanford thinks:

He was surrounded by Africans with beautiful fuzzy heads and booming tones They had all come to Paris to gather culture. Here they were, screaming for worm-powders. What was to be done? Great sweet turbines of black flesh innocently cutting slices of Keats or Rimbaud for their evening meal. A wholesome cannibalism when you thought of it. *O Grand Sphincterie des Romains*! O spice routes of the poetic mind which lead to the infernal regions below the subliminal threshold. Metaphors too big for their boots, literature of the S-bend. Wind in an old chimney – fatherly flatus? (L, 205)

Sadly, Blanford and Sutcliffe are often racist and anti-semitic in their eloquent discourses. The anti-Jewish flavour of much of *The Avignon Quintet* is problematic in a series of novels which deal with the infamous Nazi era. Irony is uppermost, of course, in Durrell's novelist protagonists, but all too often the irony cannot undermine the racism of the conversations. As Sutcliffe ruminates, in anti-semitic mode:

The future is more visible from France than anywhere because the French push everything to extremes. An audio-judeo-visual age is being born – the Mouton-Rothschild epoch where the pre-eminence of Jewish thought is everywhere apparent, which explains the jealousy of the Germans. (L, 174)

Of course, Durrell (appears to) despise Nazis and fascism, but there are problematic devices employed in *The Avignon Quintet*. For instance, the General, von Esslin, is a major character, he has whole chapters to himself. We do not see the Jewish viewpoint in similar detail. There are characters such as the Jewish psychoanalyst, Schwartz, but the Jewish, gypsy and homosexual viewpoint is not as powerfully represented.

In the *Quartet* too anti-semitism raises its ugly head: Pursewarden rails against Jews (C, 132), while in an interview Durrell said: 'the thing I have not marched well with is all the hebraic giber we have incorporated into our view of Christianity.'[9] In fact, Durrell is wrong here: another view suggests that Christianity contaminated Judaism, for there are many aspects of Christianity that are heresy and unthinkable for Judaism. For instance, the crucifixion of the messiah, the blasphemous identification (by St Paul) of the worshipper with God, the bizarre idea that the messiah died but did not die, that the messiah 'was actually God sacrificed to God'. These notions of early Christianity were 'preposterous and blasphemous in Judaic terms. They were also preposterous and blasphemous in classic Greek terms.'[10]

So often Durrell attacks Jews and Judaism, as if they were the cause of Europe's (and the world's) many ills. Durrell merely replays the age-old system where Jews are eternal scapegoats. Not only is his view politically offensive, it is also intellectually and historically untrue.[11] It is too easy and too simplistic to 'blame' the Jews, or the 'brilliant Jewish thinkers' who seem to dominate world philosophy (C, 319). Matters of European history are infinitely more complicated than that. Durrell is at his worst when he is prating about such political notions.

Another meeting of 'real' and 'fictional' people occurs in Vienna when Pia and Sutcliffe meet Sigmund Freud. They meet one of the most extraordinary women of recent times, who had an affair with Friedrich Nietzsche and Rainer Maria Rilke, and studied with Freud. These three names are enough to send Durrell's head spinning. Nietzsche, Rilke and Freud! It's incredible, but Lou Andreas-Salomé knew them well.[12]

---

9 Durrell, in Kenneth Young, 3
10 Weston La Barre, 1972, 608
11 Durrell may be right about monotheism, though: for monotheism marks the dramatic change from a panoply or pantheon of deities to just one, all-powerful deity: 'the great definitive point of sheer cleavage in the evolution of the European psyche seems to have come with monotheism', Durrell writes in *Caesar's Vast Ghost* (78).
12 see Angela Livingstone: *Lou Andreas-Salomé: Her Life and Works*, Moyer Bell, New York 1984

Anaïs [Nin] just sent me a biography of Lou [Andreas-Salome] by [H.F.] Peters which is marvellous [wrote Durrell in 1973], it was Lou who started off this whole thing in Geneva – her wicked sexy spirit – the spirit of the Great Instigators, like that of Anaïs herself!' (DML, 466)

Durrell wrote, in a letter to Anaïs Nin, in 1972:

I have always thought of you as a sort of incarnation of Lou Salomé in your knowledge and feeling for artists. Why has not more justice been done to her name?[13]

In *Livia* (published in 1978) Durrell depicts Andreas-Salomé as 'a dramatic and beautiful Slav whose extravagant and fleshy *ampleur* was somehow wholly sexy and composed' (187). She was an inspiring woman, quite brilliant, who ignited Rilke poetically as well as sexually. She knew Hugo von Hofmannsthal, Arthur Schnitzler, Jakob Wasserman, Richard Wagner, Leo Tolstoy, Ivan Turgenev and George Brandes. 'Europe's cultural élite paid homage to Lou Salomé', wrote H.F. Peters.[14]

Friedrich Nietzsche was besotted with Andreas-Salomé, calling her 'sharp-sighted as an eagle and courageous as a lion'.[15] French feminist Sarah Kofman has wondered whether Lou Andreas-Salomé was a model for that narcissitic woman which men love, the type that demand to be loved. Kofman considers this narcissistic woman in relation to Nietzsche, and wonders whether Lou Andreas-Salomé was the mediator of the theory of narcissism between Nietzsche and Freud.[16]

Lou Andreas-Salomé was the only erotic/ philosophic focus in Nietzsche's otherwise celibate experience of women.[17] Andreas-Salomé's notion of the narcissistic woman, and her thoughts on the artist, influenced Nietzsche. She was an independent thinker, quite the equal of any of the intellectual minds with which she came into contact. 'She was strikingly beautiful,' writes Rilke's biographer, Donald Prater, 'although thoroughly

13 quoted in Nin, *Journals*, vol. 7, 252
14 H.F. Peters: *Rainer Maria Rilke: Masks and the Man*, University of Washington Press, Seattle 1960, 52
15 Nietzsche: *Briefe an Peter Gast*, Leipzig, 1924, 89-90
16 Sarah Kofman: *L'Enigma de la femme:: La femme dans les textes de Freud*, Galilée, Paris, 1980. See also Biddy Martin: *Woman and Modernity: The (Life)Styles of Lou Andreas-Salomé*, Cornell University Press, Ithaca 1991
17 Janet Lungstrum: "Nietzsche Writing Woman/ Woman Writing Nietzsche", in Burgard, 144

'liberated' in ideas and scornful of convention, had led a life in which, despite appearances, heterosexual love played no part.' (37) The fiercely individual Lou Andreas-Salomé is surely one of the models for Durrell's Sabine.

Andreas-Salomé's creative woman is a type Durrell has much sympathy with: the Nietzschean (male) artist, if he is lucky, can aspire to the creativity of the women, to become a 'birther' (*Gebärerin*), which may make him 'more whole, more organic, fused... with what he creates, just as woman is,' said Andreas-Salomé in her essay "Die in sich ruhende Frau", 'and maintains him as it were in a joy of spiritual pregnancy, which lives deep within itself.'[18] These Saloméan-Nietzschean notions of the self-birthing of the artist and woman are central to Durrell's post-Rankian economy of creativity. ('One is growing with one's books', says Durrell (Mon, 121).

The Rilke-Andreas-Salomé romance has affinities with the spiritual, idealistic – and incestuous – affairs in Durrell's fiction. Rilke and Andreas-Salomé went about Russia hand in hand; they were, Andreas-Salomé said later, 'like brother and sister, but from primeval times before incest became a sacrilege';[19] they were, according Andreas-Salomé, a Neoplatonic unity: 'body and soul indivisibly one' (ib., 9). For Rilke, being with Lou Andreas-Salomé was a very rich, even an ecstatic experience. It enriched him and his art immensely. She was very much his Muse as well as lover, a profound inspiration on his art (Blanford sees Livia in the same adoring light, and also Darley with Clea).

Lou Andreas-Salomé's views on sexuality, too, were individualistic, and chime with some of Durrell's views. For instance, Andreas-Salomé distinguished between physical sex and spiritual bonds: 'I have never been able to understand why people physically in love with one another get married', she wrote.[20] As the relationship waned, Andreas-Salomé extracted herself gently from it.

Rilke, meanwhile, was far more deeply in love with her than she was with him (again, a situation common in Durrell's work). For Rilke, love was a spiritual occurrence which needed to be celebrated with 'deep and quiet festivals':

18 Andreas-Salomé: "Die in sich ruhende Frau", in *Zur Psychologie der Frau*, ed. Gisela Brinker-Gabler, Fischer, Frankfurt, 1978, 295-6.
19 Lou Andreas-Salomé: *Lebenstrückblick*, ed. Ernst Pfeiffer, Insel-Taschenbuch, Frankfurt 1974, 138
20 Lou Andreas-Salomé: ib, 288

It is not enough for two people to recognize one another, it is enormously important for them to find each other at the right time and celebrate together deep and quiet festivals in which they can grow together in their desires, if they are to be united against the storms of life...[21]

Again this is a view of love found in Durrell's work, particularly in *The Avignon Quintet*, where, towards the end of the sequence, the lovers (Constance and Affad, Constance and Blanford) learn how to celebrate love with 'deep and quiet festivals' (there is a depth and silence, for instance, symbolized in the early morning swims in the river, where Constance and Blanford are breathing softly among the lilies).

Lawrence Durrell includes 'real' characters, such as Adolf Hitler and Heinrich Himmler, Maurice Chevalier singing a song, Edith Piaf's cracked voice, the poet Giuseppe Ungaretti, who mix with the fictional characters. He includes too characters from earlier fictions, such as Balthazar (S, 2), Pursewarden, Brigadier Maskelyne, Mountolive, etc (C, 149). Melissa, Darley's lover in *Justine*, appears: Affad returns to Alexandria, to his home town, and finds Melissa staring out to sea, like the French Lieutenant's Woman.[22] They go back to his flat, and make love (S, 45). Through sex, then, Affad is connected to Darley, Justine, Pursewarden, Nessim, Capodistra, the cast of characters from *The Alexandria Quartet*. By sex too, through Affad, the cast of the *Quartet*'s characters are connected via Constance to Blanford, Livia, Hilary, Sam, Smirgel, etc.

In Lawrence Durrell's art, characters are connected sexually, as well as in other ways.[23] Thus, Justine sleeps with Nessim, with Pursewarden, with Darley; Nessim sleeps with Melissa; Melissa sleeps with Cohen, Darley and Pursewarden; Darley sleeps with Clea, as does Pursewarden; Mountolive sleeps with Leila, the ballet dancer and Liza. Similarly, in *The Avignon Quintet*, Constance has sex with Sam, with an undergraduate, with Affad, with Schwarz, and with Blanford. Blanford has sex with Livia, with the nurse in Egypt, with the British student, the hop-picker in Kent, and with

21 Rilke: *Briefwechsel Rainer Maria Rilke und Lou Andreas-Salome*, Inser Verlag, Leipzig, 1975, 26
22 Like many novelists, Durrell has said: 'I like to think that there is a family feeling about my books and here and there a character from an early book may stray into a later book' (FEB, 7).
23 'for Mr Durrell [sex] has immense and mysterious importance.' (Cecily Mackworth: "Lawrence Durrell and the New Romanticism", W, 33)

others; Livia has sex with Hilary, Blanford, Felix, Smirgel; Sutcliffe has sex with Pia, Trash and Sabine. The main characters in Durrell's art have sex with each other in various permutations, forming love-triangles, squares, and circles.

This is an old technique: Durrell's *The Avignon Quintet* thus becomes a continuum with *The Alexandria Quartet* and *The Revolt of Aphrodite*. Other British writers who have created alternative universes featuring characters from previous fictions include Michael Moorcock with his Jerry Cornelius series and Anthony Powell with his *A Dance to the Music of Time*, a series with many similarities with Durrell's fiction.

Many writers have noted that their characters often become 'real', and start living lives of their own.[24] The puppets walk and talk. Fiction occupies a psychological, cultural space, and we live in psychological, cultural spaces as well as physical, biological spaces. So it's no surprise to see Durrell extending the actuality of his characters into 'real' life. Much of our environment is psychological and cultural, as French philosophers and feminists note.[25] If we do live more in cultural spaces than 'natural' or biological ones, that is, if we live in a mental state, where thinking and feeling is crucial, then it's quite easy for one character from one fiction to slip into another fiction. Durrell breaks very few rules when he has Pursewarden appearing in the *Quincunx*.

To compound the relation between art and life, Durrell includes in *The Avignon Quintet* various 'appendixes', such as *The Last Will and Testament of Peter the Great,* which aim to add authenticity to his fictions. A more light-hearted 'appendix' is the menu of the Prince's banquet on the Pont du Gard, printed at the back of *Livia* (265). A more tricksy device is where Durrell has Pursewarden place an asterisk in a novel which refers the reader to a blank page (B, 120), and Durrell himself does this in his *The Alexandria Quartet*. André Gide began his writing career by referring to

---

24 Durrell enjoyed 'minor' characters, he valued the myth-making that created those second rank fictional characters – P.G. Wodehouse's Jeeves rather than James Joyce's Stephen. In his unpublished essay "The Minor Mythologies" Durrell wondered 'how delightful a book on the minor mythologies of the age could be', and cited fictional figures such as Bulldog Drummond, Raffles, Captain Nemo, Dracula, Frankenstein, Fu Manchu, Holmes and Captain Blood (15).

25 Simone de Beauvoir says that 'women are made, not born', while Julia Kristeva, Hélène Cixous and Alice Jardine go even further, claiming that 'woman' does not 'exist': 'she' is a 'writing-effect', existing only in language.

the act of writing. For instance, in his first work, *Paludes*, Gide's narrator included a space for the reader to add to a list of 'Most Remarkable Phrases'. [26]

Like the readymades of Marcel Duchamp or the multi-media 'paintings' of Jasper Johns, Durrell's fictions, like Gide's *The Counterfeiters,* destroy the diegetic effect of fiction, its naturalism and 'believability'.

To cover himself for attacks that he has played around with history, Durrell includes a note at the end of *Livia*: '[r]eaders who remark a slight divergence between so-called "real" history and the order of events adopted in this novel will, it is hoped, accord the author a novelist's indulgence.' (L, 264) This note is of itself an odd thing, as if Durrell could foresee critics leaping on his 'mistakes'. But the note also contains Durrell's own ironic view of 'truth', when he calls history 'so-called', and includes quotation marks around the word 'real'. Indeed, the word 'real' should always have quotation marks around it, and especially here in this novel sequence which pivots so much on the relation between the 'real' and the imagined. 'Art is what the artist *invents*', says Constantine Cavafy (my italics). [27] And Mallarmé said that the aim is 'to suggest and not to describe.' [28]

These appendixes and notes reveal how much reading and research Lawrence Durrell did in order to make *The Avignon Quintet* more interesting and 'authentic'. Indeed, he includes a note at the beginning of the key novel of the series, *Constance*, which states:

> This book is a fiction and not a history, but it is based on innumerable conversations and a residence of fifteen years in Provence; though here and there I may have taken a liberty with the chronology of an ignoble period, the sum of the matter has a high degree of impressionistic accuracy as a portrait of the French Midi during the late war. I have also studied serious historians like Kenward but owe more to French sources like the books of M. Aimé Vielzeuf of Nîmes.

'Impressionistic accuracy' describes well Durrell's aim, for clearly he is mixing in *The Avignon Quintet* his own recollection of the war and that of other people, both people he's known and people he's read. Happily Durrell mixes sequences of what could be autobiography with pure fiction.

---

26 André Gide: *Paludes,* Secker & Warburg 1953, 95
27 Cavafy, in Alithersis, 41
28 Mallarmé, in Anna Balakian: *The Fiction of the Poet*, Princeton University Press 1992, in *Sulfur*, no. 34, Spring 1994, 224

For instance, during the writing of the *Quintet* in the Seventies, Durrell went down the Nile and back to Egypt with a film crew. These 'real life' events are echoed in the texts. Durrell spent time in many of the places he describes in the *Quintet*: Geneva, Paris, Bournemouth, India, Cairo, and of course he lived in Provence for years.

For Henry Miller, the artist 'and his work are one' (DML, 309), a notion rejected by postmodernism and cultural theory. Some critics wonder, in that tiresome modernist fashion, whether Durrell himself 'is' this or that character.[29] Usually they see Durrell in Pursewarden, the weary, ever-ironic English writer; and Darley, of course, and also, perhaps, Jacob Arnauti. In fact, as Durrell admitted to Anaïs Nin, 'I am Justine'. Further, he is everybody in the novel, as a writer is all her/ his characters. If one wants to play the biographical game, then Durrell is just as much 'in' Clea as in Pursewarden, just as much Justine as Arnauti.

The most sensational fusion of Durrell's life and his fictions has been the allegations of incest with his daughter Sappho. The incest issue which surfaced in 1991 has caused much controversy in critical circles. It throws into confusion once again the relation between art and life. Can an artist be an absolute bastard in private but produce great art in public? Does it matter if an artist has had an incestuous affair? The hypocrisy of the whole matter is found everywhere. Politicians, for instance, are not allowed to have affairs. Presidents and ministers must be 'pure' and faithful. Many writers, though, have been horrible to people in private while presenting faces of genius to the public. If Durrell had physical relations with his daughter, does it invalidate all his art? Can a rapist be a great artist? Can a murderer produce great art, or any kind of art? Should we consume art that has been created by communists, marxists, fascists, terrorists, murderers, rapists? These are vexed questions, which trouble a society desperately trying to police itself.

Durrell's own views are that some artists are awful in private.[30] They can be a mess, while their art is great. D.H. Lawrence is one example. Modigliani was a debauched man in his private life, but does that mean that his paintings, which are greatly loved by many, must be made void?

Adulterous affairs, getting into fights, boozy living and drug-taking are all OK. These activities are sanctioned by society. Pop musicians, for instance, are revered if they throw a few television sets out of hotel windows when

---

29 Durrell said: 'they are my pets, my toys, my inventions, my recreation' (Durrell, W, 158)

30 'I do loathe artists with so few exceptions.' (Ald, 64)

they're on tour. Bands such as The Who, Led Zeppelin and The Rolling Stones were 'wild', creating havoc in hotels. David Bowie, Keith Richards and Lou Reed took heaps of heroin and cocaine during the 1970s but they are exalted as 'rock stars'. It's the same with writers: Dylan Thomas drank, Samuel Taylor Coleridge took drugs, Charles Baudelaire lived in debauchery with his 'Black Venus' and Paul Verlaine and Arthur Rimbaud played out their 'tempestuous' relationship across North Europe.

The Sappho-Durrell incest, though, goes too far in the eyes of society. Having sex is good for a writers' image, as is domestic violence, drinking, drugs, but not incest, not rape, not murder. These things are going too far. Hence all the fuss kicked up about Durrell having an incestuous affair with his daughter. It is an allegation that would topple a politician into the mire very swiftly. No president or minister would survive it.

What's interesting about the incest case is that some critics have said that what's important is Durrell's work, as if his fiction were more valuable than people. His image as a person is tarnished, as is Sappho's, but for some people his books are more important. The charge of incest gives Durrell a certain notoriety, perhaps the wrong kind of fame. Certainly it is ironic that he is charged with incest when incest is such an important part of his fictions, in the Byronesque brother-sister love in *The Alexandria Quartet*, and the love-triangle in *The Avignon Quintet* between Piers, Sylvie and Bruce. Also in *Quintet* is the incest between Hilary and Livia, though this is not developed.

Barbara Robson, Sappho's 'literary executrix', has made connections between the 'real life' incest of Sappho and Durrell and that of his characters (Pia, Livia and Sylvie). This sensationalist media link adds to the already complex poetic web of connections between art and life in the novels. Ultimately, perhaps, the furore surrounding Durrell and incest will enhance his texts. For if the text is primary and the author is dead, as Roland Barthes attests, then it doesn't matter what the author does. The author could be a chimpanzee or a computer, it doesn't matter in the postmodernist view. If biography is invalid, then it doesn't matter what the author is like in private. This problem confuses people. Was D.H. Lawrence homosexual? Was Shakespeare? Does it matter? Leonardo da Vinci was homosexual, but how does that alter his art?

In the postmodernist/ cultural theory view, the artwork – whether painting, sculpture, magazine, book, dance or performance – is not a 'person' or an individual, but a series of gestures, surfaces, motions, materials, signs, words, and so on. The link between artist/ author and artwork/ text is often very tenuous. As Toril Moi writes: '[w]hen the text no longer offers an individual grasped as the transcendental origin of language and experience, humanist feminism must lay down its arms.' (1985, 80)

The artwork in cultural theory is not a direct extension of the artist, even though it is manufactured by and from her/ his body, however indirectly. When the text is primary, the notion of an artist/ author dies. Roland Barthes writes:

> Once the Author is removed, the claim to decipher a text becomes quite futile. To give a text an Author is to impose a limit on that text, to furnish it with a final signified, to close the writing.[31]

The death of the author, it seems, is the death of humanist criticism. Most criticism of Durrell has been humanist in bias to date.[32] In *The Avignon Quintet*, Durrell makes the journey into postmodernism, where intertextuality is a factor, where a text's ability to relate to other texts is necessary for a full understanding of the overall work. *The Avignon Quintet* makes a concrete connection with, for instance, *Lady Chatterley's Lover,* with Stendhal's *De l'Amour*, with Denis de Rougemont's *Love in the Western World*, E.M. Forster's *Alexandria*, the collected works of Freud and Jung, and various books on Gnosticism, the Knights Templar, sex magic and psychoanalysis. (The *Quartet* intersects with Byron, Bonnard, Claudel, Coleridge, Patmore, Swedenborg, Tolstoy, Wordsworth, Paracelsus, Demonax, Aquinas, Pope, Chaucer, Augustine, Donne, Plotinus, Trollope and Descartes, among others).

There are connections too between the *Quintet* and Sir Thomas Browne,[33] one of the richest writers in the English language, whose books (*Hydriotaphia, Urn Burial, Christian Morals, The Garden of Cyrus* and *Religio Medici*) reveal the author's vast learning in every sentence. Few

---

31 Barthes: *Image Music Text*, tr. Stephen Heath, Fontana 1977, 147
32 Durrell knows how critics recreate the subjects of their criticism: '[n]or really does the 'meaning' of a work of art, either big or small, finally reside in something that can be paraphrased. I like and respect critics and criticism, but the best always seem to have more to do with the insight of the critic and his expression of his own understanding than anything else. The work under review is only the springboard for a new creative enterprise.' (Durrell, letter to Alan Friedman, 18 October 1964, Friedman, 189)
33 Alan Friedman, "Introduction", CE, 8

writers as as dense yet lucid as Browne. It is in Browne's *Garden of Cyrus* that the structure of the *quincunx*, the 'Quintuple number of Trees' that make up 'the sacred letter X' (175, 222), is explored so lyrically.[34] *The Garden of Cyrus* has the wonderful sub-title: *Or, the Quincunciall, Lozenge, or Net-Work Plantations of the Ancients, Artificially, Naturally, Mystically Considered*. Browne speaks of various quincuncial shapes, such as the 'single Quincunx of the *Hyades*', or the 'crucigerous stone of *S. Iago of Gallicia*'.[35]

Browne's omnivorous mind swallows huge chunks of the world. He is interested in so many things, and is learned in so many things. His disquisitions range from speaking of seeds in alchemical, Paracelsian terms, to musing on the burial rites of ancient Egyptians, Romans, Saxons and Chaldeans (ib, 195). Sir Thomas Browne's conjectures on monuments and funerals is wholly in keeping with Durrell's death-conscious philosophy.[36] What Browne has to say at the end of *Urn Burial* is echoed in many of Durrell's works, with its emphasis on the need to *be* in the now, not in some future immortality or memory:

> To live indeed is to be again ourselves, which being not only an hope but an evidence in noble beleevers; 'Tis all one to lye in St. *Innocents* churchyard, as in the Sands of *Ægypt*: Ready to be anything, in the ecstasie of being ever, and as content with six foot as the Mole of *Adrianus*. (*Urn Burial*, ib., 139)

Sir Thomas Browne also speaks in Gnostic terms when he states that '[l]ife is but the shadow of death... The Sunne itself is but the dark *simulacrum*, and light but the shadow of God' (ib, 221). It is not only the ideas of Sir Thomas Browne, startling as they are, that Durrell employed, but also his rich prose style, with its abundant, idiosyncratic and well-learned vocabulary. This quiet, meditative extract from the end of *The Garden of Cyrus* will suffice to show how ornate yet also direct and simple Browne's style was. It has that 'punch and nuance' that Durrell admired in the Elizabethans:

> But the Quincunx of Heaven runs low, and 'tis time to catch the five ports of knowledge; We are unwilling to spin out our awaking thoughts

[34] W.L. Godshalk: "Durrell: Death, Love and Art", OMG II, 105
[35] Sir Thomas Browne: *Religio Medici and Other Writings*, Dent 1906, 189
[36] Piers recites Akkad's position in which one becomes an adult at the realization of one's own death (M, 42)

into the phantasmes of sleep, which often continueth præcogitations; making Cables of Cobwebbes, and Wildernesses of handsome Groves. Beside *Hippocrates* hath spoke so little, and the Oneirocriticall Masters, have left such frigid Interpretations from plants, that there is little encouragement to dream of Paradise itself. Nor will the sweetest delight of Gardens afford much comfort in sleep; wherein the dulnesse of that sense shakes hands with delectable odours; and though in the bed of *Cleopatra*, can hardly with any delight raise up the ghost of a Rose. (ib., 229)

Durrell often acknowledges D.H. Lawrence's notion of the death of 'old stable ego'. In *The Alexandria Quartet* Durrell explored the shape-shifting nature of the self – he wanted to 'break up the personality and show its different facets'[37] – but in the *Quincunx* he goes much further.

"What always bothered me was the question of a stable ego – did such a thing exist? The old notion of such an animal was rather primitive, particularly for novelists with an itch to explain this action or that. Myself, I could hardly write down the name of a character without suddenly being swamped by an ocean of possible attributes, each as valid and as truthful as any other. The human psyche is almost infinitely various – so various it can afford to be contradictory even as regards itself." (L, 37)

For Durrell, the notion of character has been fragmented by modern psychology and science.[38] Asked why he didn't set his novels in the 'present time', Durrell replied that it doesn't exist, that the present is an 'absolute illusion', and it is precisely this everyday, present time that the fictions were aiming to upset with their cultivation of the precarious, the insecure, the ambiguous. If the *Quartet* did not quite ram this message of uncertainty home, the *Quintet* certainly did. Not only the ego, but also the 'old stable novel' (Durrell paraphrasing Lawrence) has been displaced by a new palimpsest-type, multi-layered novel, where characters blur into one another.[39] 'Everything and everyone comes closer and closer together,

---

37 Durrell, in Curtis Cate: "Lawrence Durrell", *Atlantic Monthly*, vol., CCVIII, December 1961, 69.
38 Julia Kristeva writes: a "fixed identity' is a 'fiction, an illusion – who among us has a 'fixed' identity'[?]', "A Question of Subjectivity: an interview", *Women's Review*, no. 12, 1986, in Rice & Waugh, 1992
39 Durrell's aim, he wrote in a notebook, was 'the poetic substance detached from the narrative line – the sullen monorail of story and person' (Som, inventory no. 1344, 86)

moving towards the one.' (Q, 99)[40] And Sutcliffe scribbles in the margin of a book: '[t]he same people are also others without realising it' (S, 8). As Arnauti puts it in *Justine*: '[f]or the writer people as psychologies are finished.' (100) The primary notion in this series of novels is that all characters are part of each other, that they fuse into a unity.

> All the characters are aspects of *one* character, Constance, and if they could be realized in 'the reality prime' of Blanford's final statement in *Quinx*, they would be fused into an ideal concept. (Med, 110)

This idea is introduced in the first book of the *Quintet*, *Monsieur*, where Sutcliffe is writing a book about the novel's events, but Sutcliffe is Blanford's creation, and Blanford is Durrell's creation. *Monsieur* becomes a series of Chinese boxes in itself, a novel about the making of the novel. In the *envoi* to *Monsieur*, Durrell marks out the family tree history of the novel: 'So D./ begat Blanford/ (who begat Tu and Sam and Livia)/ who begat Sutcliffe/ who begat Bloshford' (296). "In the end", says Purse-warden "everything will be found to be true of everybody." (B, 13)

'Be ye members of one another' – the Biblical allusion is central to *The Avignon Quintet*,[41] but, by the end of the five novels, the unity of personality is more like the cosmological unity of the Tao, for the whole series of books moves from Western physics and psychoanalysis to Oriental philosophy and mysticism. The novels progress from Aristotle and Freud to Chuang-tzu and Milarepa (another favourite philosopher of Durrell's), from Christ to Buddha. Durrell uses the image of a European (4-sided) cathedral contrasting with an Asiatic (5-sided) pagoda. The church has a centre (the altar) whereas the Eastern mosque or pagoda does not. Durrell's anti-Christianity advocates a Classical paganism of Existential awareness of life as neither good nor evil, a denial of the Fall and Original Sin, and an emphasis on unity of soul and body. The health of the body (Buddha's rounded tummy) replaces self-denial and the Christian denigration of the flesh and sexuality (Christ as a 'squirming frog' on the Cross).

Durrell's *The Avignon Quintet* (the 'Indian novel' [S, 201]) is part of a

---

40 This merging into one character Durrell also applies to acts: there may be, after all, just one primal act. William Stekel had noted, in a passage that Durrell marked in his copy of *The Homosexual Neurosis,* how close tabooed desires (incest, criminality, homosexuality) are to each other (Stekel, *The Homosexual Neurosis*, Emerson, New York 1950, 18)
41 Personality is not seen as whole and self-contained, but a fragment of and in other selves. (Veldeman, 9)

general trend in some circles of philosophy where Western metaphysics and Oriental mysticism merge. The novels are planted at the 'point of tangence between these two cultural principles' (FEB, 9).[42] East and West merge, says Durrell, after Freud destroyed what Lawrence called 'the old stable ego' and when Einstein evaporated matter (Ald, 75). 'It is striking to see physicists, and specialists in theoretical physics, reconstructing a universe in which God has his place, and also the idea of a cosmogony, of Creation', writes Mircea Eliade (1984, 131-2).

Other examples include the books on quantum mechanics and Taoism by Fritjof Capra, or Aldous Huxley's *The Perennial Philosophy* (cited in Durrell's *Key to Modern Poetry*, 85), D.T. Suzuki's *Essays on Zen Buddhism*, Alan Watts' *Tao: The Watercourse Way* and *The Way of Zen*, C.G. Jung's *Psychology East and West,* Catholic theologian William Johnston's *The Inner Eye of Love*, R.C. Zaehner's critical *Mysticism Sacred and Profane* and many others.[43] In Durrell, though, as in Zaehner, Huxley, Watts, Jung, Capra, Johnston, Bancroft *et al*, a Westerner cannot wholly take on Eastern philosophy without also remaining very much a Westerner. It's not simply a case of ditching Descartes and Derrida for Shankara and Suzuki. You can't slip off the Occident like a mantle and take up the Orient. Durrell shows that the influx of Eastern mysticism must be a dialogue with the West, as expressed in the debates of Constance and Affad, or Blanford and Max. The movement from East to West is fraught

---

42 Durrell saw himself as both Eastern and Western: 'I am both, at least I feel both' (Som, *Cercle*)
43 Lawrence Blair: *Rhythms of Vision*, Paladin 1976; Anne Bancroft: *Twentieth Century Mystics and Sages,* Heinemann 1976; Agehananda Bharati: *The Light at the Center: Context and Pretext of Modern Mysticism*, Ross-Erikson, Santa Barbara 1976; Fritjof Capra: *The Tao of Physics: An exploration of the parallels between modern physics and Eastern Mysticism*, Flamingo 1983; William Johnston: *The Inner Eye of Love: Mysticism and Religion*, Collins 1985; Willard Johnson: *Riding the Ox Home: A History of Meditation From Shamanism to Science*, Rider 1982; Thomas Merton: *Seeds of Contemplation*, Burns & Oats; R.C. Zaehner: *Mysticism Sacred and Profane*, Oxford University Press 1957; Alan Watts: *The Way of Zen*, Penguin 1980, *Tao: The Watercourse Way*, Cape 1976. See also: Gary Zukav: *The Dancing Wu Li Masters: An Overview of the New Physics*, Rider 1979; Amaury de Riencourt: *The Eye of Shiva: Eastern Mysticism and Science*, Morrow, New York 1981; Paul Davies: *God and the New Physics*, Dent 1983; Michael Talbot: *Mysticism and the New Physics*, Bantam, New York; Heinz R. Pagel: *The Cosmic Code: Quantum Physics as the Language of Nature*, Simon & Schuster, New York 1982

with problems, some of them of life-threatening proportions. After all, Piers, after immersing himself in the Gnosticism of the Near East, commits suicide.

Yet one has to try to subsume the Orient, Durrell says. In a speech at one of the 'Durrell Conferences', introducing his work, Durrell contrasted his Western Protestant upbringing with his encounter with Buddhism in his Indian childhood:

> Life being so short, it was clear that we really had to hurry up and try to achieve a kind of realization to hook in with reality, and to start using it, instead of moving along parallel tracks. The yogic asanas seemed to me to relate absolutely directly to that, and, if Buddhism was more satisfying than the Protestantism of my parents, it was because you could check it on your physique. (OMG, 13)

The aim with *The Avignon Quintet* was to unite the four dimensions of the West with the five *skandas* or sensibilities of the East, a 'mystical marriage' of four and five, Einstein and Buddha (Q, 198).[44] The progression to the Orient is embodied in the fiction in, among other people, Max, Galen's butler, who, in a remarkable transformation, becomes an Indian *yogi* or 'yoga-maker', a *saddhu*, a holy man. His sudden appearance in amongst the cold grey Lutheran/ Protestant gloom of Geneva is an amazement for Constance. '"Ah been in India a while now and ah've learned a new science. Better than the old one-two!"' says Max (S, 24). There follows an induction into yoga for Constance. Max has her buy a yoga mat. She joins his yoga classes, which complements the Oriental teachings of Affad. '"Our classes are full of young people suffering from stress and tension of spirit – on their way to crack-ups we help them to avoid [Max tells Constance]. In India they'd be surprised, since there's no ego to get mentally stressed up with"' (S, 26).[45]

This is the point of the Oriental yoga for Larry Durrell, this distressing of the tensed-up Occidental ego. Throughout the *Quintet*, Durrell emphasizes

---

44 The 'four' of the West was the Freudian four elements in an erotic relationship: the man, the woman, the 'female' in the man, the 'male' in the women. (Durrell, in Peter Adam: "Alexandria Revisited", Mac 3, 400)
45 Durrell's characters often pontificate on 'young people', usually in a gloomy fashion, prophecizing a psychic decline. Thus Marchant in *Tunc* says: 'And then, what do you make of the faces of the young? As if they had smashed the lock on the great tuck-box of sex only to find the contents had gone mouldy.' (224) It's typical of Durrell's post-Freudian-Reichian analysis to see sexuality at the heart of the decay of modern civilization.

the problems an inflated ego or self cause: sleeplessness, he says, is in the first instance due to 'simply exaggerated self-importance' (S, 105). The stressed-up ego[46] creates the problems in so much of Western art: the lovelorn lover in courtly love poetry and in Francesco Petrarch's *Canzoniere*, the *hubris* and arrogance in Shakespeare's Leontes, Othello and Macbeth, the self-delusions of many a painter, composer, sculptor, poet and novelist. The inflated self annoys Sutcliffe mainly: it is Sutcliffe who keeps criticizing psychoanalysis, because his wife, Pia, is in Geneva having expensive therapy. Often Sutcliffe grits his teeth and lays into Schwarz, the analyst companion of Constance:

> "...you know damned well, Schwarz, that the subconscious is fished out – there's hardly a sprat left. So you are driven back to base, my lad, with the old fashioned mind-fuck machine of an electro-convulsion-therapy jag. Any poet will tell you that the basic illness is the ego which, when it swells, engenders stress, dislocating reality. Then the unbeknownst steps in with its gnomes and *Doppelgängers*; but once you realise this simple fact your positivism falls from you like a cloak. The penny drops, the *jeton* engages, and you have the Dalai Lama himself on the wire; what comes out now is poetry – that highly aberrant act of nature!" (C, 133)

Max jumps into Constance's life with a sense of joy and repose. He has got 'it', the point of the whole business. What business? Life itself, of course.

> "And now?" she asked.
> "Bless you, I'm jest happy without any kind of after-thoughts. They showed me how one could meditate sweetly and gradually harmonise with the goings-on of the whole wide world!"
> "It sounds great!"
> "It certainly is. I'm telling *you*!" (S, 28)

The poem 'The Outer Limits' offers another take on Durrell's Oriental philosophy, where the 'pure form... must be the silence', which is a 'real reality realising itself' (CP, 291). Where does fiction end and life begin Durrell wonders: '[w]here do people end?' Blanford muses. 'Where do their imaginations begin?' (Q, 33) The margins are not as clearly defined as were once thought. Einstein, Heisenberg, Freud, quantum mechanics, and chaos theory, have confused the epistemological, phenomenological,

---

46 In a 1940s notebook Durrell writes of the 'I, I, I. The Ego: the subliminal self: the id: the cosmic self rather: the astrological brother: the shadow...' (Som, in Pine, 1994, 74)

hermeneutic, existential, metaphysical, religious, psychological, and philosophic boundaries. Durrell employs the 'Principle of Indeterminacy': he says that 'facts are dreams' (the last line of *A Smile in the Mind's Eye*, 58). The *Quintet* is as much a 'science fiction' in its application of quantum mechanics as the *Quartet* was in using applied Relativity Theory (Lorenz, 1). The Theory of Relativity, quantum mechanics, the New Physics and chaos theory offer intriguing models to the novelist of ideas. Realities are spontaneously created, and multiple worlds exist simultaneously. Seen in the light of quantum and chaos theory, it is quite acceptable that the fictional worlds of Blanford, Bloshford, Sutcliffe, Tu Du, Bruce and Sylvie should all exist beside each other.

The central conceit of *The Avignon Quintet* is outlined by Sutcliffe:

> To commingle and intersperse contingent realities – that's the game! After all, how few are the options open to us – few varieties of human shape, mental dispositions, scales of behaviour: hardly more numerous than the available Christian names used by the race. How many coats of reality does it take to get a nice clean surface to the apprehension? We are all fragments of one another; everyone has a little bit of everything in his make-up. From the absolute point of view – Aristotle's Fifth Substance, say – all persons are the same person and all situations are identical or vastly similar. (C, 123)

If all people are aspects of one person, then, is there only one book to be written? Is there only one viewpoint on the whole matter? Is there just one work of art to be produced? This is the 'Tu Quoque' book, the Sut-Blan collaboration, a fiction within a fiction, created by 'paper fictions', that is, fictional characters (Q, 28).[47] With the accelerating self-fictionalizaton of the *Quintet*, everything becomes provisional, ambiguous, tentative, mobile. Images of feeling detached, set free, loosened up abound in the last two books of the *Quincunx*. The *Quintet* dissolves into a notebook format,

---

47 Sutcliffe says 'my best friends are all correspondents, people I deeply cherish because I seldom or never see them' (M, 210). In a different mood, Durrell said at Pennsylvania State University: '[o]ne creates and recreates other people and is in turn recreated by them.' ("Lawrence Durrell and John Hawkes", Mac 3, 414)

with verses, quotes, maxims,[48] fragmented images and other squibs becoming the norm (echoing the 'planned formlessness' of the island books). [49] Instead of the 'sullen' monotony of A-to-B-to-C narrative, there are anecdotes, ideas, propositions, jokes, one-liners (Q, 32). Sutcliffe's artistic uncle, Pursewarden, muses: '[i]n the end, everything will be found to be true of everybody' (B, 13). Sutcliffe muses further:

> I dream of such a book, full of not completely discrete characters, of ancestors and descendants all mixed up – could such people walk in and out of each other's lives without damaging the quiddity of each other? Hum. And the whole book arranged in diminished fifths from the point of view of orchestration. A big switchy book, all points and sidings. A Golgotha of a book. (C, 123)

As the *Quintet* progresses, characters merge into one another (Q, 26). 'Thinking is shared by all', said Heraclitus (Fragment XXXI). Durrell has long enjoyed merging characters: Balthazar merges into Scobie on one side, and Cavafy on the other; Melissa's child by Nessim becomes Justine's lost child, and so on.[50] Blanford and Sutcliffe are two sides of the same novelist, as is Bloshford. Constance too muses upon the notion of people being fragments of each other: '[t]he same people are also others without realising it' (*Sebastian*, 8). Constance joins the privileged coven of narrators who philosophize on the novels' themes. Her dialogues with Affad resonate with the Blanford-Sutcliffe dialogues.[51]

Significantly, Durrell has admitted to living more in writing than in 'real life'. In a film about the tramps of Provence, Durrell said, revealingly:

> I live much more in the work I do than in real life, which makes me rather a failure in real life. My real life is rather a failure, rather hollow. A sort of pretense.[52]

---

48 One could make a book of Durrell's maxims and sayings, as has occurred with philosophers such as Arthur Schopenhauer and Friedrich Nietzsche. A few maxims might include: Akkad, in *Monsieur* speaking of death: 'What is it after all? It is nothing. It is not enough!' (M, 139) Cunégonde in *Caesar's Vast Ghost*: 'Regard yourself as a privileged person drinking nectar on the sly from a sieve.' (196)
49 Alan Friedman: "Place and Durrell's Island Books", *Modern Fiction Studies*, 13, 3, Fall 1967, and CE, 62
50 Chiara Briganti: "Lawrence Durrell and the Vanishing Author", OMG, 43
51 William Boyd speaks of *Sebastian* having 'pages and pages of this sort of the unreadable leaden dialogue' (CE, 56)
52 Margaret McCall: "*The Lonely Roads*: Notes for an Unwritten Book", in MacNiven, 1987, 384

Durrell plays upon the initial letter of his name – D – which is both Durrell and the Devil, for *Monsieur*'s subtitle is *The Prince of Darkness*. It's a jokey comparison, but underneath the joke is the comparison of the novelist and God, and their relationship with their creation. Further, in the Gnostic system, which forms the spiritual basis of the five novels, this world is not the creation of God but of an usurper, the demiurge, the Devil. The implication, then, is that the novel itself is somehow impure and 'base matter', as the world is in the Gnostic view.

Blanford, towards the end of *Constance*, muses upon the comparison of the writer and God:

> Suppose one wrote a book in which all the characters were omniscient, were God? What then? One would have to compose it in a death-mood, as if dawn would bring with it the firing-squad. But this is what the artist *does*! (C, 359)

Throughout the five books, characters muse upon their actuality. Or, rather, Blanford and Sutcliffe do: the other characters just get on with living. Leila, for instance, 'invents' Mountolive in her letters: he becomes 'a character out of her own imagination', so that when he says he's arriving in Egypt to see her, she is annoyed that reality should impinge on her imagination (B, 65).

The marvellous Taoist philosopher Chuang-tzu, the Groucho Marx of philosophy Durrell called him, was one of Durrell's favourite philosophers.[53] Chuang-tzu explored the relation between dream and 'reality' in that famous illustration of the man and the butterfly. In a Chuang-tzu mood, Durrell writes in *Monsieur*:

> It is still a moot point whether Socrates, in fact, existed as something more than a character in a novel by Plato. And what of me, he thought? Am I possibly an invention of someone like old D – the devil at large? (281)

Durrell knows that truth is stranger than fiction, so that the more extravagant or unbelievable events in the fictions will in fact be 'true': '[b]y a simple paradox (perhaps inherent in all writing?) the passages that he

53 Chuang-tzu 'propounds doctrines with an irony.... as you can't take up an exact yes or no position with regard to anything the best thing you can do about it is to come in slightly at a slant, ironically.' (Wheldon, 1962, 124)

knew would be regarded as over-theatrical or unreal ("people don't behave like that") would be the truth, and the rest which rang somehow true, the purest fabrication.' (M, 282) His characters, Durrell claimed, 'are not "real", they are "true"'.54

The Tiresias55 of the *Quartet* (someone already multi-selved), Balthazar, proclaims: '[e]ach fact can have a thousand motivations, all equally valid' (Cl, 64). 'Truth' is one of Durrell's obsessions: throughout *The Alexandria Quartet* we hear many views of 'truth', for the *Quartet*, on one level, is about getting at the 'truth', as each layer is unpeeled from the dense narrative. As in the thriller/ detective genre, Durrell enjoyed letting his readers absorb each new revelation.56 'Truth', of course, ended up as nothing absolute, but as subjective and ambiguous. The nature of 'truth' depended not so much on subjectivity and viewpoint but on desire and one's interests. 'The angle of vision is everything. The poetic vision is manufactured to meet desire.' (L, 66)

The Avignon Quintet may be seen as another 'quest' novel, again exploring the various meanings of the term 'quest' – from Arthurian knights questing the Grail to the psychoanalyst, a modern-day Grail knight, searching for the key or hidden secret of (a) personality. For Durrell, the Templar is, like the Gnostic, a type of artist.57 In the *Quincunx*, 'truth', beloved of absolutists and religionists (of which the worst sort for Durrell are clearly Christians) is in a mess.

There is no 'final truth', no absolute reality, no 'ground of being', no God. There is instead, finally, the universe, which is the 'ultimate reality' of science. Science, too, provides no absolutes, but there is always matter out there, the universe itself. Significantly, *The Avignon Quintet*, moves from Western science and psychoanalysis to Eastern philosophy and yoga. The ambiguity of Western 'truth' is supplanted by the metaphysics of the Tao and the body, as expressed in yoga. *Monsieur* is soaked in Western philosophy; *Quinx*, the last book, is founded on Oriental thought. Constance is

54 Som, inventory no. 1346, 12
55 Cavafy is also a Tiresias figure, moving 'through the minds of the characters of the *Quartet*', Durrell said (in Adam: "Alexandria Revisited", Mac 3, 399)
56 'the understanding that prevails at one moment is replaced or modified by the understanding that comes with new information' (Lionel Trilling: "*The Quartet*: Two Reviews", W, 56)
57 see Reed Dasenbrock: "The Counterlife of Heresy", in CE, 197, 226; Michael Begnal: "The Mystery of the Templars in *The Avignon Quintet*", in OMG, 160

the key character, and her book is the key book. She is a psychiatrist who falls in love with a Middle Eastern man who practises Oriental yoga. The book *Constance,* like the character, depicts the meeting of the two main belief systems of the *Quintet*: psychoanalysis (the rational, non-religious, scientific West) and yoga (intuitive, mystical, commonsensical East.)

Monsieur begins as a naturalistic narrative, but gradually, level by level, it moves into self-reflexivity and metafiction. Like Chinese dolls, characters break open to reveal more characters. The character Tu, for instance, becomes Constance in *Livia*. Felix Chatto echoes Felix Charlock, hero of *Tunc-Nunquam*. Akkad and Affad merge, as do Sylvia and Pia and Livia. And finally, in *Monsieur*, we are thrown far into the future, much further than the end of *Quinx*, the last book of the sequence, when Blanford speaks with the Duchess in Venice but right in the last paragraph we learn that she too is dead.

This is one of the imagined futures of the characters of the *Quincunx*, in which Blanford imagines himself as a lonely old man, disabled, while Constance becomes the 'Duchess of Tu', married to someone else, with children of her own, a kindly companion to the solitary writer. In *Monsieur*, the fictional worlds become Chinese boxes, which are lifted to reveal other realities inside. If one lives more in a work of art (fiction) than in the 'real' world (as Durrell admitted doing) then which is 'truer' or more 'real', imagination or reality, fiction or 'real' life? In the post-quantum mechanical *Quintet* fictional worlds are born, grow, and split off the mother-(*Ur*)-narrative, like the 'babyverses' or mini-universes of the New Physics.

Lawrence Durrell, like most novelists, is very fussy about names. Many of his names come from old British poets: Campion in *The Dark Labyrinth*, Beddoes in *the Sicilian Carousel*. In *The Alexandria Quartet* there is even a John Keats. For his neurotic, confused women he likes theological or Latinate names, such as Pia and Benedicta. These names need no gloss. The name Justine of course conjures up the whole of de Sade, beloved guru of the French intellectuals. De Sade is the 'final flower of reason' and rationalism for Pursewarden (J, 211), and 'the most typical figure of our century' for Durrell (W, 165). Aubrey is reminiscent of early Aldous Huxley, the Huxley of *Eyeless in Gaza*, and Evelyn Waugh. There are names out of P.G. Wodehouse, and *Boy's Own*, names from Egyptian and European aristocracy, and Roman writers (Galen). The name Trash is unsubtle in racial connotations ('white trash'). Julian in *Tunc* probably echoes the Roman Emperor. Pombal evokes the archetypal pudgy, pompous, lascivious, languorous Frenchman. Durrell likes names which connote his Proustian/ Bergsonian/ Einsteinian themes of time and memory: Mnemidis, the psychopath in *Sebastian*, and Mnemjian in *Justine* echo a favourite Durrell word, *mnemonic*.

Curiously, the all-important trio of siblings, Hilary, Livia and Sam, do not have a surname. Constance, the key female character in *The Avignon Quintet*, is only ever referred to as Constance. Durrell uses Connie occasionally, not wanting to draw attention too much, perhaps, to *Lady Chatterley's Lover*. Schwartz the psychoanalyst in Geneva needs no gloss, his name being tied up with the alchemical themes of the novel sequence. Schwartz is also melancholy, the 'black bile' depressant, who eventually commits suicide.[58] Smirgel evokes a sly, smarmy, smirking character, who wriggles out of traps. Sebastian is of course the soft, gorgeous secret name of the otherwise indifferent name Affad. Names such as Robin Sutcliffe, Toby, Blanford and Pursewarden speak of Britishness. Other names in the Durrell canon – Vibart, Koepgen, Hippolyta, Leila, Clea, Banubula, Banquo, Balthazar, Arnauti, Iolanthe, Nessim – attest to the stylish, cosmopolitan nature of Durrell's characters.

Who are these people in the *Quartet* and Durrell's other fictions? Often they have an ambiguous nationality, identity and background. At times, for example, characters such as Justine and Nessim speak in English, where they would usually be speaking in Arabic or probably French. They seem to have unlimited incomes, no ties or responsibilities, an ability to travel wherever they wish, whenever they wish. (Durrell's fiction, like many fictions, has its unbelievable moments. One of the more unbelievable events (there are many, really) in the *Quartet* is where Clea eavesdrops on an argument between Mountolive and Liza. Not only does she manage to keep them in the sights of Nessim's telescope, Clea is also a skilled lip-reader, enabling her to tell Darley what the arguers said [Cl, 100]).

In Durrell's art, it's all done with mirrors.[59] At the end of *Monsieur* and

---

58 Schwarz's suicide is ironic, for one of his insights is this: 'Socrates sought suicide like Jesus, but did not want to take the blame for the act. What a contrast to Buddha who thought that felicity and the rounded tummy were best!' (S, 177) A Freudian-Rankian psychoanalyst, Schwarz cannot quite shake his psyche free of its origins in the negative elements of European culture, which Durrell defines as sin, the Fall, the ego, birth trauma and the Will.

59 in Jean Montalbetti, 84

the beginning of *Livia*, the change over to self-reflexivity occurs. The third chapter, "Sutcliffe, The Venetian Documents", brings humour and parody centre stage. It is one of Durrell's most enjoyable sequences, where his Wodehouse/ Antrobus component takes flight. In chapter four, "Life With Toby", the text breaks up into short passages, phrases, squibs, maxims and poems. This is a notebook-style format that Durrell excels at: this is how *Livia* begins. Durrell's book of poems *The Red Limbo Lingo* is a collection of notes, maxims and aphorisms (Novalis, Pascal, Nietzsche and La Rochefoucauld have written in this way).

By the beginning of *Livia*, Durrell has decided on the form and style of his five novel sequence. His two novelists, Sutcliffe and Blanford, discuss it on the telephone. At this point they haven't met, although it is and is not possible for a novelist and his creation to meet. Blanford and Sutcliffe can of course meet, because they are both, finally, figments in Durrell's text.

When they do meet, in *Constance*, Sutcliffe retires to bed with a cold. He was supposed to meet Blanford at the airport, but mutinies: Blanford realizes that his control of Sutcliffe is incomplete ('damn him', C, 331). At the start of *Livia*, they talk on the telephone. They try out various versions of the book they are going to write together, or separately. At one point, Blanford asks Sutcliffe to bring along his novel, to help him with his own. It's an intriguing notion: the fictional novelist (Sutcliffe) helping the novelist who created him (Blanford). More bizarre still is Blanford admitting that Constance sneakily looked at his novel, and found out what was going to happen (C, 342).

Throughout the *Quintet* Durrell tries out different futures, different lives, different actions for his characters.[60] The 'unholy trinity' of lovers, Sylvie, Bruce and Piers, for instance, pop up from time to time, with slightly altered names, in slightly altered circumstances. In *Livia* Blanford provides another version of *Monsieur*: 'So the Sutcliffe he invented for his novel *Monsieur* shot himself through the mirror in the early version? "I had to," he explained, pointing to Blanford. "It was him or me."' (L, 3) In another take, Durrell/ Blanford writes: 'Sutcliffe, in writing about him, or rather, he writing about himself in the character of Sutcliffe, under the satirical name of Bloshford in the novel *Monsieur*' (L, 5).

Who invents whom? The question recurs: Sutcliffe asks Blanford: '"What would you give me if I wrote a book to prove that the great Blanford is

---

60 'Seen in continuum you do... see people in sort of allotropic states, all divine, all perverse, all good-bad.' (Durrell, Ald, 75)

simply the fiction of one of his fictions?"' (L, 53)[61] Durrell merely extends the cultural theory/ post-structuralist notion that the reader 'writes' a novel as s/he reads it. Criticism is called 'reading': one 'reads' television, or 'reads' a painting. Reading becomes writing, so readers create characters, just as much as authors. Indeed, the reader is essential, for some critics. For, without readers, the characters would not come alive. The fictional people need the 'real' people to live. Without us, culture does not live.

Hogarth, the psychologist in *The Dark Labyrinth* remarks:

> "In a very real sense we do create the world around us since we get it to reflect back our inner symbolism at us. Every man carries a little myth-making machine inside him which operates often without him knowing it." (193)

Hélène Cixous writes that 'the mystery is that we confuse invent and believe.'[62] Clearly Durrell enjoys the complexity his various levels of fiction create; he enjoys meshing the fictive worlds and the 'real' worlds (which has to be so carefully done, otherwise readers will make mistakes in perceiving the 'real' and the 'fictive' worlds). One fiction on top of another. We all present 'selected fictions to each other', remarks Justine in Anaïs Nin mode (Cl, 48). No particular world is more important than another: each is given precedence, each has its possibilities.

For some, the shifting perspectives create disappointment and alienation: the reader's first disappointment in *The Avignon Quintet* comes two thirds into *Monsieur*, as William Godshalk notes.[63] But ever since his first 'major' fiction, *The Black Book*, Durrell has been layering fictional worlds on top of each other, to create that 'sliding-panel' effect, as Pursewarden calls it. In *The Black Book*, though, the self-referential asides are awkward. In *The Avignon Quintet*, Durrell is fully in control of what he's doing. Since *The Black Book*, too, Durrell has included himself in his own fictions. For example, Tarquin says he borrowed Durrell's car in *The Black Book* (200),

---

61 Mephisto: 'O Yes, I am as real as you like to imagine.' (*Faust*, 40)
62 Hélène Cixous: *Jours de l'an [First days of the year]*, 1990, in Cixous, 1994, 185
63 'I was confused and upset by the realization that the narrative of Bruce, Piers, and Sylvie is a secondary fiction, not the primary reality of the novel... I was annoyed by Durrell's game, thrown off balance, perhaps a little angry.' (Godshalk, in OMG, ed, 189). Robin Rook, in *Lawrence Durrell's Duble Concerto*, writes: 'Durrell seems to be denying the artist his autonomy to create a fictional world of his own because his fiction would be building on what was already fictitious.' (53)

while in *Nunquam* a line of poetry comes from 'the best of our modern poets' (267), and in *Justine*, Durrell raids his poetry for imagery: '[t]he smell of satin and leather. The horrible feeling of some great impending scandal' (J, 91), which comes from 'The Anecdotes' (CP, 206). For Durrell, writing the *Quincunx* was a heroic gesture, to counter the banality, as he saw it, of contemporary fiction:

> Up to now the feedback idea has been purely temporal as a notion; but I am trying to feed back second-degree fictions into field inhabited by first-degree ones. Will the result be over-contradiction and chaos – ('reality over-determined'!)? Or will they marry and settle down happily ever after like nouns and verbs in the same poem? I'm curious to see. It felt that if somebody didn't do *something* the novel was going to be about as modern as morris-dancing to flageolet & drum soon! If the bloody thing works however it will give a new flavour to fictional reality. (DML, 508)

Even as he aims for being 'modern', Durrell's fictions remain conservative and Romantic. The seemingly 'high brow' theoretical notions that powered *The Alexandria Quartet* (the journey from the 'psychological' novel *Justine* through the 'philosophical' *Balthazar* to 'objective' *Mountolive*)[64] turn out to be far less important than the emotional and spiritual explorations of the tetralogy. Durrell's talk of relativity æsthetics turns out to be a sop for the critics, something for critics to dig their talons into, while the novelist is actually exploring 'human love', as he calls it.[65]

Durrell also uses personas and masks in his poetry. There is, for instance, Melissa, Pursewarden, Sutcliffe, and the philosopher Conon in Durrell's poetry who is a sort of Greek Chuang-tzu. As with *The Alexandria Quartet*, Durrell prefaces his poems sometimes with a note, explaining his intentions.[66] The note before the poem 'Conon in Exile', where Conon's physical exile on the island mirrors his internal exile, Prospero-like,[67] reads:

Conon is an imaginary Greek philosopher who visited me twice in my

---

64 Jean-Paul Hamard: "L'espace et le temps dans les romans de Lawrence Durrell", *Critique*, 16, 1960, 387-413
65 Robert L. Stromberg: "The Contribution of Relativity to the Inconsistency of Form of *The Alexandria Quartet*", in OMG I, 246-256
66 John Press wrote that the poems were the best introduction to the *Quartet*, and the best explanation of the *Quartet* was to be found in the *Collected Poems*. (1963, 204)
67 'I think that the real 'foreigner' in an anglo-saxon society is the artist' (Lab, 41)

dreams and with whom I occasionally identify myself; he is one of my masks, Melissa is another; I want my total poetic work to add up as a kind of tapestry of people, some real, some imaginary. Conon is real. (CP, 107)

Absolutely typical of Durrell to add 'Conon is real', when he has just stated that 'Conon is an *imaginary* Greek Philosopher' (my italics). Durrell's whole work can be seen as a 'tapestry of people, some real, some imaginary', as he terms it. 'We do exist; we are fictions', says Tarquin in *The Black Book* (37). The poetry must be regarded as a continuum with the novels. But so are the travel books part of this continuum. One might think Durrell's travel books might be 'documentaries', factual texts. No. They are fictions, in which Durrell selects and reshapes the world according to his own vision.[68] In the travel books Durrell alters reality to suit his own tastes. They are subjective, personal, 'impressionistic' accounts of Sicily, Corfu, Rhodes, Cyprus and Provence. The travel books contain seemingly real people, sometimes given initials, sometimes given odd names. We are led to believe these are 'real' people that the narrator, Durrell, meets and talks to on his travels. In fact, they are fictional characters, even when the initials disguise 'real' people such as Durrell's wife Nancy (who is 'N.' in *Prospero's Cell*).

'Real' and 'Fictional': More on Blanford and Sutcliffe

At times Blanford gets bored with his creation. Predictably, he tries to kill him off:

> I did a Sinbad in the hope of ridding myself of Sutcliffe – you will have noticed my various attempts to dispense with him, to make him commit suicide for example, using the bridge as a symbol. I had to have my spine shot into holes before I realised that the only way to deal with the Socratic Voice is to concretise it, let it live, manifest itself. Then it becomes a harmless ghost, it passes off in a fever, it writes the classic phrase for you. (S, 5)

68 The writer of subjective prose should first and foremost surrender her/himself to the associative movements of the topic or object they're writing about', Durrell says in *Key* (45)

For the writer, her/ his characters are 'paper creations', who keep him company. In the poem 'Orpheus', Durrell says that writing/ art is 'a paper recreation of lost loves' (CP, 234). Durrell speaks of 'this damned pen-pushing which lives in a sort of amo-odi relationship to life!' (May 1958, LJF, 28) Darley sees his former lover, Melissa, the 'Bee-Goddess' of the *Quartet*,[69] as a creation of the 'acid-bath of words': she becomes all text in his memory, which is itself compounded of words. Melissa becomes 'simply a nexus of literary cross-references scribbled in the margins of a minor poem' (Cl, 35).

Blanford gets attached to his characters, much as, one supposes, Durrell got attached to Mountolive, Pursewarden, Darley, Justine, Gregory, Campion, Felix, Benedicta *et al*.

> If lonely people have a right to talk to themselves couldn't a lonely author argue with one of his own creations – a fellow-writer, Blanford asked himself. (L, 8)
> He was filled with a vague sense of insufficiency at having at last decided to say goodbye to his creations – they had been together for a couple of years now and he had, inevitably, become fond of them and reluctant to part from them. (M, 275)

On the one hand the author's characters are simply bits of paper, offering no consolation, finally; on the other hand, the characters are psychological realities, perhaps even (why not?) flesh-and-blood realities. On the one hand there is loneliness, on the other a strange kind of companionship. On the one hand there is no connection other than through letters and words: 'I really came here because I was lonely,' says Sutcliffe in his "An Astonishing Letter", 'These are the penalties of a paper life; my best friends are all correspondents, people I deeply cherish because I seldom or never see them.' (M, 210) Blanford has the same sentiments: 'He would write poems in invisible ink, then, and post them to himself.' (L, 185) On one level, artistic creation counters Lacanian lack and Kristevan absence: the act of writing staves off emptiness and loneliness by filling up the psychic space. As Julia Kristeva wrote in *Freud and Love: Treatment and Its Discontents*:

> If narcissism is a defence against the emptiness of separation, then the whole contrivance of imagery, representations, identifications and

---

69 James A. Brigham: "The Uncommon Ground", Ker, 28

projections that accompany it on the way towards strengthening the Ego and the Subject is a means of exorcising that emptiness. (1990, 257)

At the same time, the author's characters can provide much amusement, even a kind of spiritual solace. There is no direct emotion expressed between Blanford and Sutcliffe, because they would despise mawkish sentiments in the Disney style. They do, though, cherish each other. They are, after all, 'versions of one another set upon differing time-tracks', as Sutcliffe puts it in *Constance* (341). There are moments when Durrell sends up his conceit even as he endorses it. For instance, in the background to the telephone conversation at the beginning of *Livia*, Blanford hears 'the voice of a girl. He could not imagine her face as he had not yet invented her. That would come, he supposed. O God!' (L, 25-26) Blanford often makes fun of Sutcliffe's predicament, being dependent upon him. From time to time, Sutcliffe gets worried and asks his 'creator' if he is 'real'. After Trash sleeps with him - naked under furs - Sutcliffe says:

> "I am ringing to tell you that I have been raped by Trash - very enjoyably but against my will. Pure rape!"
> "It is not possible; you are fictions."
> "Have we no future, then?"
> "You have contexts, but no future and no past."
> He laughed and then recited:
>   "Tell me, how do fictions fuck?
>   All our swains commend their pluck!" (C, 340-1)

Even though they speak at length at the beginning of the second novel, *Livia*, Sutcliffe and Blanford do not meet until the end of the third novel, *Constance*. Significantly, it is the central female figure of *The Avignon Quintet*, Constance, who keeps questioning Blanford about Sutcliffe. For a while it is not certain whether Sutcliffe is 'real' or not. But when the couch from Freud's Viennese consulting rooms appears, Sutcliffe achieves a heavier reality (C, 19). It is apposite that a totem of psychoanalysis, one of the symbols prime of the new Freudian religion, is the object that makes concrete the reality of Sutcliffe. For so long he is an alter ego, sometimes a Jungian shadow, then he gains 'reality'. And the question is raised, who is writing whom, who invents whom?

> "Remember, Rob," Blanford retorted, "that everything you write about me is deeply suspect - at the best highly arguable. I invented you, after all."

"Or I you, which? The chicken or the egg?" (L, 10)

In the psychoanalytic view, the artist, *à la* van Gogh or Rimbaud or Michelangelo, is driven by his/ her compulsions. So it's quite possible that the fictional character creates the 'real' character. Indeed, this is exactly what happens, in the psycho-cultural view: our environment shapes us, we are shaped by what we consume, we align our readings with those of other people, etc. So Blanford may indeed be formed by Sutcliffe, much as Durrell will be formed by his characters. Why not have the writing process going both ways, flowing not only from author to text by from text to authors. Texts affect us, so why not characters? (And books are also characters in themselves: they have 'minds of their own'. Authors frequently speak of books 'writing themselves' – the author simply follows the book. Of *Monsieur*, Durrell complains of his 'exasperating book which keeps trying to dictate to me like a bloody schoolmistress' [DML, 460]).[70] In one of the many moments in his letters where Durrell is ruminating about *The Alexandria Quartet*, Durrell personifies his novel as another authoritarian figure, a refined English gentleman:

> My big book is there all right – it hasn't gone. I looked into myself yesterday and it was sitting there, smoking a pipe and looking back at me. I made a sign to it and asked it to wait a bit, and it nodded and smiled as one who might say, 'In your own good time, old boy, I'm in no hurry. I can wait." (DML, 205)

And in *Monsieur*, the Blanford-Sutcliffe exchanges provide some of the best moments in *The Avignon Quincunx*. Some of these conversations are vicious, like this typical, misogynist one:

> He broke off and said suddenly: "*Et le bonheur?*"
> "Exactly."
> "It cannot be impossible to find. It must be knocking about somewhere, just out of sight. Why don't we write a big autobiography? Come on, punish everyone!"
> "The last defence! All aboard for the last alibi!"
> "What does a man say when his wife leaves him? He cries out in an agony of fury: 'Thrice-tritrurated gasometers! Who will burn sugar to this tonsil-snipping tart?'"
> "Or seek the consolations of art: the little choking yelp of Desdemona

---

70 Durrell said that *Monsieur* was 'a terrible muddle because it's got all the themes in it, it's an old suitcase full of all themes I intend to develop.' (in Carley, 1979, 46)

is pleasant to dwell upon."

"Or he will become a widow and in desperation take up with some furry housemaid who will in due course be delivered of some rhubarb-coloured mite." (L, 16-17)

Much of Blanford and Sutcliffe's talk revolves around such 'men talk', the kind of barely-disguised woman-hating talk that goes on in pubs and men's clubs. Sutcliffe and Blanford can be tiresome in the extreme, their sexism relentless, their jokes sour and their handling of life's complexities becomes stereotypical.

But Blanford and Sutcliffe also announce the major themes of the *Quincunx*, and together they plan a series of five novels.

> "We will write a book."
> "Of what will it treat?"
> "Of the perennity of despair, intractability of language, impenetrability of art, insipidity of human love." (L, 15)

The form of the novels is spatial, they are joined together like five sides of a pentagon, or like the five trees which mark where the Knights Templar treasure is buried. The five novels of *The Avignon Quintet,* 'the Q novels' as Durrell calls them, are 'a Quincunx which is the magic pentacle' (DML, 492),[71] are not sequential, Blanford maintains, but linked spatially. Blanford explained:

> "Well, squinting round the curves of futurity I saw something like a quincunx of novels set out in a good classical order. Five Q novels written in a highly elliptical quincunxial style invented for the occasion. Though only dependent on one another as echoes might be, they would not be laid end to end in serial order, like dominoes – but simply belong to the same blood group, five panels for which your creaky old *Monsieur* would provide simply a cluster of themes to be reworked in the others. Get busy, Robin!"
> "And the relation of form to content?"
> "The books would be roped together like climbers on a rockface, but

---

71 Durrell envisioned Western (Freudian) psychology as based on the square (constructed from male, female, conscious, unconscious), and upon this four-sided configuration he placed the Eastern pentagram with its five skandhas (interview, BBC radio, 29 May 1985) The five skandhas or 'compartments' represented the Indian (Oriental) ego or self (Sanavio, 59). For Durrell the (Western) four was a question of counterstatement and paradox: the artist has to transcend the paradoxical stage in order, as Durrell put it, *'to cross the gulf which lies between the emblem and the symbol.'* (Ill, 42, 8, 1)

they would all be independent. The relation of the caterpillar to the butterfly, the tadpole to the frog. An organic relation."

Sutcliffe groaned and said: "The old danger is there – a work weighed down with theoretical considerations."

"No. Never. Not on your life. Just a *roman-gigogne*." (L, 11)

This is Durrell's problem, this over-theorizing of the novel. But all novels, all works of art, have æsthetic foundations of one sort or another. The art object itself is not a 'natural' occurrence, but a human, cultural one. Only humans make art, it seems. So Blanford's hope of an 'organic' form of the novel is not possible. The notions of time, space, sequence, viewpoint, content, form, etc, are all human-cultural notions. At the same time, *The Avignon Quintet* does seem to develop 'organically', that is, it grows and expands and improvizes in an open manner. As with *The Alexandria Quartet*, Durrell improvizes, jazz-style, on a number of themes. He can do this endlessly, it seems, conjuring up one love affair after another, moving from an exploration of one city after another. The reader, too, is invited to join in the game of creating alternative narratives: Durrell includes not only the 'Workpoints' at the end of each of the *Quartet* books, but other material which the reader may use if s/he chooses. Like post-Renaissance forms, Durrell's novels are 'open' forms, resisting closure, inviting improvization.[72]

For some critics of *The Alexandria Quartet*, Durrell was being too clever in his explorations of '4-dimensional' (DML, 272) post-Einsteinian space and time and relativity. As if one can be 'too clever'. Isn't this jealousy? Can one be 'too clever'? Isn't that like being too good, too kind, too pure, too tender? Why is cleverness a bad thing in an artist? Because artists are meant to be animals of instinct, like Vincent van Gogh, madly pursuing their inner daemons. No cleverness! Because it is 'pretentious' to be clever, to deal with grand themes. Durrell, it seems, is disliked for his cleverness, yet you might see Thomas Hardy and William Shakespeare as clever, and as tackling 'grand themes'. But Hardy and Shakespeare are humble, while Durrell remains arrogant, a little self-important, a little too smug, which critics hate.

Whatever the critical response, though, Durrell happily weaves in æsthetic and philosophical discussions into the narrative. The novel, said D.H. Lawrence, was the 'bright book of life', and one could put anything into it. Durrell's *The Avignon Quintet* is open enough for all manner of elements

___
72 George Steiner: "Lawrence Durrell: The Baroque Novel", in W, 1962, 15

to be woven in: satire, essays, travel writing, perorations, arguments, and so on.[73] One has to think openly, as Blanford notes:

> "I think the trouble is that you are thinking one-dimensionally all the time, like an old-fashioned novelist. You do not seem to be able to envisage a series of books through which the same characters move for all the world as if to illustrate the notion of reincarnation. After all, men and women are polyphonic beings." (L, 41)

Anaïs Nin pursued this notion of multiple personalities within one person, and may have influenced Durrell in the 1930s in this area.

The precursors of Blanford and Sutcliffe's Gog-and-Magog relationship are many: John Middleton Murry and D.H. Lawrence, Friedrich Nietzsche and his sister Elisabeth, Sigmund Freud and Carl Jung, Plato and Socrates (Durrell supplies most of these allusions). Sut and Blan appear more like Laurel and Hardy at times, which is not a criticism or demeaning of their writerly relationship, for Laurel and Hardy are highly prized comic artists. Samuel Beckett enjoyed them, and used their comic exchanges as a reference point in *Waiting For Godot*. Indeed, Sutcliffe and Blanford are often like Vladimir and Estragon ('Nothing happens! It's awful!'; 'What's the carrot like?' 'A carrot'; 'Shall we go?' 'Yes, let's go'. But, like Sutcliffe and Blanford, they don't go anywhere, they stay right where they are).

Other allusions in the Sutcliffe-Blanford relationship are to God and the Devil, where either is mistaken for Monsieur, the Prince of Darkness. And of course there is the Faust myth, with both Sutcliffe and Blanford taking the part of Mephistopholes. Sutcliffe often winds up gloomier and more grudgeful than Blanford. For Blanford exists, Sutcliffe moans, while he is only a figment, reliant on other people, namely Blanford, to make him appear (S, 144).

> "What more would you like to hear from me if I bring you back you life?"
> "About Tu; about Livia; about Hilary the brother and Sam. About the lake, and about Tu Duc and the Avignon of those early days. About us, the real ones."
> "Then let me ask you one question," said Blanford sternly. "Just how real do you feel to yourself, Robin Sutcliffe?"
> "I have never stopped to think," said his only friend after a pause.

[73] In the *Monitor* interview, Durrell said that the propositions about humanity and the cosmos were 'now so fantastic and so confused and so complicated that it does now seem to me worth the attention of a novelist to have a look at them.' (Mon, 122)

"Have you?" (L, 26)

The Blanford-Sutcliffe dialogues provide a commentary on the five novels of *The Avignon Quintet*. They reveal the narrator's disappointment with his creation. They are extra-digetic voices which disrupt the flow of the narrative even as they add to it. They are two old codgers leaning on a fence, discussing the flow of action from a distance, even as they are embroiled in it. But they can do this precisely because so much of the 'action' of the *Quintet* is discussion, is ideas and cultural commentary. In Durrell's art, as in Shakespeare's plays, dialogue is action, and much of the 'action' revolves around sparky dialogue. Blanford: "'You know full well that there is always something going on in the room next door and you often find yourself wondering what it might be. But it's never what you think.'" (S, 143) Schwarz, later on, adds: "Moreover it will prove surprising, totally unpredictable, and more often than not unpalatable!"

5

Philosophy

We are in the realm of magic, of course.

Lawrence Durrell, *Caesar's Vast Ghost* (38)

What is Lawrence Durrell's philosophy? Well, he started out with the notion of 'the heraldic universe', developed in the Thirties, which preoccupied his critics for a while. The 'heraldic universe' is that realm of subjective, affective and mysterious experiences and ideas, aligned with symbolism, rather than objectivity and causality.[1] In an early letter to Miller, Durrell said that 'in heraldry I seem to find that quality of magic and spatial existence which I want to tack on to art' (PC, 23). The 'heraldic' moment was the very moment of artistic creation, which Durrell was trying to isolate and explore. He admitted: 'for myself I am beginning to inhabit this

---

[1] Durrell, *Personal Landscape*, in W, 39-40. The key (and somewhat confused) letter explicating the 'heraldic universe' was written in Spring 1945 to Miller, where Durrell speaks of the 'purity of the symbol', and outlines in a table the plus and minus sides of his philosophy of heraldic 'Oneness' (PC, 200-4)

curious HERALDIC UNIVERSE when I write' (ibid.).[2]

The 'heraldic' dimension was really another version of the Neoplatonic 'essence'. It is the 'sigil' or 'sign' of a thing, the thingness of a thing, the "mandala' of the poet or of the poem', a 'chemical sigil or signature of the individual', Durrell explained in *A Smile in the Mind's Eye* (53). It's rather like Rainer Maria Rilke's notion of *innigkeit* or 'innerness'.[3] Rilke's sense of 'thingness' celebrated in his *New Poems* of 1906, and in poems such as 'The Panther', 'The Bowl of Roses' and 'The Torso of Apollo', was derived partly from his study of sculpture with August Rodin.[4] Durrell's 'heraldic universe' was similarly a product of Durrell's youth, of his first forays into literature. For Durrell's philosophy changes throughout his writing career. Just as Rilke moved from *innigkeit* to the Nietzschean Angel, so Durrell moved from the heraldic universe to Georg Groddeck's It, and finally to Taoism.

Blanford outlines his new life-philosophy in *The Avignon Quintet*, which is about being free, and fearless, and all-round healthy, a living in awe (Q, 174), with a cosmic viewpoint, a lack of European Will and sin and ego. 'You cannot help hugging yourself once you realise that there is no such thing as a self to hug! And you have all the time in the world' (Q, 94). Even Lord Galen gets to philosophize in the Blanfordian manner: '[t]he only art to be learned was how to cooperate with reality and the inevitable!' (Q, 191) In this Buddhist-Taoist philosophy, nothing is wasted, nothing is lost, and there is plenty of time for everything to take place. With every breath, heartbeat and thought 'the whole universe invests its strength in reality' (Q, 52). All this cooperation with the universe takes time to learn, however, and one of the most poignant of the many maxims and squibs in the *Avignon Quintet* is this from *Quinx*:

> "It's too short. It's the only criticism one can make of life. It's too short to learn anything." (Q, 210)

In the *Quincunx*, the narrator tells the reader time after time his views

---

2 'It is not making what goes on outside, I have discovered. It is what occurs in the inside spirits, where the great beings make their territory and the words cannot touch them', says the narrator of *Asylum in the Snow* (SP, 266)

3 Henry Miller was more sceptical about essences: 'who gives a fuck finally about the actual thing-in-itself? That is a philosophic problem, not an artistic one.' (PC, 22)

4 see Rilke: *Selected Poems*, tr. Stephen Mitchell, Picador 1987

on the universe. The universe is a big hug with no arms, says the narrator; the universe doesn't say anything precise, it merely hints (Q, 95); the universe is simply playing, improvising, there is no 'plan' or deity a work (Q, 167); '[t]he universe simply does the *next thing*' (Q, 38); the universe is not 'for' or 'against' anything, it is 'completely merciless' (Q, 39); 'life is on nobody's side' (L, 3). There is no formula for achieving this repose, Durrell's narrators know. 'Try as you will, there is no explanation for madness, happiness or death' (T, 173).

Lawrence Durrell's poetry is full of capitalized words, words as big symbols, as personifications, words found in Neoplatonism, Classic philosophy, mediæval theology, alchemy, etc. In Durrell's poem 'Cities, Plains and People' (1946) we find typical philosophic terms such as 'Time', 'Here and Now', 'Man', 'Sex', 'Consciousness', 'the One' and 'Spirit'. These are the terms Durrell employs, throughout his work. He is constantly searching and testing, setting up generalized terms such as 'Time' or 'God' only to destroy the simplicity of them, as they fragment into subtle shades.

The philosophy behind *The Alexandria Quartet* is basically Freudian psychoanalysis. This informs the psychological study of sexual relations, the 'investigation of human love', as Pursewarden calls it.[5] Durrell's metaphysics unites seemingly disparate elements: the psyche and the 'It', the individual and collective unconscious, the phenomenal and noumenal realms, individuality and tradition, science and psychology, Einstein and Lao tzu, Plato and Milarepa, East and West.

In *Key to Modern Poetry* Durrell cites Lao tzu and St John of the Cross, T.S. Eliot and Rainer Maria Rilke, W.H. Auden and John Donne, not quite as various a group of thinkers as he would later embrace – *Key* was written in mid-career (the late 1940s): Durrell came to appreciate many more philosophers after that time. The 'common ground' of Durrell's *philosophia perennis* (Gottfried Leibniz's term) incorporates a multiplicity of belief-systems. Yet there are other philosophies at work in *The Alexandria Quartet*. One of these is Georg Groddeck's theory of the 'It', which has something in common with Martin Buber's 'I and Thou'. Durrell wrote a Foreword to an edition of Groddeck's *The Book of It*, and the notion of the 'It' working through characters is most apparent in that 'non-human' character in the *Quartet*, Alexandria itself (DML, 195). In the

---

5 In his Foreword to Groddeck's *Book of the It*, Durrell rewrote Descartes thus: 'I am, therefore I can love' (xi).

characters, not just in Justine, the 'spirit' or 'Nous' or soul of Alexandria manifests itself. In 1946, Durrell wrote enthusiastically to Henry Miller of Groddeck: '[a]h! if only we had known about him in Paris! *This* is all that we felt was missing from Howe and Rank and Jung!' The idea is to cure oneself by finding 'a less painful mode of self-expression' for the 'It' (x). This is (partly) what the characters in the *Quartet* are trying to do. A few years later, though, in 1950, Durrell has changed his views after discovering another psychoanalytic guru: Francis J. Mott:

> I think his books are as big a step forward from Freud as Freud's Dream Analysis was from the psychology of the Victorians... he knocks Rank, Jung and Groddeck cold by the breadth of his vision. (DML, 248)

Durrell employs the psychoanalysis of Otto Rank at many points in the *Quartet*, particularly in the story of Darley's growth and transformation into being 'an artist'.[6] In *Key to Modern Poetry* Durrell writes at length of the significance of Rank's psychoanalyzing of the artist (88f). Psychoanalysis, whether derived from Freud, Rank, Jung, Groddeck or Mott, is central to Durrell's philosophy, if his views can be thought of as a 'philosophy'.

Throughout his fiction psychoanalysis is applied to human relationships. In *Tunc* and *Nunquam*, psychoanalysis is broadened to include all of civilization. Durrell calls *Tunc* 'very St Augustine and I hope a little Petronius too' (DML, 396). The analysis in *The Revolt of Aphrodite* is Freud filtered through Oswald Spengler, another longtime favourite of Durrell and Henry Miller. Spengler is a great metaphysical thinker in the tradition of Immanuel Kant, Johann Wolfgang von Goethe and Georg W.F. Hegel. But it was Spengler's discussion of æsthetics that Durrell really used in his double-decker – the way Spengler discussed the decay of 'cultures' into 'civilizations'. *The Revolt of Aphrodite* was all about decay. The setting of *The Revolt of Aphrodite* in the 'present' (1960s) adds to Durrell's interpretation of societal decay,[7] for his other fictions are set in the past, which is inevitably idealized. Set in the present, in the era of

---

6 Ray Morrison: "The Influence of Otto Rank on Lawrence Durrell's *The Dark Labyrinth, Sappho* and *The Alexandria Quartet*", OMG II, 135f

7 *Tunc-Nunquam* is all about being to the end of millennium, at the end of a certain trajectory of Western culture. Benedicta: "'[i]t's a terrible thing to feel that one has come to the end of one's life-experience – that there is nothing fundamentally new to look forward to: one must expect more and more combinations of the same sort of thing."' (T, 271)

cinema and mass advertizing, Durrell didn't need to exaggerate the decay, because it was present, he thought, in every trashy commodity, every banal TV advert, every capitalist political act.

The psychic decay is due to the 'death of God' culture we live in, as Mircea Eliade terms it.8 This is precisely Durrell's point too: that we live in a society of total desacralization. For Durrell, as for Eliade, a sense of meaning, which is vital, has been lost. This is a spiritual loss and decline:

> The crises of modern man are to a large extent *religious* ones, insofar as they are an awakening of his awareness to an absence of meaning. (ib, 148)

In *The Avignon Quintet* Freudian psychoanalysis is pitted against the other main metaphysical trend in Durrell's work, Oriental mysticism. For a long time Durrell espoused a loose Taoism. In a 1937 Paris notebook Durrell wrote about Taoism and Lao tzu as dissolving opposites, black and white, a 'wingless flying' (the Zen 'doing without doing') that transcends Western dualism: notions of 'ratiocinative principle' and taboos are also jettisoned when oppositional dualism is transcended (Ill, 42, 8, 1).

One of his favourite philosophers was the Tibetan mystic Milarepa (1052-1135) 'Mila Repa... I had known since I was sixteen', he said (*Smile*, 33). Another Tibetan slant is the sub-title, so to speak, of *The Alexandria Quartet*: the 'Book of the Dead', 'a Tibetan-type novel', Durrell calls it.9 Of course, in the tetralogy, set in Egypt, Durrell is also going for resonances with the Egyptian Book of the Dead. In the end, *The Avignon Quintet* turned out to be much more Eastern and Tibetan than the *Quartet*.

Writing to Durrell about his 'influences', Miller said:

> True, I've read [Freud] well, but as for "influence", I'd rather say that of Rank and Jung, if any. Bergson belongs to my "youth"... The great influences were Nietzsche, Spengler, yes, Emerson, Herbert Spencer (!), Thoreau, Whitman – and Elie Faure... This ties up with the progression, as you put it, from Bergson-Spengler to Chinese-Hindus. I think I've passed that too now. The key-word is Reality... The nearest philosophy to my heart and temperament is Zen... (DML, 229)

---

8 Eliade, 1984, 151: 'the theology of "the death of God" is extremely important, because it is the sole religious creation of the modern Western world. What it presents us with is the final step in the process of desacralization.'

9 Durrell: *On Miracle Ground: The Fourth International Lawrence Durrell Conference*, Pennsylvania State University, April 1986

There are many correspondences with Durrell's philosophy, and with the way Durrell, like Aldous Huxley and Alan Watts, moved from West to East. All this is summarized neatly in one of Durrell's best books, if not his best book, *A Smile in the Mind's Eye.*

A Smile in the Mind's Eye is perhaps Durrell's best book because it does everything Durrell wants from a book. It describes landscapes; it conjures up Eastern mysticism; it discusses food; it contains journeys; it is ironic; it talks about love; and it features 'real' and 'imaginary' people, not the least of these being the author himself. In *A Smile in the Mind's Eye,* Durrell writes himself into the text, as in the travel books, creating a carefully edited version of himself, as well as a female companion, called 'Vega'. In *A Smile in the Mind's Eye,* Durrell presents and mixes the two traditions of thought: Oriental philosophy, represented here by the writer Jolan Chang, Chinese cooking, memories of Lhasa and Tibet, and Taoist sex-mysticism. The Western tradition is embodied in discussions of the love affair of Francesco Petrarch and Laura de Sade, the Friedrich Nietzsche and Lou Andreas-Salomé relationship, Christianity, French wine, Freud, Empodecles, Epicurus, Faust, etc. The meshing of East and West in *A Smile in the Mind's Eye* is deft. Durrell is a clever writer, and he has never written in a better mode of syncretism and synthesis than in *A Smile in the Mind's Eye.*

Durrell's view of Taoism is that it is an open, relaxed life-philosophy, a state of 'total availability' and total involvement in the present moment (SME, 1). It is *'a perfect spiritual detachment'*, being *'content to 'be' as fully as possible' (Pied Piper of Lovers,* 233-234). It is something that cannot be pinpointed and pinned down by language or rationality. It is not this and not that: '[h]ere you are in the region of the Indian *not-this-not-that business'* (ib., 8).

Durrell continually emphasizes the 'poetic' quality of Taoism. It is, for him, the most poetic of world religions. Indeed, he sees it partly as 'an aesthetic view of the universe rather than a purely institutional one' (8). Durrell speaks, like Alan Watts, D.T. Suzuki, Aldous Huxley *et al,* of 'right attention', 'is-ness', 'refinement', 'enlightenment', 'spontaneity' and 'bliss'. 'Congruence, appropriateness, it was our job to capture the whole thing when it was bliss side up, so to speak' (10). The idea is to grasp 'the impossible' (happiness, justice and love), perhaps not even waiting for the woman to follow (Som, inventory 1345).

Like Taoism, Durrell's form of Gnosticism, as expounded by Akkad in *Monsieur,* encourages spontaneity. One begins to improvize, and existence becomes 'extremely precarious, vertiginous, hesitant – but truthful in a way that you never thought you could be' (M, 167). When Durrell discusses, via Jolan Chang, Taoist sex yoga, he speaks of 'the vital Taoist essence', 'rapport', 'attachment' and 'the whole precious transaction'. All of this Taoist lore was pumped into the *Quintet*, in particular the last three novels. It's all about getting into a deep rapport with the significant other, an enmeshment that encourages Taoist immortality; it's about cultivating essence and love, to evoke insights and intensity (SME, 18). Durrell's 'Tao of sex' is a lovemaking of chiming orgasms and blissful amnesia (20).

Durrell and Science

An eternally curious soul, Lawrence Durrell, like Goethe, Shakespeare, Novalis, Hardy and Dante, was fascinated by natural science, by the knowledge that biology, medicine, chemistry, astronomy and physics uncover. The use of Einsteinian relativity in *The Alexandria Quartet* was only one part of Durrell's general scientific curiosity. Notions of space and time have always fascinated Durrell. Durrell's use of Albert Einstein is to indicate one area of science that might impinge upon the 'modern novel'. Throughout his work, Durrell explores, in an amateurish, intuitive way, the development of theories of space and time: from Classic Greek space, which was finite and spherical, to Euclidian geometry, with its notion of three dimensional endlessness. In the cosmology of Classical Greece, space, that is, the universe, was 'finite and spherical, with no endless stretch of emptiness beyond.'[10] Renaissance science and philosophy, however, destroyed this sense of finite space. Michel Foucault suggests that

> the real scandal of Galileo's work lay not so much in his discovery, or rediscovery, that the earth revolved around the sun, but in his constitution of an infinite, and infinitely open space.[11]

Euclidean geometry changed Classical cosmology: after Euclid's *The Elements of Geometry* and *Optics*, space was re-ordered. Renaissance

10 F.M. Cornford: *Plato's Cosmology*, Harcourt, Brace, New York 1937
11 Foucault: "Of Other Spaces", *Diacritics*, vol. 16, no. 1

perspective built on Euclid, with the concept of the 'cone of vision'. At the same time, in the midst of this endless space, with its notions of emptiness underneath things so central to post-Renaissance culture, is the individual observer. What sets alight Renaissance space, makes it work, is the homocentric, egocentric, subjective observer.

> The effect of monocular perspective [writes Victor Burgin], however, is to maintain the idea that this space does nevertheless have a centre - the observer. By degrees the sovereign gaze is transferred from God to man. With the 'emplacement' of the medieval world now dissolved, this ocular subject of perspective, and of mercantile capitalism, is free to pursue its entrepreneurial ambitions wherever trade winds blow.[12]

This is the position of Durrell's narrators: they are individuals who see things in terms of an idiosyncratic subjectivity. Each character has her/ his own viewpoint, which does not match up with that of others. Durrell also uses the notion of phenomenology and Werner Heisenberg,[13] namely that the observer affects directly what is being observed. Subject and object are thus part of a continuum: the detached onlooker is no longer tenable: every one affects everyone else.[14] The very act of studying something changes the thing and the observer.[15]

For Durrell, the New Physics, quantum theory, particle physics, superstrings, babyverses, black holes, cosmology and so on, offer intriguing metaphors apposite for the era. These new scientific theories have a poetry to them which is hard to ignore. After all, the term *quark* comes from James Joyce, from *Finnegans Wake* ('Three quarks for Muster Mark'). Murray Gell-Man found that Joyce's phrase fits roughly with the recipe for

---

12 Victor Burgin: "Geometry and Abjection", in Fletcher, 1990,106
13 Even Durrell's appraisal of Heisenberg, though, is given an anti-semitic slant, for Durrell asserts that the 'fruit of Jewish monotheism was the scientific rationalism which afflicts us, for the Jewish intention was to exploit matter by smashing it anatomically and extracting its marketable energy to yield gold!' (CVG, 38)
14 'In recent decades, the Heisenberg "principle of indeterminacy" has been seized upon by this desperate infantilism of man (theology always distorts the facts) as purporting to prove that the prestigious physical world itself behaves in ways that we would like to believe true also of ourselves. What is astounding is our duplicitous distortion and stubborn misapprehension of the evidence itself - always in the direction of our desire!' commented Weston La Barre (1972, 333).
15 see Rodaway, 8; D. Seamon: "Doing phenomenology", paper, Association of American Geographers, Colorado, 1983

making a neutron ('take three quarks').[16]

The new cosmology is instantly poetic and mysterious, and Durrell does not pretend to understand it: he reacts to it as an artist, looking for its æsthetic potential. 'If anyone says that he can think about quantum mechanics without becoming dizzy, that only shows that he has not understood anything whatever about it', said Niels Bohr.[17] At the same time, though, Western æsthetics, perspective and sense of space have not changed that much since Euclid, Galileo and Newton:

> The cosmology of modern physics has nevertheless had little impact on the commonly held world-view in the West, which is still predominantly an amalgam of Newton and Aristotleanism – 'places in space', a system of centres of human affairs (homes, workplaces, cities) deployed within a uniformly regular and vaguely endless 'space in itself'. (Victor Burgin, op. cit., 107)

The Universe of Death

Death is central in Lawrence Durrell's philosophy. It occurs throughout his fiction and writing. The significance of death is everywhere apparent in Durrell's *œuvre*. He speaks continually of people 'stepping behind the curtain', of people speaking the truth from beyond the grave, of the dying and the dead questioning the living. Just looking at the number of people who die in his books suggests an emphasis on death: Pursewarden commits suicide, as does Campion, leaping into the Mediterranean without being able to swim; Sacrapant throws himself off a building ('[t]he suicide of Sacrapant... is a warning, like the Capitoline geese, to the two lovers who

---

16 Murray Gell-Man: *The Quark and the Jaguar*, Little, Brown 1994; Lewis Wolpert: "Hunting the quark", *The Sunday Times*, 19 June 1994, 7, 4
17 In Gell-Man.

witness it', Med, 91);[18] Piers is given poison in a 'Gnostic' suicide[19] (Piers' 'Gnostic' suicide is mirrored ironically by the chief psychopath of the War, Adolf Hitler, who suicided in the bunker after his dream of creating a modern, occult Knights Templar came to nothing, and the head of the Pompey brought back by the Crusaders failed to utter any prophecies); the psychoanalyst Schwarz poisons himself; Julian falls to his death from the Whispering Gallery of St Paul's Cathedral; Sam is blown to pieces by shells; Affad is stabbed to death by the psychotic Mnemidis; Melissa dies, as does Cohen; Capodistra fakes his death, while Clea nearly drowns; Iolanthe dies; Sipple the clown is murdered; Scobie is beaten to death by sailors. And so on.

The catalogue of deaths in Durrell Land is not simply a cheap gimmick to create sensational material, but a deep fascination with death that runs throughout Durrell's worldview. The number of deaths Constance has to endure is large: her sister, Livia, commits suicide; her brother, Hilary, is executed by the Germans; her husband, Sam, is killed in a British artillery accident; her lover, Affad, is murdered by her psychotic patient; her co-worker and mentor, Schwarz, suicides; her friend, Nancy Quiminal, is killed by the French mob.

Suicide has a place of importance in Durrell's art: suicide is a popular way of dying in Durrelland. Why? Because committing suicide is the most 'romantic' act, and especially for an artist. The central suicide of *The Alexandria Quartet*, of Pursewarden, is given a number of interpretations, from political intrigue, to sacrifice (making way for Mountolive's marriage to Liza). The major function of Pursewarden, though, is as an *artist*. It is as an artist that Pursewarden utters all his insights and views.[20] He has an exalted view of the artist ('the creative person is charged with the difficult responsibility of being more human than others', he claims, in Nietzschean

---

18 The 'fall' is a gnostic 'fall into matter', echoing the Fall of Adam and Eve into original sin; the Oriental twist on the fall is that it is a mystical leap into the 'beyond', as Chuang-tzu called it. 'Yes, there is always The Leap! The Avignon bridge symbolises it', muses Blanford (Q, 92). Nature itself can also 'jump', not slowly evolve, from one thing to another, Durrell notes (FEB, 8)
19 The gnostic death (suicide) is meant to re-establish the 'self-perpetuating cycle of joy which was the bliss of yesterday', Akkad says (M, 142), evoking a new slant on the nostalgia for an ancient, mythic Paradise which is so central a myth to Western culture.
20 Critics have doubted Pursewarden's abilities, as demonstrated in the *Quartet*, to 'make an artist of any kind at all' (in Boris Ford, 7, 526)

mode),[21] and so his suicide must be seen, finally, as an æsthetic act. 'Pursewarden's suicide is the sacrifical suicide of a true cathar', says Durrell in "The Kneller Tape" (W, 168), although it is not presented as such.

For Lawrence Durrell, the Gnostics and Cathars were artists; just as modern artists are the heretics of our time, going against the flow, eternally rebellious and anti-establishment, so the mediæval Gnostics, Templars, courtly love poets and Cathars rebelled against the status quo. Pursewarden's suicide thus combines all the major themes in Durrelland: love, art, time and religion. Mythologically, Pursewarden is Osiris, a Dionysian god, a Falstaffian expounder of 'belly worship', that is, a lover of pleasure, wine, women, humour. *God Is a Humourist* is the (bad) title of Pursewarden's last book, and so God is, finally, the Joker, the 'Trickster God', an ancient type of deity who delights in usurping the social and moral order. Pursewarden's function is to overturn the establishment, to upset and subvert the social order. Pursewarden's image as the Trickster God is echoed by his *magnum opus*. That is, the joke, the Great Cosmic Chuckle (the Taoist laugh) is at the heart of things – the unexpected, the Principle of Indeterminacy.[22] Pursewarden as the Trickster God is endlessly phallic. Pursewarden, like Zeus in Greek mythology, fucks all the woman in the *Quartet*: he fucks Melissa, Justine and Liza (and nearly fucks Clea). He tups all of Darley's women, and does it better than Darley. As Osiris or Dionysus, the ancient gods of fertility and creativity, Pursewarden is endlessly resurrected.

The ancient oak-kings, as Robert Graves calls them in *The White Goddess*, the 'Green Man', Robin Hood, May King, or Jack-in-the-Green, as he is known in British folklore, must be sacrificed each year. So Pursewarden, like the Fool of Tarot cards,[23] like the king of 'primitive' tribes, is sacrificed then resurrected, exactly as described in J.G. Frazer's *The Golden Bough*. (One huge sacrifice involves the burning of Pursewarden's greatest achievement, his love letters to Liza – he and Liza are compared to Isis and Osiris).[24] Pursewarden's resurrection is, naturally for a writer, mainly as a writer: each character resurrects Pursewarden in

---

21 Lee Lemon: *Portraits of the Artist in Contemporary Fiction*, University of Nebraska Press, Lincoln 1985, 10
22 Lee J. Lemon: "Durrell's Major Works", in K, 161
23 Pursewarden is linked with the ancient Trickster God (in the Tarot deck scheme of the *Quartet* he is the Fool).
24 Carol Peirce: "That "one book there, a Plutarch": Of *Isis and Osiris* in *The Alexandria Quartet*", in OMG, 83

their own manner: each character has their own Pursewarden anecdote, as they do about Scobie. It is a resurrection into art (for Durrell art is religious, and vice versa).

The importance of Pursewarden for the narrator of the *Quartet* is clear from the first third of *Clea*: as the narrator relates Darley's return to Alexandria, Pursewarden's wry comments are cited constantly. The narrator writes 'as Pursewarden said', or 'which recalls Pursewarden's motto', and so on. Even though Pursewarden has been dead some three or four years, or whatever the time is that Darley has been away, he remains a key figure, vividly remembered by the characters. The first of the major sections in another narrative voice in *Clea* is Pursewarden's "My Conversations with Brother Ass", which Durrell regards as important.

In fact, Henry Miller wrote perceptively about Pursewarden in letter of 7th September 1959, saying that he didn't think Pursewarden was that interesting a character, and he didn't believe Pursewarden was the great writer the narrator and all the characters in the *Quartet* think he is. For Miller, Pursewarden's literary/ philosophical remarks were 'sententious and tedious and feeble sometimes' (PC, 361). I can't help agreeing. Durrell's narrators are wary of artists when they start preaching; after all Pursewarden dislikes this in D.H. Lawrence, yet it is what Pursewarden does more than anything else! Pursewarden can't help berating every character with his Deep Thoughts. He lectures Clea, Darley, Mountolive, Nessim, Justine. No character escapes from a Pursewarden metaphysical diatribe. Durrell seems to have made a rule that every time Pursewarden opens his mouth, some joke, witticism, dictum or philosophical attack should fall out. It's a terrible (and embarrassing) burden Pursewarden's character has to sustain, this constant humorous/ metaphysical discourse. No one stands up to Pursewarden's apparently towering intellect. No tells him to *shut up, you're a lecherous, sexist, modernist, out-of-date, Anglo-Saxon, generalizing, ineffectual wind-bag.*

Pursewarden is indelibly romantic, utterly, excruciatingly romantic. It is his final spiritual creed. When Mountolive appears in his beloved sister's life, it is the moment for him to extricate himself from his incestuous relationship. Yet how typical of a writer who is an inheritor of death-obsessed Romanticism, from de Sade and Byron through Baudelaire and Bataille, that Pursewarden should conceive of his withdrawal in terms of death. Yes, death is, in a sick, twisted way, Pursewarden's 'wedding present' to Liza (Cl, 149). Pursewarden has swallowed the whole sex-and-death metaphysics of the European Romantic so completely he thinks his suicide will set Liza free! And she half believes it, in her confusion and sorrow. It is extraordinarily pathetic. Pursewarden's act of suicide, conceived in the novel as the ultimate 'romantic act', is in fact pathetic. Not 'pathetic' in the grand, tragic manner, but 'pathetic' in the cheap, silly, childish manner. One feels like saying, 'oh, come on, Ludwig: *grow up!*'

Aligned with Durrell's poetic Gnosticism is his notion of the significance of the negative, the paradox, the counterstatement. One of the key phrases in Durrellian philosophy is: 'I move through many negatives to what I am'. This Gnostic negative outlook chimes with Durrell's death-consciousness, his enshrining of figures such as Paracelsus and Faust in the West and Milarepa and Chuang-tzu in the East, and his Taoism and Buddhism. The *via negativa* of in *An Irish Faustus* is described by Margaret:

So that somehow one must turn oneself
Into a place of visitation, refining by negatives
Until the void, abhorred by nature, is filled by it,
Rushing in to expel the categories of the mind? (12)

A sentence Durrell found valuable in Ford Maddox Ford's *The Good Soldier* is also pertinent here: '[q]ualities are inherent in their negatives'.

Durrell's Spenglerian/ Gnostic view is that civilization has become perverted or corrupted at its heart, via the Gnostic view of the 'fall' into matter. Creativity is thus inverted, and becomes decay.[25] Durrell calls for a 'Science of Death,' a sort of tragic Nietzschean awareness of the vicissitudes of life (*The Dark Labyrinth* contains an epigram from Plato's *Phaedo* on the reality of life and death). Poets ought to get close to death (and childbirth) Durrell said (like Rainer Maria Rilke), for 'these two great basic experiences... are the workshop of poetry' ('Asides of Demonax', Som, 7).

The death-consciousness of Lawrence Durrell's owes something to D.H. Lawrence, to Nietzsche, and to Gnostic philosophers. The concern with death is there at the beginning of Durrell's writing career, in books such as *Panic Spring* and *The Black Book*, with its living death of 'the English death', and early poetry such as 'The Death of General Uncebunke'. For Durrell, the dead are all around us, exactly as a novelist's characters surround her/ him. In his fiction, Durrell's characters communicate with the dead exactly as a writer communicates with her/ his fictional creations.

25 Ian MacNiven: "Steps to *Livia*", OMG, 334

One thinks of Blanford talking to the empty alcove in the restaurant at the end of *Monsieur* – he is talking to the dead Constance. Sutcliffe regards himself as partly dead, and begs his creator, Blanford, to bring him back to life. The author, then, is also 'D', the Devil, the one who brings death, who orchestrates the living and the dead. Just as Balthazar is described as 'some goat-like apparition from the Underworld' (B, 15), so the author/ narrator in Durrell's fiction is a latter-day god, guiding people back and forth over the River Styx, bringing them to life, then quenching their life.

Death, says Durrell, is so central to life children ought to be acquainted with it from an early age. If Durrell was world president, a visit to the morgue would be on every school's curriculum:

> Fundamentally, our education, the whole business of our ethos, or culture, should begin with death and with birth... All education should really start with death, and the proof of our enormous repression about this matter is that we put a screen around the dying. (OMG, 15)

For Durrell, things would be a lot better if people assisted at the delivery of children, and helped people to die. Getting in touch with death and birth in such a 'hands on' manner, Durrell claims, would balance people. Instead of repressing/ suppressing death and the actualities of the human condition, they would become normalized and balanced. Durrell reckons that directly facing birth and death is what poets do, and is what Eastern philosophy, in the form of yoga, is about. Discussing a seminar he took, Durrell said that

> the fact of helping to deliver a few babies and helping shut the eyes and lay out a couple of people deepened their feeling of reality, which engaged them immediately on the poetic path, which, like yoga, starts from there' (ib., 15)

Like D.H. Lawrence, Durrell reckons we hide too much of these important events and experiences. Like Lawrence, Durrell advocates a culture of reawakening. 'Here I am, lost in wonder at the self-evident', he writes in a late poem, 'Les Saintes' (CVG, 79)

One of the key phrases of Durrell's art is: 'it *hurts* to realize'. Or 'realization hurts'.[26] Artistic rebirth is thus seen as being potentially as

---

26 'The new is the most frightening thing. It's like being born all the time you know' (Durrell, in Margaret McCall: "*The Lonely Roads*: Notes for an Unwritten Book", MC 3,

painful as actual birth. Rebirth is literally an 'en*light*enment', that is, coming in to the light after years spent in darkness. It is literally a re-awakening after a sleep that resembles death. This is why when Darley is saving Clea's life he feels he has hit his head on the roof of the universe: his own rebirth as a creative individual is seen as physically (symbolically) painful as Clea's actual coming back to life after nearly drowning. Speaking towards the end of Durrell's *An Irish Faust*, the magus says:

> For the first time I knew I was in reality.
>   Most of the time
> We are not, d'you see, life as we
>   Know it is a conditional state,
> And reality prime – why, it hurts. (70-71)

One way of reawakening or rebirth is yoga; another for Durrell is creativity. Thus, he makes the artist the central character of *The Avignon Quintet* and *The Alexandria Quartet,* artists who are embarked upon a quest of reawakening,[27] of rebirthing themselves, being their own midwife and mother and foetus.[28] For the Western world, which does not have ancient and still thriving practices which involve the whole body and mind such as yoga, art is one of the nearest things that may also do the trick of reawakening. Others try aromatherapy, crop circles, Tarot, hypnosis, astrology, Amercan Inidian shamanism, palmistry, numerology, tassomancy, homeopathy, creative visualization, herbalism, geomancy, Qabalah, meditation, runes, acupuncture, reflexology, etc. These areas of thought, now termed New Age/ hippie/ underground/ alternative, are not far from Durrell's own do-it-yourself view of life.

For Durrell, Protestantism, Catholicism and the Anglican faith are simply not enough. They repress and suppress the body, which is only present in the bizarre god-eating ritual of the Mass, the blood and body of Christ. His hatred of the 'blood-stained package' is apparent throughout all his work. In *Caesar's Vast Ghost* he speaks of '[g]uilt, original sin, circumcision, atonement. And all symbolized by the blood-spattered crucifix with its

---

27 J.R. Nichols speaks of 'the necessary yet self-defeating nature of cyclical rebirths' ("The Paradise of Bitter Fruit: Lawrence Durrell's *Alexandria Quartet*", OMG I, 231)
28 In his Egypt and Corfu notebook, Durrell spoke of the (Greek) sea as a womb, a dreaming sea, in which the bed of the dreamer (or foetus), the room, the house and the sea were all womb-images (Som). These are typical ideas of Durrell in the 1930s and 1940s, the era of Miller with his womb-fixation, and Durrell's exaltation of Otto Rank.

nailed-up symbol of man's divinity, the holy predicament of twentieth-century man!' (78) Durrell was turned off the slaughter and cannibalism of Christianity at a early age;[29] the move into Buddhism and Taoism was inevitable for a person of his temperament, it seems, as with Aldous Huxley and Alan Watts.[30] Naturally shiatsu, Tai Chi, *I Ching*, yoga and other Oriental pathways would interest Durrell (though Blanford is berrated by Sutcliffe in *Quinx* for carrying so much 'brain-wearying lumber' around, all the philosophic baggage which Sutcliffe calls 'this brain-mash of Hindu soul-fuck' [Q, 83]).

The trajectory of Durrell's fiction, then, is away from the repression/ suppression of 'the English death' of the early novels, a life-denying world-view, towards that of yoga and the holistic, 'whole body' philosophies of the East. The general metaphysical movement towards the Orient, though, is balanced by any number of sidetracking shifts into the arcane realms of Western thought. Durrell has been intrigued by astrology, numerology, alchemy, psychoanalysis, Tarot, Qabalah, Gnosticism, meditation, vampirism, Satanism and ophitism, all of which appear in his novels. Caradoc in *Tunc* founds his notion of architecture, in his Parthenon speech, upon notions of geomancy and Chinese *feng shui*, a system of making buildings in harmony the Earth's energies ('[a] real piece of building must be responsive to the emanations of the ground upon which it stands' [N, 211]), while Justine uses Tarot cards (J, 160), and Durrell used the Tarot pack to delineate his characters.

Durrell employed the Ryder-Waite and Marseilles Tarot decks chiefly,[31] and relates each volume of the *Quartet* to the four elements (the fire of sex in *Justine,* cerebral air in *Balthazar,* Egypt's earth magic in *Mount-olive,* and the watery transformations in *Clea*).[32] Melissa is the High Priestess card, virginal, Artemis-like; Pursewarden's The Fool; Balthazar's the hermetic doctor and Hermit; Darley is the would-be Magus, the artist;

29 Durrell's dim view of Christianity is expressed in one of his late poetry books, *The Red Limbo Lingo*: 'the extraordinary blood-spattered figure of a man nailed to a wooden cross, like an expiring frog' (10-11).
30 'Beginning in 1938...the perennial philosophy appears increasingly, so that the bulk of Durrell's verse constitutes a document of nonattachment', writes James A. Brigham ("The Uncommon Ground", K, 28)
31 Durrell's characters are sometimes seen as deriving from pantomime, or the circus, or Jungian psychology (*anima, animus* and shadow figures), or mediæval mysteries and plays (knight-errant, clown, dwarfs and grotesques, damsels/ princesses, deposed kings, whores, etc.
32 Carol Peirce: ""Intimations of Powers Within": Durrell's Heavenly Game of the Tarot", CE, 202

Nessim and Justine are the Emperor and Empress; and Capodistra may be The Devil. The elements of esoterica such as alchemy, Gnosticism and the Qabalah are obvious from any reading of *The Alexandria Quartet* or *The Avignon Quintet* (Mountolive, for example, is related to the charioteer of the Tarot pack, to Pilate, and to Antony, which recalls Shakespeare and Plutarch). As he embraces Oriental philosophy, and dives into the underworld of Western metaphysics, Durrell also collects folklore, everyday sayings, mottoes, and superstitions. He employs the local or folklore view most obviously in the travel books, but the homely and quotidian slant also provides a commentary on the narratives in the fiction. Durrell's travel books are in one sense collections of local colour, superstitions and folklore knitted together with lyrical descriptions of landscapes. What Durrell's embracing of Oriental philosophy lacks is precisely the sense of detail and folklore which is apparent in all his fiction. The Oriental philosophy is presented with big, broad brushstrokes, while the descriptions of Greece or France or Egypt are full of 'local colour', nuances and details.

The love of depravity, 'perversity', sterility, vacuity, and other extremes of feeling and experience in Durrell's work is explained by his life-philosophy of achieving wholeness through an embrace of *every* aspect of life. Not just the lovely, pretty bits, but also the nasty, disgusting bits. Only by embracing the hearty, fleshly, erotic, smelly, dirty side of life can people be whole, says Durrell. 'It's only with great vulgarity that you can achieve real refinement, only out of the bawdy that you can get tenderness' (in Andrewski, 60).[33]

Durrell's 'vulgarity', his use of clowns, bawdy humour, squalor and excrement is part of this Rabelaisian movement towards tenderness. Henry Miller, John Cowper Powys and Arthur Rimbaud also worked through squalor to sacrality. In John Cowper Powys's fiction there is a dual religion, as in Durrell's work, of the ecstasy of excrement and the excremental dimension of ecstasy. In Durrell's output, the two poles of human life, sex and death, ecstasy and excrement, spirituality and materiality, are united only by excessive indulgence. Like Rimbaud, Durrell advocates a

---

[33] Even so, 'Durrell's is an astonishingly lovely world', as Gerald Sykes notes ("One Vote For the Sun", W, 154). The more one reads of the scorching beaches, the dazzling blue skies, the silk-warm seas, the sailing trips, the dolphins, the Greek languor, the more wonderful seems the world of Durrell's characters (SP, 66, 79-80)

'deschooling/ disordering of the senses', but not for the sake of debauchery.

There is always a spiritual goal in Durrell's art, so sex is never just sex, but something more. Love, says Durrell, is '[o]f all experiences the new sublime'.[34] The dive into extreme sensuality is precisely in order to cultivate the spiritual dimension. Each Durrell character is on a vision quest which involves travelling through the labyrinth of disgust and decadence, in order to reach refinement and the sacred.[35] 'I must work through the dross of my character and burn it up,' says Justine (J, 64).

Alexandria plays its part, like other Durrell locations, from Athens through Istanbul to Bournemouth and London, in this unification of mud and mysticism, death and divinity: always Alexandria is a place of dualities, of ontological polarities, always described in the 'Big City Poem' (as Durrell called his *Quartet* [W, 159]) as both a place of ecstasy and excrement: 'royal city and anus mundi' (C, 63), 'a city at once sacred and profane' (B, 83), an 'impossible city of love and obscenity' (B, 183), a city like a whore and virgin, a city like 'some old reptile' (C, 14), a Kundalini serpent, the central image of Tantrism.[36]

Each character is on a religious journey through the Underworld of Alexandria (life) in order to be reborn. Rebirth is the key theme of *The Alexandria Quartet*,[37] and of all Durrell's work, a theme which can be stated in different ways (you might see it as transcendence, as Jungian individuation, Lawrencean 'coming into being', Rilkean death-consciousness, Rimbaudian seer-hood, Taoist wholeness, etc).

The underwater near-drowning scene and the love scenes were 'really a mime about rebirth', Durrell said, in which 'the breakthrough to poetic illumination' and 'artisthood' is made – through breathing, and through the carnal knowledge sex brings (W, 166). The aim is to become a genius, which is simply 'the self awake'; 'poetic illumination' is Durrell's non-religious term (though it is a 'religious' term) for this spiritual awakening or *hieros gamos*. This cathartic enlightenment is 'the unrecognized Happy Ending that people look for at the end of a work of art' (W, 161). It is this

---

34 Durrell: 'State of Lovers: Aix', in Med, 128
35 All Durrell's characters are on a quest of some sort or another. 'My real objective has always been a sort of religious quest', Durrell said in the late 1980s (Pine, 1994, 55).
36 David M. Woods in OMG, 108f
37 James Nichols: "The Paradise of Bitter Fruit: Lawrence Durrell's *The Alexandria Quartet*", in OMG I, 224f

fairy tale-like 'happy ending' he invokes at the end of the *Quartet* when he has Darley write *once upon a time*. Although *Clea* 'ends' like this, it doesn't really 'end': Clea's letter trails off into a series of dots...[38]

Even as Darley is developing as a person he is understanding new things about the people he lived with for years. His growth inhibits the realization of certain things at certain times: his growth in sclf-knowledge parallels his knowledge of events.[39] Darley travels a course of psychic transformation, following 'classic' lines, from weakness to strength, low self-esteem to self-confidence, ignorance to knowledge, restlessness to repose (Nichols, ib., 224).

It is a simple, mythic development, as found in the myths of Orpheus and Eurydice. For Rainer Maria Rilke, the key was to embrace silence and death, to become so 'death-conscious' that reality becomes lucid and transparent. For Rilke, flowers live partly in the Underworld, they are open to 'the Open', as lovers are. In early poems such as 'The Prayer-Wheel', Durrell wrote of the void which surrounds people. (CP, 82)

For Rilke, as for Durrell, love and art and spirituality are the three main methods of achieving pellucidity and wholeness. Durrell's characters use other methods – incest, violence, political power, Qabalah, Tarot – which are all related to, and parts of, the basic theme of rebirth. In *The Alexandria Quartet*, Balthazar outlines the metaphysical dialogue between the twin polarities of Durrell's theme:

> ...to work here [Alexandria] at all ...one must try to reconcile two extremes of habit and behaviour which are not due to the intellectual disposition of the inhabitants, but to their soil, air, landscape. I mean extreme sensuality and intellectual asceticism... It is the national peculiarity of the Alexandrians to seek a reconciliation between the two deepest psychological traits of which they are conscious. That is why we are hysterics and extremists. That is why we are the incomparable lovers we are. (J, 87)[40]

Whether the way to transcendence is religion, science, art, politics or

---

38 As John Weigel rightly notes: '[t]he book never properly ends. There are no 'endings' in curved [Einsteinian] space!' (89)

39 Lisa Schwerdt: "Coming of Age in Alexandra: The Narrator", Cartwright, 211

40 Of the two sides of the Egyptian character, Durrell, sitting beside the Sphinx, says: '[y]ou get the immense æstheticism absolutely side by side with an absolutely agonising sensuality.' (in Peter Adam: "Alexandria Revisited", Mac 3, 401) Surely that should be 'immense *asceticism*', not 'æstheticism'?

sex, the key is to *'indulge but refine'*, as Balthazar says (J, 89). This is the key dictum of all Durrell's characters. It is the dictum of the Romantic, Symbolist artist: Verlaine, Rimbaud, Gide, Hölderlin, Lawrence, Byron, Shelley, Keats – they all preached a gospel of extremity and indulgence, in one way or another. For Durrell's characters, one must always go to extremes: that's where knowledge lies. In Durrell's world, love 'is an absolute which takes all or forfeits all' (J, 93). One might substitute the word 'religion' or 'art' for 'love' here, as one can do throughout Durrell's work.

Some Lawrence Durrell places. This page: Bournemouth, England.
(Photos by J.M. Robinson)

Paris, left, at
Montmartre.
Avignon, above, lookin
towards the Popes'
Palace during the
Festival.

Corfu, above.
Cairo, below.

Modern day Alexa
Egypt, including so
Lawrence Durrell
settings: Pastroudi
top, and the tower,
below.

6

Personal Landscapes

Many commentators have discussed Lawrence Durrell's notion of landscape or 'spirit of place'. 'I firmly believe in the theory that landscape shapes people and behaviour patterns', Durrell said. (BS, 90) For Durrell, landscape (expressed in flora and fauna, trees, plants, smells) is one of the guiding principles or forces that humans must respond to (*Nunquam*, 211). For Durrell, 'man is only an extension of the spirit of place' (*Justine*, 156); the narratives of the *Quartet* are controlled by the city (J, 23), so that '[w]e are the children of our landscape; it dictates our behaviour and even thought' (J, 36). Thus, people in the Mediterranean are 'simply the landscape-wishes of the earth', which also produces the wine, food, sunlight and sea.[1]

The key text here is the essay "Landscape and Character", where Durrell describes the process of sitting quietly in a place in order to sniff out the essence of it. "Landscape and Character" is pure proto-hippy philosophy: Durrell speaks of 'tuning in', idly, to the landscape, in order to experience that 'mysterious sense of *rapport*, of identity with the ground' (SP, 162). One should be able to do this poetic absorption anywhere, Durrell says, whether having a quiet drink in a Parisian *bistro*, or sitting under the Tree

---

1 Durrell: "Women of the Mediterranean", SP, 371

of Idleness, or beside the *omphalos* at Delphi, or the Mena House pyramid at sunset (SP, 157-8). Durrell even recommends going to Stonehenge and watching the sun rise – a 'dull and 'touristic' thing to do' he says, but a good way of reaching the heart of England. (In fact it is not possible to sit in the actual stone circle of Stonehenge anymore, as hippies know to their dismay).

Durrell speaks of being a 'residence writer', that is, someone who lives in a place not as a tourist or visitor (SP, 156). Like any number of other (travel) writers (Paul Bowles, Bruce Chatwin, Paul Theroux, Rose Macaulay), Durrell thinks of himself as a resident in foreign climes. The condition of being decentred, displaced, 'unhoused', in exile, is central to the work of writers such as Beckett, Borges, Naipaul, Chatwin, Nabokov, Pynchon, Kafka and Rilke.2

Durrell thought of himself as essentially permanently in exile, homeless, without a hearth or personal space that was his own for more than a few years. He was a typical writer in exile, cast adrift from his loved and loathed 'Pudding Island'. He was also, he said, exiled from himself, as in the Rimbaudian 'Je est un autre'. As Durrell put it, 'je suis un refugiée de moi-même'.3 He was a mixture, he said, both Eastern and Western, with 'an English father, an Irish mother and India as a cradle'.4 When it suited him, Durrell would stress his Irishishness, saying he was really an Irish writer; or his Englishness; or, later in life, as he become nostalgic for India, Lhasa and Tibet, his Indian origins.5

One critic does not see Durrell as a typical ex-pat, a writer in exile. He does not have an ambivalent attitude towards 'home', because he is a writer without a 'home'. Instead of being a 'traveller', and a writer of 'travel books', Durrell is perhaps a firmly 'centred' writer, who fixes on certain places and then writes about them (in what he called 'residence books', as opposed to 'travel books' – all his books can be seen as 'residence books' – '[m]y books are always about living in places', Durrell says [SP, 156]).6

2 see George Steiner: *Extraterritorial: Papers on Literature and the Language Revolution*, Atheneum, New York 1971; Reed Way Dasenbrock: "Centrifugality: An Approach to Lawrence Durrell", OMG II, 202
3 Durrell, interview with Jean-Luc Moreau and Jean-Didier Wagneur, late 1980s (Som)
4 Durrell, *Les nouvelles littéraires*, 1978
5 For some critics Durrell 'remained unshakably the child of the Empire' (Brown, 1987, 95)
6 see Gregory Dickson: "Lawrence Durrell and the Traditional of Travel Literature", OMG II, 43f

A colonial, born in India, raised in England, who escaped to Paris, and Corfu, and Egypt, and ended up in South France, Durrell seems to have no 'centre', no place he can call 'home'. He has, however, a number of creative or spiritual centres. London and England remain one creative centre ('I'm as English as Shakespeare's birthday' he says [KT, 163]); Paris and France is another creative ground; Greece and India are two spiritual homes. Durrell is in fact at the centre of Western culture (running from Petronius through Petrarch and Shakespeare to Joyce and Eliot), even though the man himself has lived in many different places.

Durrell's narrators, though, are often exiles, ex-pats, colonials, much as Durrell regarded himself and his companions in Cairo during the Second World are as 'castaways',[7] 'displaced persons', 'migrants'.[8] The sense of displacement is paramount in Durrell's art: all his characters are displaced in one way or another, most obviously emotionally and psychologically. (At the same time, Durrell invents many places, and all his evocations of 'real' places, such as Venice, Istanbul or London, are also inventions. This distinction between 'real' and 'fictional' places is made clear by the water-colourist Paul Hogarth, who tried to find the 'original' of Durrell's places, and often couldn't find anything remotely like them.[9])

Lawrence Durrell developed Bertie Lawrence's 'spirit of place',[10] mixing it with Sigmund Freud and Oswald Spengler, folklore, and an amateur anthropology.[11] Like Lawrence, Durrell makes the usual generalizations about 'London', 'the Mediterranean', 'Italy', and so on. Like Lawrence, Durrell made landscape primary. Lawrence employed landscape as a setting and a symbol: he did not choose landscapes simply for their 'beauty'. The settings of Lawrence's fictions add much to their meanings. The snowy countryside of the short story "Wintry Peacock", is central to the story; the environs of Eastwood, so loved in *Sons and Lovers* and *The Rainbow,* are so much of the impact of the novels. As with *Wuthering Heights, Great Expectations* o r *Tess of the d'Urbervilles,* you couldn't take away the

---

7 Introduction, *Return to Oasis*, in Selwyn, 1980, xxv

8 Durrell, "Bernard Spencer", *London Magazine*, January 1964, 456

9 Paul Hogarth: "The Artist's Journal", in *The Mediterranean Shore*, 137

10 Lawrence W. Markert: "Symbolic Geography: D.H. Lawrence and Lawrence Durrell", in OMG I, 90f

11 Since Durrell's development of his 'spirit of place' theory, landscape and geographical studies have developed further, so that a 'sensuous geography' must include the 'smellscape', the 'soundscape' of acoustic space, the 'bodyscape', the haptic and spatial senses. See Paul Rodaway's excellent study *Sensuous Geographies.*

settings without altering much of the meaning.

> As a poet of historic consciousness I suppose I am bound to see landscape as a field dominated by the human wish – tortured into farms and hamlets, ploughed into cities. A landscape scribbled with the signatures of men and epochs. Now, however, I am beginning to believe that the wish is inherited from the site; that man depends for the furniture of the will upon his location in place, tenant of fruitful acres of a perverted wood. (J, 100)

The most piquant use of landscape as character is Alexandria, the 'Capital of Memory' (J, 166), a 'super-character', a 'metaphoric protagonist', 'a place quickened into a character', a 'framing symbol', a place where 'private and historical mythologies' meet and embrace, a 'condition of being'.[12] The inhabitants are simply the products or puppets of the city, their acts are simply the manifestation of the city's desires and repulsions: 'a city like a human being collects its predispositions, appetites and fears', muses Darley, wandering around the backstreet brothels of Alexandria (J, 166). Darley sees the whole Alexandrian narrative 'not as a personal history with an individual accent so much as part of the historical fabric of the place' (J, 168).

In Durrelland, there is complete continuity between past and present, so Justine and Cleopatra become interchangeable, and the inhabitants of two thousand years ago walk around the modern day city. For Darley, Alexandria is a spirit, a ghost haunting him, a Goddess. Like a Goddess, it is simultaneously desired and loathed, like the beloved woman, like the mother. 'It was as if my imagination had become subtly drugged by the ambience of the place and could not respond to personal, individual assessments' (J, 168). Writing of Alexandria becomes, in part, an exorcism of the city-spirit's hold on him. 'Perhaps Durrell, like Darley, eventually breaks the city's deadly spell by recreating it.' (Goulianos, 1969, 673)

Durrell's 'spirit of place', like other theories of landscape, is an æsthetic construct, determined, like any artwork, by the usual panoply of social, political, psychological and symbolic forces. Landscape is a 'cultural

---

12 Jacques Vallette (*Mercure de France*, Nov 1958, March 1959), Paulette Michot ("Lawrence Durrell's *Alexandria Quartet,*" *Revue des Langues Vivantes*, XXVI, 1960) and R.M. Albérès (*Combat*), W, 180; Mackworth: "Durrell and the New Romanticism", in W, 28; Alan Warren Friedman, 1970, 183; John Weigel, 1965, 97; Eleaner Hutchens, 1962, 57; Roger Bowen: "The Artist at His Papers", in MacNiven, 1987, 475

image', [13] a symbolization, always imbued with meanings and feelings,[14] not simply 'a kind of backcloth' to human actions.[15]

Durrell and Painting

Lawrence Durrell makes many references to painting in his works. He writes like a painter at times. In *Livia* the narrator muses that words are about casting spells and gaining mastery, *à la* Merlin and Faust, over something, which in painting is not so 'treacherous' (L, 245).

Like Henry Miller, Durrell produced figurative watercolour paintings that look something like a cross between Marc Chagall and Paul Klee (though that is probably flattering Durrell and Miller, for they were distinctly amateurish painters - enthusiastic certainly, but nowhere near the accomplishment of Chagall or Klee). Durrell painted under his pen name Oscar Epfs.

Henry Miller's ideas about painting are so close to Durrell's - they exchanged ideas about painting in their talks and letters. Both Miller and Durrell loved modern art, and also painters such as J.M.W. Turner, who was (is) without question England's greatest painter. In a late poem, 'Elsie at Nîmes', Durrell writes:

You told me how a picture by Turner
Upset your reason and digestion by its
Unexpected force of vision: adding that art
Should do just that, outrage and disturb,
Not just contrive and move but really punish! (Med, 13)

Miller describes the effect Turner had on him in *The Waters Reglitterized*: he relates 'the night I stood with Joe O'Regan in front of a department store window - on Livingston Street, Brooklyn, I believe - and took in with all my senses the Turners hanging there.' (PHM 113) Durrell describes the Turnerian enlightenment in his Foreword to *The Paintings of Henry*

13 D. Cosgrove: *Social Formation and Symbolic Landscape*, Croom Helm 1984, 1
14 E. Relph: *Place and Placelessness*, Pion, 1976, 122
15 J. Appleton: *The Experience of Landscape*, Wiley, 1975, 2

Miller:

He himself has best described the first major experience that woke him up to the reality of the painting experience. The passage, which is perhaps in *Black Spring* or another of the early works, concerns the omnipresent Joe O'Regan and their joint stumbling into a Turner retrospective in New York. It was like bursting into a jewel case, he said, or like diving into a tropical sea. Even long afterwards he would describe this first experience to friends in Paris, and when he did a rapt expression came over his face at the memory of those great canvases smouldering away in the gloom, glowing like fire opals. (PHM, 17-18)

The more one reads Miller on painting, the closer his ideas chime with Durrell's: both Miller and Durrell, as painter-writers, exalt the Taoist codes of spontaneity, naturalness, nowness, going with the flow. The following passage by Henry Miller is wholly in tune with Durrell's Taoist æsthetics:

The greatest joy, and the greatest triumph, in art comes at the moment when realizing to the fullest your grip over the medium, you deliberately sacrifice it in the hope of discovering a vital hidden truth within you. It comes like a reward for patience – this freedom of mastery which is born of the hardest discipline. *Then*, no matter what you do or say, you are absolutely right and nobody dare criticize you. (PHM 117)

This is how Durrell works in *The Avignon Quintet,* his most self-consciously 'painterly' fiction. He is working at the height of his powers, and has that lucidity and total control and fluidity that Miller describes. Arthur Rimbaud had achieved this fullness in his *Illuminations*, when he was 18. In *The Avignon Quintet*, Durrell forgets all he knows about writing in order to reinvent writing, and to reinvent himself. *The Avignon Quintet* is a sequence where Durrell is in control, for he has spent decades learning how to know when to stop, when to hold back, and when to let go. In the *Quintet*, Durrell appears to have gone through the cultural grinder and he comes out the other side with his senses still intact. Not only intact, but refreshed. After all, Durrell, like most writers of his age when he started the *Quintet* (around 60 years old) knew a trick or two about writing. As Henry Miller writes:

I know every trick – where to use a semicolon instead of a dash, when to give a short stabbing thrust, and when to wax loquacious or even circum-locuitous – *even when to stammer*! (PHM, 117)

In *The Avignon Quintet,* Durrell knows when to stammer, when to appear halting and hesitant. Miller in *The Waters Reglitterized* is here sounding much like Durrell in *A Smile in the Mind's Eye* – indeed, Miller's *The Waters Reglitterized* reads as a parallel to the relaxed, informal philosophizing of Durrell's Taoist book:

> It doesn't matter what route one travels – every route brings you eventually to the goal. All roads lead to heaven is the Chinese proverb. If one accepted that fully, one would get there so much more quickly. One should not be worrying about the degree of "success obtained by each and every effort," but only concentrate on maintaining the vision, keeping it pure and steady. (PHM, 119)

Miller's discussing watercolour painting here, but his analysis applies to all artistic creations. In his foreword to Miller's books of paintings, Durrell explained his and Miller's painterly technique, which Miller called 'The New Instinctivism', and Durrell coined the term 'Epfsistentialism, for Durrell's *nom-de-plume* when painting was Oscar Epfs, another of Durrell's many characters who are more than half-real. The Miller-Durrell painterly technique's affinities with Taoism are inevitable, really, for their way of painting was derived in part from the tradition of Chinese landscape painting, where intuition and the calm of emptiness plays a large part:

> If you wished to draw an arm of a chair or an airplane, you closed your eyes and wished for it to form under your brush; also, of course, you used whatever resources you had of memory or drawing skill. But the main effort was just to will the image, and quite often (though not always) this image would actually form itself under your brush. You seemed to project it mentally without going all to all the trouble of building it up from rule and precept, by constructing it as one does in a life class. Yes, often the desire was answered and the coveted object was brought to light quite miraculously, or at least so nearly suggested that a waking touch was enough to finish it, to "situate" it in the painting's context.

Durrell's descriptions of landscapes have often been termed 'painterly' or vivid. The visual dimension is crucial in Durrell's writing, although he makes few direct references to painters. In *The Avignon Quintet* we find the major painting reference to be to J.M.W. Turner, when the Prince courts his beloved at the church overlooking the Thames, where Turner supposedly once sat. Other painters are referred to in the *Quintet*, most notably to Clement's painting of *Cockayne*. Other references include

Giorgio de Chirico's *The Parting* and Poussin. Images of paradise, a lost Eden, lie behind *The Avignon Quintet*, in the lengthy evocations of Provence, for instance, which is envisaged as a pastoral realm inhabited by gypsies and figures from folklore. In modern day Provence, Durrell says, you can find images straight out of Classic literature. Shepherds, a man on a donkey, and maidens. Durrell's images of Arcadia are, like the Arcadia of ancient Greece, fictions created to flatter the wishes of people.

> ...in Greece you feel the pagan world is very close. Where I live now in the South of France, you feel something equally strong – you feel Nostradamus, the Provençal singers, the intense savagery, and a different sort of mysticism. (in Kenneth Young)

In *Livia* Durrell allows himself to go wholeheartedly pastoral and Arcadian, writing of Constance's wilderness-style garden at Tu Duc, with its holm-oaks, fruit trees, and strawberries; the scents of the sea from the Carmargue, and thyme and rosemary inland; Hilary taking a shower from the water pump at Aimargues; Livia doing her yoga in the garden; swimming at dawn in the lily pond with the two young women who looked like 'young Graces who had slipped out of the pantheon' (L, 111-3).

At the heart of Durrell's pastoral Provence lies hidden treasure, the Templar treasure, which is not just any treasure, but may contain the very vessel Christ used, the Holy Grail. Nicolas Poussin is connected with the Templar treasure: his painting *Et in Arcadia Ego* is thought to be a key in the chain of mysteries which reveal where the treasure is buried.[16] The whereabouts of the Templar treasure is a symbol of the vision quest every character is on: indeed, it is this treasure quest that unites all the characters in the *Quintet*, when, at the end of the sequence, they go into the caves. In Durrell's *Quintet*, the pastoral bliss of youth is destroyed by the harsh realities of war. Before the war starts, though, death has already occurred in the *Quintet* landscape: Piers' suicide. Continual shifts describe Durrell's view of paradise, for, how can this Earth be Paradise if, as the gnostics believed, it is 'evil', made by the Devil?[17] The Grail may be the answer, hence the quest for it. In Durrell's art, though, as in Jung's work, the Grail

---

16 see Michael Baigent, Richard Leigh & Henry Lincoln: *The Holy Blood and the Holy Grail*, Corgi 1983
17 In a mode at right angles to Gnosticism, Durrell said: '[y]ou mustn't ask what's right or wrong. We must ask what's fruitful and what is unfruitful.' (in McCall, op. cit., OMG, 3, 384)

is simply the ultimate metaphor, the most grandiloquent metaphor in a Christian society. A metaphor for whatever you like: integration, wholeness, transcendence, realization, beingness.

Tapestries are part of scenes, particularly related to Sylvie's rooms. The tapestries add an air of mediæval art to Sylvie's character, which is apposite, as she and Bruce and Piers are involved in a scenario out of courtly love poetry, which itself was deeply associated with the Cathars, Templars and other mediæval heresies. Sylvie at Monfavet lives in a mediæval dreamworld, which is seemingly lit by a 'soft brumous Italian skyline'. In this languid, Gothic, misty scenery of the tapestry violence erupts; the hunting of a stag. As with Benedicta and her falconry in *The Revolt of Aphrodite*, Sylvie's mediævalism sets chivalry and courtly love against bestial violence. The *mise-en-scène* of mediæval culture - the horses, chivalry, knights, falconry, castles, etc - turn out to be the surface gloss which hardly hides the violence underneath. Benedicta, like Sylvie, is presented as a mistress of love out of the Middle Ages, but she turns out to be a murderer too - she watches her husband die in a swamp.

Lawrence Durrell has long loved hunting and shooting - there are photographs of him at Corfu, gun in hand. Like Ernest Hemingway, he liked the 'manly' pursuits of hunting, shooting and sailing. Like Hemingway, and D.H. Lawrence at the beginning of his novel exalting male violence, *The Plumed Serpent*, Durrell wrote enthusiastically of bullfights - the horror, ritual and nobility of the *corrida* of Nîmes and Arlès (in *Caesar's Vast Ghost*, and the poem 'Feria: Nîmes'). Hunting particularly forms some of his most memorable scenes (the duck shoot at Mareotis in the *Quartet*, for example). The most savage scene of hunting is related in *Quinx*, where Sabine tells a story of a aristocrat who loved to hunt women, especially women weening young children (another manifestation of the hated 'phallic Mother').

Lawrence Durrell is a well-travelled writer, as we have mentioned: always his texts move through global spaces, at home, though in exile, in South America, the Near East, Indian, Europe, and so on. This cosmopolitan ease is shown in the titles of his poems: 'Carol on Corfu', 'At Corinth', 'On Ithaca Standing', 'In Europe', 'Elegy on the Closing of the French Brothels', 'Bere Regis', 'Sarajevo', 'Delphi'. By far the most poems are about Greece ('Eleusis', 'Near Paphos', 'Acropolis', 'Seferis', 'Patmos', 'Lesbos', 'At Epidarus', 'In Arcadia', 'Exile in Athens'), which emphasizes the all-pervasive significance of Greece in Durrell's work.

The landscapes of *The Avignon Quintet* are international and cosmopolitan, as we come to expect from Durrell. The characters move around
these landscapes with ease: Provence, Venice, Paris, Geneva, Cairo, India,
Egypt, and London. In *The Alexandria Quartet* Durrell chose the city
Alexandria because it was rich enough in symbolism, background, history
and topology to carry four novels. In *The Avignon Quintet,* Avignon itself
was clearly not enough. Despite being a City of Popes at one time, it was
not as rich as Alexandria. So Durrell extended the novels to include
Geneva, London, Paris, Cairo, Alexandria and India. Indeed, Geneva features
so much that one might retitle the series *The Geneva Quintet.* Most of
Constance and *Sebastian* occur in Geneva.

Pudding Island and 'The English Death': England

*Fuck the English eh? Henry the English are everywhere, all around
me – like mutilated black beetles... I hate England... Henry fuck the
English.*

Lawrence Durrell, letter to Henry Miller (DML, 92-93)

*In England... what is killing is the spineless and revolting life they
have built up around themselves, the habits, the boredom, the lack of*
bonne chere. *No belly worship!*

Lawrence Durrell, *Paris Review* (37)

Lawrence Durrell's England in *The Avignon Quintet* is the usual England of
his fiction. Scotland, Wales and Ireland are not mentioned (even though at
times Durrell fancies himself as a Irish writer, and reckons the best writers
in England are really 'Irish'). Durrell's England is the 1920s and 1930s
Blighty of schoolboy adventure comics, the hated yet loved homeland. He
calls England 'Pudding Island', a phrase which neatly describes his view of
England as a land of shopkeepers, of cricketers, of old landladies hiding
behind net curtains, of Oxford University, of the old cafés of Soho in

London (Durrell played piano in a jazz club in Soho). Blanford lives in Tu's house when he hears of her death, at the beginning of *Livia*, the nice, cosy Home Counties, Tory Country, and of course it is November and it's snowing. At the beginning of *Constance*, Blanford is asked what does England mean to him?

> He closed his eyes upon the word and saw a sort of jumbled composite picture of grey buildings, low hills, and wrinkled rivers, and backing them all the romantic image of the golden Kentish Weald, raised like a golden buckler to heaven. (C, 9)

Oxford is another reference point, of course. Durrell's fiction is firmly a part of the public school-Oxbridge circuit, where characters call each 'old boy' or 'chum'. Toby is an Oxford don, and Aubrey and his chums go to Oxford. Bournemouth features in Sutcliffe's extremely 'humble beginnings'. Again, Durrell lived there. Bournemouth features in *Prospero's Cell*, as the place where Durrell and his mother and family left when they went to Corfu. In *Livia* we hear of Sutcliffe's escapades as a teacher of a convent in Bournemouth. Sutcliffe is given a sketch of a background, which changes throughout the *Quintet*: 'Sutcliffe might get born somewhere north of Loughborough, say, to decent Quäker parents. Millers of grain? He was a scholarship boy who had won an Exhibition to Oxford, and then, like so many others, had found himself thrown upon the slave market of pedagogy.' (L, 54-55) Durrell's Bournemouth is typical of his love-hate view of Britain:

> Hymendale was a suburb of Bournemouth, that salubrious south coast resort, which even then was geared to the retirement requirements of professional and colonial civil servants. Privet hedges, eyes peering from behind curtains, a draughty gentility; silent streets awoken only to the clip clop of the milkman's little van. It was a fine place to develop inner resources – so he told himself grimly as he grimly did his daily walks, twice round the sewage plant and once there and back along the cliffs in the rain. Ah! the eternal rain! (L, 55)

Durrell makes fun of Britain, but it is an erotic irony, as Thomas Mann wrote.[18] Really, Durrell can't help liking aspects of Blighty. After all, many of his characters work abroad for their country. They are diplomats, working for the Foreign Office, or some other hallowed British institution, as Durrell too worked for the British government abroad. The stupid rituals and quirks of the diplomatic service in fact provide Durrell with much of his material. Not only in the Wodehousean *Antrobus* stories, but also in *The Alexandria Quartet* and *The Avignon Quintet*. The problem Felix has with the British flag in Avignon, where he is stationed, is typical of the silly stiff upper lip stories the diplomatic service generates when Durrell gets hold of them.

Durrell delights in detailing the finer points of Felix's life in the service in Avignon: he lists all those bizarre books, for instance, that the young officer is issued with (*The Foreign Service Guide to Residence Abroad*). Felix unpacks a crate sent from Blighty, with items such as 'a tin of Bumpsted's Bloater Paste... a bottle of Gentleman's Relish and Main-wearing's Pickel Mix... Imperial Anchovies, Angostura Bitters. Pork and Beans, Imperial size. Lea and Perrin's Sauce' (L, 97). These are the products of beloved Blighty, home of retired colonels who live in Cheltenham, Eastbourne and Surrey and write xenophobic letters to *The Times* and *The Telegraph*, home of football hooligans (football has replaced mass hanging as a spectacle, says Durrell sarcastically [M, 186]), home of greasy, rainy streets with their terraced houses.

It's practically a test for writers to evoke the cold and drear of an English Autumn and Winter. Durrell revels in the task. In an early work, *Panic Spring*, Durrell employs the usual metaphor and imagery of a British Fall: rotten leaves, bonfires, smoke, damp. However, the closer one looks at Durrell's archetypal rendering of Autumn (culled from the Elizabethans through Kelley and Sheats to the Georgians) one sees just how much Durrell's narrator in *Panic Spring* emphasizes the sense of decay and ruin: 'crush of rotten, sweet-smelling leaves', 'pitted and perforated', 'littered', 'burnt out', 'heavy and patched with decay', 'rotten', 'burn up', 'eating away', 'burning up the body', 'death' – all these phrases are found in one

---

18 Some of Durrell's unpublished anti-British sentiments are, as one would expect, more vicious than those he included in his fictions: 'one cannot deal with the British artist without a great deal of tender pity – such as one extends to a terrible street accident', 'anything without an explicit morality which can be objectively stated is automatically suspect to Anglo-Saxons', 'the one thing on which the sun ever sets is British hypocrisy' (Ill, 42, 19, 10, 42, 11, 1).

medium-length paragraph (SP, 204-5).

In many articles (some collected in *Spirit of Place*) Durrell feels ashamed about being British, about the lack of artistic endeavour in Britain, about the repressive attitude to sexuality, and the inability of the British to really let go and enjoy themselves.[19] The French, Durrell says, really care about artists, and, further, many of the French are engaged in some creative pursuit or other (SP, 315, 372).

Durrell's bitterest attack on Blighty appears in the mouthpiece of quasi-lit'ry guru Pursewarden, who loathes the debased once-great Albion of Anglo-Saxon puritanism, stifling religion of curates and churchwardens, simplistic nationalism (football replacing hanging), sexual repression, grey twilights around Westminster, the Britain of crappy food and crappy weather and po-faced people. As youths, the wannabe D.H. Lawrences came to London from the provinces with suitcases bulging with manuscripts, dreaming about illuminative poems in the manner of Rimbaud, only to find the muezzin of the trade, London's lit'ry publishers and critics, were waiting for the next stodgy-prosed Trollope (Cl, 110).

At times Durrell's banging on about the ugliness of Britain recalls D.H. Lawrence's incisive descriptions of the horrible industrial Midlands, which appear in *The Rainbow, Lady Chatterley's Lover* and *Women in Love*. Richard Aldington wrote in his introduction to his friend's *Selected Essays*:

> The three pieces on England ["Whistling of Birds", "Nottingham and the Mining Country", "Dull London"] may give the impression that Lawrence had little but hostile criticism to make of his native island, but all his earlier novels and stories abound with passages of the tenderest love for country England, and even in Australia he longed for the primroses and bluebells of an English spring. But his hatred of the blind industrial destruction of the old rural England was vehement and implacable. (9-10)

In his essay about his hometown, Eastwood in Nottinghamshire, "Return to Bestwood" (1926), Lawrence describes the familiar feelings of nostalgia and revulsion that many a homecoming has initiated in people of all ages and countries: 'I feel at once a devouring nostalgia and an infinite repulsion' (146). This is also how Durrell feels about England. Like Lawrence, Durrell feels bitter about it, about the mess into which it's slipped. In his essay: "Nottingham and the Mining Countryside", Lawrence writes: 'The real

---

19 Like Lawrence he [Miller] exclaimed: "O why do the English fence off the great wild scope of their natures?!" (AO, 17)

tragedy of England, as I see it, is the tragedy of ugliness. The country is so lovely: the man-made England is so vile.' (SelP, 108) He's right, of course. Durrell concords with Lawrence, as he does in so many other ways.

Unlike dear old D.H. Lawrence, who was often so solemn about his pet hates, Larry Durrell always employs humour when writing about Britain and British life. He loves to get his talons into it, and it's such a soft target. So, gleefully, he describes the sordid bachelor life of Sutcliffe and Toby, Sutcliffe with his washable 'Eversafe' condom, his dingy digs, his piles, his furtive affair with Effie:

> When he was overcome with depression he sometimes went down into the town and for ten shillings and a Devonshire Tea gave Effie a furtive caress, which only increased his sense of despondency and alienation. Effie was a barmaid at The Feathers and a good enough little soul, very modest in her demands upon life. She was indeed sweet but O the cold apple tart between her pale-frog-like legs. (L, 57)

In its laconic misogynism, this sequence is reminiscent of Samuel Beckett. Beckett's characters have this kind of sordid, loveless relationship with women. For Beckett's derelict men, being with a woman is 'like fucking a quag', as one of his characters puts it. In the famous Beckett *Trilogy*, a character wonders whether he's had anal sex by mistake: 'is it true love in the arse?' he wonders. Durrell is not as vicious as Beckett. He is altogether much softer in his irony.

When Blanford buries his mother, though, Durrell makes sure to tease out the ugliness of the cremation:

> The suburban church architecture of the chapel was of a glacial coldness and infernal ugliness. The altar with its cheap cathedral-glass saints wallowing in the crepuscular gloom shed a dreadful Sunday School light upon them. (L, 181)

This awful English funeral, veritably the 'English death' that so obsessed Durrell in the 1930s, is contrasted with the more Gothic romance of the pagan/ semi-Catholic burial of Piers in *Monsieur*. At the heart of 'the English Death' is a sense of vacuity or void, an 'obsessive attempt to cover up or repress nothingness'.[20]

That fucking English system! No repose about it. Takes you ages to

20 David M. Woods: "Love and Meaning in *The Alexandria Quartet*", in OMG, 103

unlimber in Europe.[21]

Durrell's England lies in a similar spiritual space as D.H. Lawrence's England (though Durrell's upbringing – colonial India, Canterbury, Bournemouth – was distinctly middle class, while Lawrence's – mining community, Nottingham teacher training college – was working class). But Lawrence and Durrell share a common origin in their disgust/ affection for Britain, a place, as Lawrence wrote in "Nottingham and the Mining Country", between the 'old England and the new', between 'industrialism and the old agricultural England of Shakespeare'.[22] Lawrence wrote a number of pieces describing his feelings on returning to England. It feels deathly, quiet and claustrophic ("On Coming Home").[23] England is dull, dull, dull. It deadens the spirit. It's so 'nice' and safe and utterly boring ("Dull London"):[24]

> It begins the moment you set foot ashore, the moment you step off the boat's gangway. the heart suddenly, yet vaguely, sinks. It is no lurch of fear. Quite the contrary. It is as if the life-urge failed, and the heart dimly sank... the first half-hour in London, after some years abroad, is really a plunge of misery. The strange, the grey and uncanny, almost deathly sense of *dulness* is overwhelming... you are haunted, all the time, sleeping or waking, with the uncanny feeling: It is dull! It is all dull! this life here is one vast complex of dulness! ("Dull London", 122)

For D.H. Lawrence, coming back to England is like being indoctrinated into 'a dead muffled sense of stillness, as if nothing had any resonance.'[25] Wherever you go, there is the sordid sense of humanity.'[26] Lawrence always did exaggerate.

But Durrell is a romantic, much more romantic, in a way, than Lawrence (though both writers are often hopelessly idealistic). For instance, Durrell used some of the grander aspects of Britain in his other fictions, settings which suggest an ancient England, a historic, Imperial Albion. There is the set-piece on fogbound Salisbury Plain, where amidst the military tests Felix and co. come upon Stonehenge. And *The Revolt of Aphrodite* culminates in the Hitchcockian setting of St Paul's Cathedral, so like the end of

21 Durrell, 4 November 1957, Ald, 32
22 *Selected Essays,* 114-7
23 Lawrence: *A Selection From Phoenix,* 139, 141
24 *Selected Essays,* 123-4
25 "On Coming Home", *A Selection From Phoenix,* 139
26 Lawrence: "On Coming Home", in ib, 147).

Hitchcock's films (Mount Rushmore in *North By Northwest*, the Statue of Liberty in *Sabotage*, Big Ben in *The 39 Steps,* the tower in *Vertigo*. And when it comes to creating a thriller story, Hitch is much more skilful than Durrell).

And in *Livia*, in that key telephone dialogue between the two novelists, Blanford tells Sutcliffe about his childhood:

> how happy it made one just to squander one's youth, lying about in the deep grass eating cherries. The velvet English summers of youth, deep grass, and the clock of cricket balls marking the show hours of leisure between classes. The distant clapping when someone struck a ball to the boundary merged with but did not drown the steady drizzle of crickets. We slept in the bosom of an eternal summer. (L, 10)

Again, a litany of names helps to sketch in the quintessential post-adolescent British experience: urban Bohemia after suburban family life, the cafés and clubs and pubs of London, the evocations of 'smoky Euston' and the dreary south London suburbs:

> "It is the small things which build the picture."
> "London."
> "Yes, and the places we frequented in London most of which have disappeared – wiped out one supposes by the bombings?"
> "Like the Café de Paris?"
> "Yes, and Ciro's and The Blue Peter, the Criterion Bar, Quaglino's, and Stone's Chip house, Mannering's Grill, Paton's. The Swan…"
> "Good, Robin, and then the night-clubs like The Old Bag O' Nails, The Blue Mantern, The Black Hole, and Kiki's Place… We simply never slept… Just before dawn Lyon's Corner House, everyone with yellow exhausted faces, whores, undergraduates, all-night watchmen and workers setting off on early jobs. The first newspapers appearing on the icy street. Walking back in the pale nervous rinsed-out dawn, the whole way back across London – over Westminster Bridge and into the baleful suburbs of the capital… (L, 30-31)

Critics have noted how old-fashioned and nostalgic Durrell's England is, how stuck it is in the inter-war years. One sees this old-fashioned Britain in the language, the tone, the attitudes, the imagery and poetics of Durrell's fiction. 'Durrell's mind is a museum-piece', said one critic.[27] Durrell's characters are not as wholly top-hole and spiffing as Wodehouse's toffs, calling each other 'old sport' and 'old fruit', but they do address each other frequently as 'old boy'.

---

27 Martin Green: " Lawrence Durrell: A Minority Report", W, 132

The Dark Crystal and the Blue Silence:
Italy, the Mediterranean, and Greece

The extraordinary thing is that Greece has somehow remained exempt from the flavour of such disappointments. Much has changed, yes, but more has remained obstinately and invincibly the same. The radical feel and temper of the land and its people are still what they were for me at twenty.

Lawrence Durrell, "Oil For the Saint: Return to Corfu" (SP, 286)

Greece is the Paradise of Lawrence Durrell's youth, the place of his second (spiritual) birth,[28] the place of pure escape, the 'miracle ground', where the infinite blue sky and the warm blue sea forge a huge space in Durrell's soul. The second birth-place is 'where you really wake up to reality'. Greece is this place of reawakening, where the poet's inner life came alive. The shrine of St Arsenius (in Corfu) is Durrell's second, spiritual birth-place (BT, 22). (Other paradises in Durrell's fiction include 'the Roof of the World', where a new Adam and Eve live in *Cefalû* (*The Dark Labyrinth*), and the South Seas island, where Caradoc winds up, becoming a Tiresias figure, suckling two children). In *Blue Thirst*, Durrell speaks of the incredible light of Greece, the way it bounced around from rock to rock, an electric, magnetic light which remains one of the most memorable aspects for him of Greece (18).

> Tread softly, for here you stand
> On miracle ground, boy.
> A breath would cloud this water of glass,
> Honey, bush, berry and swallow.
> This rock, then, is more pastoral, than
> Arcadia is, Illyria was. (CP, 111)

This stanza from 'On Ithaca Standing' is the archetypal Durrell poem. For a long time Durrell exalted Greece as the birthplace and cradle of Western civilization. In poems such as 'Delos', 'In Arcadia', 'At Epidaurus', 'Eternal Contemporaries: Six Portraits', 'Lesbos', 'Eleusis', 'Io' and 'Aphrodite', Durrell celebrates aspects of Greece in his distinctive, dry, ascetic verse.[29]

---

28 Alfred Perlès wrote: 'Larry, perhaps the only really civilised person I've met, has his cultural roots in Greece.' (AO, 40)
29 'The best English poetry about Greece is certainly Lawrence Durrell' reckons Peter Levi (Levi: "Lawrence Durrell's Greek Poems", Lab, 101)

The problem is that Greece is so beautiful that 'one tends towards purple prose all the time' (BT, 11).

> The pure form, then, must be the blue silence
> And the archaic shape of whiteness posed
> On blueness utterly bemused, a sort of coyness
> Which garners the wind of the four quarters.
> ('Limits: Mykonos Windmills')[30]

Greece is the place where one whiles away hours under the 'tree of idleness'. One has to learn how to 'do nothing', in the Taoist sense; that is, in doing 'nothing', one does 'everything.

> The fulness of being is not in refinement,
> By the delimitation of the object, but
> In roundness, the embosoming of the Real.
> ('The Anecdotes', IV: 'At Rhodes', CP, 204)

This is where Durrell's Oriental repose comes from, Greece. In one of the mid-period 'island books', *Reflections on a Marine Venus,* Durrell wrote of repose: '[e]ach moment to itself entire, populating a whole continuum of feeling.' (123) In the letters to Miller, Durrell speaks of a desire that could apply to many writers:

> Simple needs this time. A girl who really fucks with the heart and soul and buttocks; an olive tree, a typewriter, and a few great friends like you. (DML, 170)

This is a Durrellian goal, this kind of erotic, creative bliss in a Mediterranean landscape. It is a dream of wine, women and creativity set amongst the Provençal *garrigues* or the Greek islands.

> How about a year in Poros now [Durrell asks Miller, trying once again to entice the American to stay in Europe or the Mediterranean] – baked hard rock and glittering sea... No more writing but lying about and taking a long myopic and unbiased view of the universe. (DML, 169)

---

30 In Durrell: *The Mediterranean Shore*, 144

And not just Greece, but also India,[31] for it was in India, Durrell says, that he first encountered the calm and repose of Buddhism:

> It is something that is extraordinary when the national ethos of a country is devoted to seeking out states of calm and states of harmlessness and states of good nature, because after all if you want those sorts of results you must really work for them. Goodness can't just be inherited; it's got to be earned, in a way. If you live in a Buddhist country, it is so extraordinary. You wake up without being afraid of you neighbour, as you do in the countries we inhabit. The whole of nature seems permeated by a sense of harmless good will, and it opens a field for self-development which is not accessible in a country where you have very rigid, theologically oriented people with a national ethos that's repressive or restrictive in any way. ("Overture", in OMG 13)

Durrell makes generalized statements about the differences between East and West, and it's clear which he regards as the closest to paradise ('one feels that real bliss, the smiling silence of pure transcendence, is Asiatic.' CVG, 14) The important difference, for him, is spiritual, a question of 'one's angle of inclination to the universe', as he might put it, echoing E.M. Forster's description of Constantin Cavafy. In interviews, letters and other places, it is the *religious* aspect that is crucial for Durrell in defining the East and the West. Not climate, economics, politics, race, but religion. 'Durrell is a very religious writer' said James Nichols.[32] The last religion, says Julia Kristeva, is art: 'we are all the faithful of the last religion, the esthetic one. We are all subjects of the metaphor.'[33]

Greece is important for Durrell philosophically too. It is the birthplace of Western philosophy. As he listens to the sound of water (a key metaphor in Chinese mysticism), Affad muses upon the way Greece distilled the thought systems of India, Tibet, Persia, Egypt, Israel and Iran. From these countries Greek philosophy was born (in Heraclitus one finds Persia, in Empodecles Egypt, in Pythagoras China, and so on [S, 43]). His friend, the Greek poet George Seferis, wrote of Durrell:

31 But not, though, South America, which did not feature in Durrell's fiction (as it did in Graham Greene's); which is odd, because for a while Durrell seemed quite enthusiastic about Rio and Brazil: 'the most fantastic country in the world... It's completely hallucinating.' (1947, SP, 92-93) After a while, though, Durrell began to dislike many aspects of South America, as he viewed it from his lecturing post in Buenos Aires.
32 James Nichols: "The Risen Angels in Durrell's Fallen Women", in OMG, 179; also Reed Way Dasenbrock, 1980, 16
33 Kristeva: "Throes of Love: The Field of the Metaphor", *Tales of Love*, 279

He is not a landscape artist. He is mirrored in his *living eye*, he and his private domain. In other words, he uses the GREEK OBJECT (in its widest possible meaning) to measure his own problems and desires, as a man and as a poet of our times, tortured by our Western culture.[34]

This picture painted in 'The Anecdotes' of Rhodes is another typical Durrellian scene: the languor, the boats, the cicadas, the figs, and Spring:

> Anonymous hand, record one afternoon,
> In May, some time before the fig-leaf:
> Boats lying idle in the sky, a town
> Thrown as on a screen of watered silk,
> Lying on its side, reddish and soluble,
> A sheet of glass leading down into the sea...
>
> Down here an idle boy catches a cicada:
> Imprisons it, laughing, in his sister's cloak
> In whose warm folds the silly creature sings. (CP, 204)

Durrell's Greece certainly sounds fabulous. In many letters and poems Durrell does not bother to disguise his absolute love of Greece.

> Full moon. We bathe in a little half-moon of green water under the tiny shrine to St Arsenius: clean pebbles like baby's hands; sheer straited lime-stone metamorphic up to ceiling; water so warm it is like silk; hornets; silence; ache of noon-blue heat. (July 1938, PC, 126)

You enter Greece as if entering a dark crystal says Durrell. (SP, 187) He is talking of sailing from Italy to Corfu, a voyage of no great distance, but, culturally, the jump is a major one. It is a journey, from Europe to the beginning of the East, that haunts Durrell's work. It is the journey – down the string of towns of Italy like a necklace to Brindisi, then over the sea by ferry to Corfu, that lurks behind the other journeys described in Durrell's work. 'Somewhere between Calabria and Corfu the blue really begins', writes Durrell in "A Landmark Gone" (SP, 187).

The leap from Italy to Greece, between two seas (Adriatic and Ionian) is partly what contributes to Durrell's idiosyncratic vision. He is not a Euro-pean resident travelling about the Near East then returning to Blighty to write up his travels. He is, rather, a resident of the countries which form not just the 'backdrop', but the very heart of his works: Cyprus, Rhodes, Corfu, Egypt, France.

---

34 Seferis: "The Greek Poems of Lawrence Durrell", La, 85

Greece has a landscape that Durrell utterly adores: it is 'unchanging, uncompromising, ravishingly pure and vertical' ("Delphi", SP, 273). Returning to Greece is a rebirth; one feels 'renewed'.

Then Greece [Durrell writes in *Reflections on a Marine Venus*]: the vertical, masculine, adventurous consciousness of the archipelago, with its mental anarchy and indiscipline touched everywhere with the taste for agnosticism and spare living. Greece born into the sexual intoxication of the light, which seems to shine upwards from inside the very earth, to illuminate these bare acres of squill and asphodel. (RMV, 183)

In Greece Durrell begins to sense the vast space that is such an important part of Oriental philosophy. In the infinite blue skies of Greece you can appreciate the Clear Light of the Void of Tibetan mysticism. It is this Greece of the 'big blue' that Durrell employs in his fictions ('Islands consuming in a sea/ Born dense with its own blue', he wrote in 'Delos' [CP, 132]). In *Blue Thirst* Durrell speaks longingly of 'the amazing blue' of Greece (34). 'Ach the blueness', Durrell wrote from Rhodes (1945, PC, 79). To T.S. Eliot Durrell wrote of enjoying 'whole fortnights of ringing blue sea-days where the mind can expand' – teasing comments to make (in October, 1946) to the denizen of rainy, dark London (SP, 87). In Greece, says Durrell, you get a feeling for absolute solitude and tranquillity, a mystical sense of calm, as this nostalgic evocation of Corfu shows:

The peace of those evenings on the balcony before the lighting of the lamps was something we shall never discover again – the stillness of objects reflected in the mirror ever so slightly swinging, its surface ungrazed by the fishes moving about its lower floors. It was the kind of hush you get in a chinese water-colour. The darkness leaked in over it all without disturbing anything; the proportions all remaining the same but the light changing. At last the sea would merge into a single warm veil.[35]

At the heart of Durrell's Greek books is a part-Epicurean, part-Heraclitean philosophy which celebrates tranquillity, the in-seeing or 'inscape' or Rilkean *innigkeit* of things, as well as flow and change. Taoism combines both – stillness/ tranquillity and movement/ change: in a letter written from Corfu in 1938, Durrell said that: 'the deepest meaning of Logos or Tao is not in a dynamic, fretful SENSATION... but in a sudden huge calm – an underground lake inside oneself' (DML, 104).[36]

35 "A Landmark Gone", *Spirit of Place*, 188
36 'Because of endless and perpetual metamorphosis Durrelland is in perpetual turmoil.' (Jean Blot: "Durrelland", Ker, 132)

Often the calm and repose of the Mediterranean world flows from water, from bathing, from being beside the sea. The typical Durrellian landscapes – Bournemouth, Alexandria, Greece – are all coastal spaces. In *The Avignon Quintet* Constance and her companions go swimming at the bottom of the garden, but Durrell takes the characters to the sea in *Quinx*, to the gypsy festival at Saints Marie-de-la-Mer. 'Water plays an important part in the *Quintet*', he said (Med, 132). In both *The Avignon Quintet* and *The Alexandria Quartet* characters go on an outing from wartime Alexandria to swim in the Mediterranean, clearly based on a Durrell's personal experience, as this extract from his letters shows:

> ...were driven out through Bourg El Arab, and slipped down through the battlefields to a long beach where the real Mediterranean comes up in great green coasters and sky is smothered down to violet, all lambent and turning your body in water to a wonderful rose. The sea citron-green cold and pure with sandy floor; for the first time in four years I felt I was in Greece. Bathing naked. (DML, 172-3)

The Mediterranean is a world of the Goddess, as Durrell makes clear in many works. Underneath Durrell's exaltation of Greece and Italy is a feminine presence, a female *jouissance*, as this stanza from an early, highly Lawrencean poem, 'Summer in Corfu', shows:

> State me no theme of misery. The season
> Like a woman lies open, is fooling,
> Secret, growth upon growth. The black fig,
> Desire, is torn again from the belly of Reason.
> Our summer is gravid at last, is big. (Med, 18)

Italy features in Durrell's work mainly as a stepping stone for Greece. Venice is usually mentioned, if any Italian city is noted. Rome and Florence hardly feature at all. 'Old Venice glittering and liquefying among her multiple reflections, wing of a thousand peacocks fired up into a sun-cloudy evening sky' (M, 187). It is Venice, the canals and Florian's Café, that Durrell uses most often in his art. In particular the Romantic/ Gothic Venice, the faded, decadent, pseudo-Byzantine capital. Venice appears thus in Pursewarden's Byronic vampire spoof in *The Alexandria Quartet*. In *Monsieur*, Venice is where Sutcliffe fetches up for a while, meandering along the alleys, a parody upon Mann's *Death in Venice*. Here he pursues Sabine, and fails to bed her.

Vaguely he hoped for a cloud-shape but he wanted it more localised in association, more specially Venetian as to colouring. He pictured thick lustrous auburn hair, a little brush repellant, a little wayward, sweeping out at the nape into a veritable squirrel's tail which one could not resist stroking. Then also a pure intellectual beauty, work of an ancient master, which would make the saliva start to the mouth. These, then, were some of the trusting demands he made upon life in that slow Venetian spring... (M, 182-3)

Durrell must have thought of Venice as a possible site for a work: there was Athens in *The Revolt of Aphrodite*, and Avignon and Alexandria in the *Quincunx* and the *Quartet*. Venice certainly has all the right credentials for a Durrellian setting: rich history, debauchery, aristocracy, violence, maritime power, art, and many artists lived there. And, of course, it's on the Mediterranean.

Durrell's series of Greek travel books compare with the Italian books of D.H. Lawrence. Durrell clearly draws on the spirit of *Twilight in Italy, Sea and Sardinia* and *Etruscan Places* in his own travel books.[37] For Lawrence, as for so many others who travelled there (J.M.W. Turner, John Ruskin, Percy Shelley, John Keats), Italy was the divine pagan land, sensuous, soft, verily a living Arcadia. Lawrence writes lovingly of Italy, much as Durrell writes of Greece:

Thousands of square miles of Italy have been lifted in human hands, piled and laid back in tiny little flats, held up by the drystone walls, whose stones came from the lifted earth. It is a work of many, many centuries. It is the gentle sensitive sculpture of all the landscape. And it is the achieving of the peculiar Italian beauty which is so exquisitely natural, because man, feeling his way sensitively to the fruitfulness of the earth, has moulded the earth to his necessity without violating it.[38]

37 On Lawrence's travel books, Durrell wrote in "Landscape and Character": 'It is not at all nonsense what D.H. Lawrence had to say in his communion with the 'ghosts' in the New World. He was within an ace, I think, of making real contact with the old Indian cultures. Genius that he was, he carried too much intellectual baggage about him on his travels, too many preconceptions; and while the mirror he holds up to Mexico, Italy, England is a marvellous triumph of art, the image is often a bit out of focus. He couldn't hold or perhaps wouldn't hold the camera steady enough' (SP, 161). Durrell himself, though, carried far more 'intellectual baggage' about with him than Lawrence. Durrell's reading (in science, psychology, occultism, architecture, medicine, etc) was perhaps wider than Lawrence's, though it was Lawrence who, finally, produced longer-lasting and more powerful works.
38 Lawrence: "Flowery Tuscany", *Selected Essays*, 140

Durrell is wholly in tune with Lawrence's emphasis on sensitivity to the landscape. Like Lawrence, Durrell was sensitive to human-made ugliness, and Italy and Greece showed a way of living in a landscape without destroying it. As Lawrence puts it: 'it *can* be done. Man *can* live on the earth and by the earth without disfiguring it.' (ib.)

For Durrell, as for Lawrence, Shelley, Byron, and all the others who journeyed to the Mediterranean, it was, among other things, the sun, the climate, the warmth, the sensuality of the life there that struck them. Throughout his travel writing and letters, Durrell emphasizes the magnetism of the Mediterranean, a world he characterizes as being marked out by the olive tree, for the Mediterranean is ringed by olive trees.

Even his book on Sicily, *Sicilian Carousel*, was really another 'Greek island book', like *Bitter Lemons* or *Reflections on a Marine Venus*. D.H. Lawrence wrote of 'the exquisite beauty of Sicily [and] the old Greek paganism that still lives there'.[39] And Henry Miller said that Durrell's 'beloved Greece was there ever as a sort of spiritual compass' (DML, 489).

For me, *Sicilian Carousel* is a potboiler with good moments, but not one of Durrell's best travel books, certainly not as deep and enlightening as *Bitter Lemons*. *Sicilian Carousel* ends up rather like the way Durrell described *Reflections on a Marine Venus*: 'literary pisspot style to épater that beautiful English public which can always recognise style – but which would be scared shitless if there was any content.' (DML, 205) In *Sicilian Carousel* one can see Durrell too obviously straining for the relaxed travel writer's touch. One sees through the padding to the travel writing machine underneath. Henry Miller, though, adored *Sicilian Carousel*, and fired off one of his ubiquitous puffs:

> What a master you are! Salut! Hail! I finished the Sicilian Travel Book this morning, feeling said that it had come to an end. I read slowly now... The slow pace made it all the more exciting. Listen, this isn't another travel book. This is *it*! One of your very best efforts. I was profoundly moved throughout; in ecstasy, in fact. (DML, 489)

---

39 Lawrence: "New Mexico", in *A Selection From Phoenix*, 126

Paris, Provence and France

The real landscape of *The Avignon Quintet* is cultural. For instance, when Blanford is in Paris the atmosphere of the capital of modern Europe is as much cultural as physical. The look of the urbanscape is sketched in:

> The old streets down at the fag end of the rue St.-Jacques which smelt of piss and stale cooking were the mere folklore of life lived in a relatively waterless capital where the women did not shave under their arms, and preferred stale scent in soapy bath water. In summer the smell of armpits in the cafés was enough to drive one mad. Yet everywhere the river winds cradled the velvet city and one could walk all night under a canopy of stars worthy of grand opera – the brilliant glitter of outer space impacting upon the shimmering brilliance of a world of hot light. (L, 172)

Towards the end of this paragraph Durrell deliberately parodies Henry Miller. For it is one of Miller's methods of writing to always make cosmic statements out of everyday material. It is the Paris of cafés and talk that Durrell is really interested in, the Paris of rapid exchanges of ideas. Idea and sex, for, typically, at the 'Sphinx' café, there is a brothel at the back of the café in Montparnasse, behind a 'simple bead curtain' (L, 172).

This is the Paris of Durrell's time with Anaïs Nin and Henry Miller, a city where, for Durrell, sex and philosophy intermingle ecstatically. Going to Paris, Durrell said in his last book,

> was like a sudden unpremeditated chord on the piano – a chord I had never struck before. The city was full of a subtle oxygen which mounted to the head. I realized I was among people who valued pleasure as a religious and æsthetic good, as soul-food! (CVG, 27)

London is contrasted with Paris, and it's clear which Blanford prefers. For Blanford, Paris is a city of cultural ferment: '[h]e had never been in such an extraordinary ambiance before, a sort of ferment of freedom and treachery, of love and obscenity, of febrility and distress.' (L, 173-4) Blanford dives into Proust, Spengler, Freud: '[i]t was the epoch of puzzling Gertrude Stein, Picasso, and the earlier convulsions of the American giants like Fitzgerald and Miller.' (L, 174)

In his letters, Durrell similarly eulogized the Paris years: 'long icy walks by the Seine with Anaïs in her cloak... walking in the Louvre like mad angels...', Edgar, Fred, Herbert Read, Raymond Queneau, Vaslav Nijinsky,

Betty Ryan, Teresa Epstein, Buffie Johnson (DML, 187-8). Paris reinforces Blanford's desire to be a writer. It is Livia, Blanford's first important love, who takes him to Paris, and it is Livia who gives him the 'gift' of being a writer:

> "I *see*," she said at last, drawing a surprised breath. "You are a *poet*." It was an unforgettable moment: she went on staring at him, staring right through him as if by some optical trick, right into his future. It was as if she had suddenly invented him anew, invented his career and the whole future shape of his inner life by the magic of such a phrase. One cannot help loving someone who divines one so clearly, throws one's whole obscure destiny into clear focus. (C, 6)

Instead of pork pies, net curtains, pubs, stiff upper lips and ape-like Anglo-Saxon attitudes, Durrell prefers French cuisine, the alleys of Montmartre and Montparnasse, cafés, sensuality and French liberalism. Baudelaire rather than Shelley, de Sade rather than Bentham.

Blanford's response to Paris is essentially the same as Durrell's response to Paris, Provence and France. Throughout his letters, poetry, non-fiction and fiction, Durrell contrasts France and Britain, and you can guess which country comes out most favourably. France, Durrell reckons, is a country where they appreciate the artist. People in France are delighted when Durrell says he is a writer, as he notes in his letters. In France, an artist *means something*, Durrell claims. The artist is treasured, not suppressed, as in Britain. Of the French, Durrell writes '[t]hen there are two other things unique of their kind – the reverence for love and the devotion to artists... I can't think of another nation quite like them at their best.'[40]

France would be the choice of residence of Pursewarden, Death Gregory, Darley, Blanford, Constance, Caradoc and Sutcliffe. Durrell's choice of a place to live after he left Cyprus in 1956 was of course France. He lived there from 1957 until his death in November 1990. Typically, Durrell lived in a part of France that could combine being French with being Mediterranean, the part of France most like Greece: Provence.

Significantly, the last of his 'foreign residence' or travel books was about his beloved Provence, Durrell's aim in the book being to 'capture the poetic quiddity of this extraordinary cradle of romantic dissent without sentimentalizing it' (CVG, 7). Durrell's Provence was a place in which present-day shepherds 'offer us Stone Age echoes in their habits', a place whose 'long roots stretch back into Greek and Roman history' (CVG, 31).

---

40 letter, July 1957, in *Spirit of Place*, 143

Provence is not all beauty: there are the 'tourist playgrounds' of the seaside towns, Nice and Monte Carlo, which is 'a ragged hinterland of skyscrapers', and 'vast unwelcome dormitory suburbs' around Avignon, Nîmes, Marseilles, Béziers and Montpellier (CVG, 9-12).

France permeates the later fiction, and the characters of *The Avignon Quintet* are always drawn back, finally, to France, rather than Egypt, Greece, Italy, Austria, Switzerland or England, the other countries of the *Quincunx*. France is the cultured centre of their lives. The characters speak most warmly of France, and Durrell's warmest and fondest thoughts are for France, as his short travel pieces collected in *Spirit of Place* show.

In Provence, Durrell can imagine himself back in his beloved Greece, the country of his second, spiritual birth (the Chinese have a notion of the 'spiritual birth'). The *garrigues*, the olives, the drystone walls, the *mistral*, the heat, these things conspire to make Provence like Greece for Durrell. In *Caesar's Vast Ghost* he writes of St-Rémy:

> I know of few villages more benign, and indeed more beautiful for a prolonged visit, say in April; its green and radiant glades give off a feeling of a perennial rejuvenating and healing force. The feeling, the light, conveys a magical playfulness, almost boisterousness; it is as if here the inhabitants wake up in a good humour every morning. It is like a corner of Greece. (151)

The 'innate purity and dignity of Provence' (CVG, 13) informs *The Avignon Quintet*, giving the novels their flavour. But it is the culture and history, as much as landscape and climate of Provence, that Durrell uses in *The Avignon Quintet*. *Caesar's Vast Ghost* is as much a historical account of Provence as a geographical, travel or personal account. As with Alexandria and Athens, Durrell writes about Avignon and Provence because of the weight of history he finds there. For instance, Provence is, like Alexandria, a place where faiths merged, syncretically. There are Stone Age, Saracen, Greek, Roman, Celtic and Cathar relics in the area.

> The long roots stretch back into Greek and Roman history, and of course through these great channels into the Mediterranean world as a cultural epic form – a masterpiece of realized memory. It is more emblematic than metaphoric, more poetry than prose! And in the heart of its historic change lies a continuity and consistence which shows the pious strength of these hills and rivers to bend man and shape him into an original thought-form – the place expressing itself through his body and mind as surely as a sculptor expresses himself in the clay he works or the stone

he carves. One can believe in Caesar and Mistral as spiritual coevals, and in the whole tapestry of its tempestuous history as all being appropriate, all belonging right there and nowhere else. (CVG, 31)

Durrell trawls Provence for its historical artifacts, and spends much of his time in *Caesar's Vast Ghost*, as in *Reflections on a Marine Venus* or *Bitter Lemons*, relating historical events, such as battles. In its own way, Provence is for Durrell a summary of the Mediterranean world: it feels like Greece; Egyptian *mummia*, fragments of mummies, are eaten; ex-votos and phalloi are found; 'the Camargue was a second Egypt' (83); the gypsies come to Stes Maries de la Mer, to celebrate St Sara, a Black Goddess who is dipped in the sea like the Indian Goddess Kali; the Knights Templar and the Cathars flourished in Provence; Italy and the Catholic Church (in the form of the Popes) lived in Avignon for a while. 'For a hundred years it was a Rome in exile', writes Durrell in "Laura, A Portrait of Avignon" (SP, 342). Avignon is the 'rose of all the world', the centre of the dual obsessions of Europe, passion (Laura) and pain (de Sade). In Avignon (or France) the two extremes of European love culture meet: the sublime, transcendent love of Petrarch's *Rime Sparse*, and the cruel, painful emotions of the Marquis de Sade (C, 353).[41]

Provence, it seems, is a compression or Stendhalian crystallization of all Durrell's landscapes. It is a landscape that sucks into itself all of Durrell's 'personal landscapes' and 'private countries'. Durrell writes of Avignon in "The River Rhône" (1960) that it is 'one of the most beautiful and romantic towns on earth'. He describes the Popes Palace in a euphoric mode: 'the tones of these marvellous palaces combine a dozen soft shades from the brown of dried tobacco or coffee to the violets and pearl-pinks of cooling lava-shades of nacre and bistre and honey according to the stoop of the sun.'[42]

He is equally excited about Vienne, with its mediæval streets, castle, and Corinthian temple. Durrell lovingly writes of the mulberries, the dusty

41 One critic sees the use of Petrarch in the *Quintet* as an important balance to the theme of original sin: James Nichols reckons Petrarch's and Dante's 'simple re-evocation of life, and sunlight, and humanity' counters the 'death-drift' of modern Europe ("Sunshine Dialogues: Christianity and Paganism in the works of Lawrence Durrell", OMG II, 133). Petrarch, though, was also, in works other than the *Canzoniere*, a decidedly ironic, sometimes cynical thinker, whose worldview was just as much influenced by the severity of St Augustine's theology as by the 'pagan' (i.e., non-Christian) philosophy of Cicero and others.
42 in *Spirit of Place*, 331-2

plains, the round-tiled houses, the blue shadows at twilight in Vienne; and he notes, as he does in the *Quincunx*, that it was to Vienne that Pontius Pilate was exiled (the patron saint of diplomats Durrell calls Pilate [SP, 329]).

Alexandria, Capital of Memory

...from Alexander to Amr; founders of this anarchy of flesh and fever, of money-love and mysticism. Where else on earth will you find such a mixture? And when night falls and the white city lights up the thousand candelabra of its parks and buildings, tunes in to the soft unearthly drum-music of Morocco or Caucasus, it looks like some great crystal liner asleep there, anchored to the horn of Africa – her diamond and fire-opal reflections twisting downwards like polished bars into the oily harbour among the battleships.

Lawrence Durrell, *Balthazar* (127-8)

Lawrence Durrell's relation with Alexandria was a love-hate one, as with England. In his letters written at the time of living in Alexandria, Durrell expresses hatred: he speaks of 'an Alexandrian frenzy of apathy' (8 February 1944, DML, 159). Again and again, Durrell recommends excessive self-indulgence (boys, women or drugs) as a way of surviving Alexandria:

The Alexandrian way of death is very Proustian and slow; a decomposition in greys and greens – by the hashish pipe or boys... First this steaming humid flatness – not a hill or mound anywhere – choked to bursting point with bones and the crummy deposits of wiped out cultures. Then this smashed up broken down shabby neapolitan town, with its Levantine mounds of houses peeling in the sun. A sea flat dirty brown and waveless rubbing the port. Arabic, Coptic, Greek, Levant French; no music, no art, no real gaiety. A saturated middle European boredom laced with drink and Packards and beach-cabins. NO SUBJECT OF CONVERSATION EXCEPT MONEY. Even love is thought of in money terms; "You are getting on with her? She has ten thousand a year of her own." Six hundred greaseball millionaires sweating in their tarbushes and waiting for the next shot of rot-hashish. And the shrieking personal unhappiness and loneliness showing in every face... Sexual provender of quality, but the atmosphere is damp, hysterical, sandy, with the wind off the desert fanning everything to mania. Love, hashish and boys is the obvious solution to anyone stuck here for more than a few years. (DML, 160, 168, 171)

It is interesting to compare the Alexandria conjured up by Durrell in his letters, and the Alexandria found in *The Alexandria Quartet*. In the letters, Durrell hates being in Alexandria, and that hatred and weariness comes over in the character Darley. The general atmosphere of *The Alexandria Quartet* is of an existential lassitude, but it is a fashionable and stylish weariness, cleverly shaped by the author into an elegant structure.

The Alexandria in the letters is a place to be escaped as soon as possible – Durrell went back to Greece (to Rhodes) after the war. In the fiction, Alexandria is a place of extremes: opulent, decadent materialism is contrasted with flea-bitten poverty, a time-honoured contrast.[43] The pageants of the ancient Ptolemy dynasty, which Durrell echoes in his over-the-top set-pieces, involved enormous spreads of pigeons, myrrh, sweetmeats, lions, elephants, gold and Indian princesses – verily overblown ceremonies in the D.W. Griffith style, with a cast of thousands (J. Pinchin, 14). In the fictional Alexandria, as in all Durrell's fiction, there is much decadence, much partying and jewels and huge cars and money.

> The master-sensualists of history abandoning their bodies to mirrors, to poems, to the grazing flocks of boys and women, to the needle in the vein, to the opium-pipe, to the death-in-life kisses with appetite. (Cl, 12)

But the decay is everywhere in Durrell's Alexandria, and the premier hotel, the Cecil, has dust on its palms. *Fin-de-siècle* decay permeates every aspect of Durrell's Alexandria – no one escapes it. *The Alexandria Quartet* is a novel of existential and societal decay, the decay of a culture into civilization, in the Spenglerian manner. Alexandria embodies that decline, and the shabbiness of modern day Alexandria is an expression of the decay, as is the sexual promiscuity and 'perversions'. *The Alexandria Quartet* is Durrell's 'Book of the Dead', and is all about spiritual bankruptcy. 'We were fellow-bankrupts', admits Darley, referring to Melissa (J, 20).

Durrell finds in wartime Alexandria a suitably ruined place for his

---

43 In his introduction to Forster's *Alexandria*, Durrell writes: 'Going ashore in Alexandria is like walking the plank for instantly you feel not only the plangently Greek city, but its backcloth of deserts stretching away into the heart of Africa. It is a place for dramatic partings, irrevocable decisions, last thoughts; everyone feels pushed to the extreme'. (xvi)

exploration of spiritual decay. In Alexandria he says in the letters 'the atmosphere of sex and death is staggering' (DML, 168). Sex and death are Durrell's chief concerns, as we have maintained, and the two are fulfilled by art. Alexandria became for Durrell in many ways the 'capital of memory', as he called it, 'the hinge of our whole Christian culture' (W, 168). It was, and is, a city of the imagination, a city built on memories, a city that only poets, it seems, can really appreciate, because, today, Alexandria reveals very little of its former glory. The glories of Alexandria have to be imagined, and the artist is the best person to do this. Thus, the inhabitants of Durrell's Alexandria are creative people – not only the writers Darley, Arnauti and Pursewarden, but also Justine and Nessim. Justine, for instance, is not a writer, but she, like all Durrell's characters, sheds petals of insight as if she were a philosopher or artist. Durrell says that 'the novel is only half secretly about art, the great subject of modern artists' (in Malcolm Cowley, 231). While writing his *Book of Friends*, and going back over his life, much as Durrell's Darley does, like any number of narrators do, Henry Miller wrote: '[t]he past is like an open book – rather, a cinerama spectacle. Nothing is ever lost, what!' (DML, 461).

Where is Alexandria? The city is made up of mythology and history, which lies not just below the surface, but deeply buried. The French and Greek city is built upon the ancient one, but for hundreds and hundreds of years Alexandria was a fishing village of some four thousand inhabitants. Nowadays, the city has been reclaimed by the Arabic Egyptians. The street names, once known in French, have been Egyptianized; the colonial glory of the 19th and early 20th centuries fades away. But it was fading fast even when Durrell lived there, in the war years. Robert Liddell writes of Alexandria:

Unreal City – for all its materialism and its hideousness, yet one of the cities of the soul. There I have known the misery and nostalgia of other exiles, 'stretching out our hands with love for the other shore'. (211)

Edmund Keeley, also, like Robert Liddell, in search of C.P. Cavafy's Alexandria, was disappointed by the present day city:

During a recent visit there, in the spring of 1973, I tried to make myself believe that the ugly reality I was seeing masked the presence of another city, more real in its way, a city open to those who could bring to it an imaginative vision, a mythical sensibility if you will, akin to Cavafy's and exemplified in recent English letters by E.M. Forster and Lawrence

Durrell. But the mask, the surface reality, was so unlike the literary images I brought with me, so immediate and harsh in its effect, that it frustrated any imaginative projection. Today's Alexandria strikes one first of all as squalid. (*Cavafy's Alexandria*, 4)

The artist's job, then, is to recreate Alexandria, to make it anew. Yet each writer who has remade Alexandria - Durrell, C.P. Cavafy, E.M. Forster, Edmund Keeley, Naguib Mahfouz, Michael Haag - has made it in their own image, and with dollops of irony. The three writers who have 'rewritten' Alexandria, so to speak - Durrell, Forster and Cavafy - have been markedly ironic artists. 'Alexandria goes on being Alexandria still', as Cavafy says, but in a very particular, æsthetic, philosophic way. Not the squalid contemporary city, or the squalid city of the 1930s, but an artistic creation, which, magpie-like, hordes bits of Alexandria picked up from any time in its history. The artists who have remade Alexandria have taken freely from 323 BC, Alexander the Great's epoch, or from Cleopatra's time, as mediated by Plutarch and Shakespeare, from Muhammad Ali's 19th century Alexandria, and from early 20th century cosmopolitan/ aristocratic/ bohemian Alexandria.

"Alexandria goes on being Alexandria still": for those who see it for what it really is - a city of the imagination, a city that satisfies the mind's eye first of all. (Edmund Keeley, ib., 3)

Durrell's Alexandria is very much the cosmopolitan city, where Greek, French, Italian, British, Jewish, Arab and Egyptian people mix. Like Durrell's beloved Corfu Town, the Greeks, Italians, French and British each made their mark on Alexandria. It is this modern city that provides the background of *The Alexandria Quartet*. But it is the mythical, historic city that lies deep underneath, that is the 'spirit' of Alexandria that infuses *The Alexandria Quartet*. It is the mythical, spiritual Alexandria that really excites Durrell. If Alexandria were merely LA or New York, a modern, mid-century city, the fascination would be much less for Durrell. Durrell's Alexandria, a distinctly fictional place, 'is completely faithful to the ancient spirit of the place'. (Robert Scholes, 1965, 24) The poet is excited by the ancient figures that still haunt Alexandria: Cleopatra, Antony, Amr and Alexander. To quote E.M. Forster on the mythic aspect of the city (here, Cleopatra) from his Alexandria guidebook:

She was the last of a secluded and subtle race, she was a flower that

Alexandria had taken three hundred years to produce and that eternity cannot wither, and she unfolded herself to a simple but intelligent Roman soldier. (28)

Alexandria was the capital of syncretic religion, where many faiths and creeds were discussed and formed, where Gnosticism and Neoplatonism was prominent. It is this philosophical richness that excites Durrell. The cosmopolitan/ colonial aspects of the city provide diverting scenes and people, but the themes of *The Alexandria Quartet* are carried on in figures such as Ptolemy and Cleopatra. The interweaving nature of the lives in *The Alexandria Quartet*, like crabs in a basket, as Balthazar puts it, is mirrored by the ancient beliefs that mingled in syncretic fashion around the time of Christ and in the first few centuries AD. The narrator of *The Alexandria Quartet* evokes the ancient city from time to time: it's more difficult to incorporate the ancient city into the present day one. But Durrell does find ways of integrating the ancient and modern: for instance, he will have a character walking down the 'Street of the Soma', even though no street in modern Alexandria bears that name (Rue Fuad appears most frequently in the *Quartet*). Or he will have characters meet near Pompey's Pillar, and he'll mention the ancient Park of Pan, in a manner that suggests E.M. Forster's historian style. Or he has Nessim undergo a series of dreams in *Justine* which include visions of the Mouseion, one of the splendours of classical Alexandria, or an army's shrine built to Aphrodite (J, 156f). Nessim's dreams are fearful expressions of the 'spirit of place': here the landscape is literally speaking through him.

Durrell might as well have chosen Jerusalem for his mythical city background in the *Quartet*. After all, Jerusalem is at the spiritual axis of the three monotheic religions. Durrell's narrator could have written 'Jerusalem!' instead of 'Alexandria!' (as was his habit with exclamation marks) and the word would have much more poetic and symbolic resonance. Of course, Jerusalem does feature in the *Quartet*, but Durrell's evocation of Israel and Palestine is very vague, distinctly off-stage. Besides, the Israel-Palestine side of Middle East politics was (is) far more problematic than Durrell's eventual choice of Egypt, the British and the Copts. Perhaps taking on Palestine, Israel, and that side of the Levant would have been too much, too complex, too inflammatory, too much to deal with.

Other cities which share this highly symbolic function include Athens and Rome, both thriving modern cities as well as historical and mythical centres. In Rome and Athens the ancient world is all around – and is very visible too. Perhaps the extraordinary debauchery of ancient Rome would have been too obvious a background for the investigation of modern sex and death in Durrell's *Quartet*.

Durrell's Alexandria and Egypt is the archetypal view of the 'Oriental' Middle East seen from the viewpoint of (white, affluent, imperialist) European society. Durrell espouses the traditional views of the Levant which have been prevalent from the Crusades onwards; the uncleanness of the people and landscape; the bestial, earthy, poor lifestyle; the internecine warfare; the many tribes, cuisines, costumes, crafts, languages, *mœurs*, beliefs; the violence; the ethnic, religious and social cross-fertilization; the beauty and mystery of the East, and so on. Durrell 'orientalizes' the East in that romantic, 'imperialist' fashion familiar from the works of Edward Said. [44] However, notions of the 'East' and 'Occident' are inventions as much for the 'real' Orient as for the 'real' West. Even as writers such as T.E. Lawrence, Richard Burton, Norman Douglas, Rose Macaulay, and Durrell romanticized and orientalized the East, writers in the Orient also romanticized themselves.

The mythical Alexandria is described by visitors such as Durrell, Robert Liddell, E.M. Forster, Edmund Keeley and Michael Haag as a city of dreams, in which one needs to dream hard to recapture its former radiance. [45] Liddell writes of ancient historic Alexandria:

> Of ancient Greek Alexandria nothing survives but the name and the site, and the Romans have only left inconsiderable remains behind them. The conquering Arabs, who were to build so magnificently elsewhere, here did nothing but destroy. A miserable village stood during the centuries where had been the city of Alexander and the Ptolemies; and of course the poets Theocritus, Callimachus and Apollonius Rhodius; of Antony and Cleopatra; of saints and heresiarchs such as St Athanasius and Arius; of learning and philosophy of the Mouseion, of Plotinus and Hypatia. The Venetians went off with the head of St Mark, the apostle of Egypt. (17)

Alexandria has to be invented to become fully satisfying. 'Art is what the artist invents', said Constantin Cavafy (*Alithersis*, 41), and this is precisely what Durrell does with Alexandria in *The Alexandria Quartet*, and what

44 see Peter Lamborn Wilson: "Orientalismo", in *Sulfur*, no. 35, Fall 1994, 233
45 One of the best writers I've read on ancient Greece is Mary Renault, a truly fabulous writer who, like Durrell, was English but lived much of her life abroad. Renault's trilogy on Alexander the Great is one of the great novel sequences of the 20th century.

his characters do.[46] All the time they are inventing – Balthazar invents, improvizing upon Darley's inventions, Arnauti re-invents Justine, just as she invents herself. Alexandria is invented and re-invented throughout Durrell's work: it looms large also in *The Avignon Quintet*, as the place where the Oriental lover and would-be mage, Affad, lives.

Durrell's Alexandria is much more than a 'backdrop' for the action in *The Alexandria Quartet*. It is invoked continually in the tertralogy as more than a mere city, more than a collection of buildings and people and climate. It is a 'spirit', a presence, the 'It' of Groddeck, which moves through the characters, mobilizes them, limits them and shapes them. Alexandria is the guiding force behind the *Quartet*. Groddeck's 'It', which is expressed in Alexandria and her people, is associated by Durrell with the Tao, in that '[t]he It is a Way, not a Thing' (Key, 79), a manifestation or a process, but not a 'thing-in-itself'. Henry Miller wrote to Durrell:

> ...the city itself, Alexandria, is the real hero. You've made it immortal. It communicates always by and through the senses. It also gives the impression of being inexhaustible – like a god... Alexandria < – *your* Alexandria – > is the whole pantheon of Homer's bloody, senseless gods – doing what they will, but *conscious* of what is done. The Homeric gods are more like blind forces, components of the now exposed psyche – atomic, in other words. Whereas Alexandria – thru and by her inhabitants, climate, odours, temperament, diversity, freaks, crimes, monstrous dreams and hallucinations (*but why imitate you?*) – gives the impression of living herself (her panthe*onic* self) out, of washing herself clean through complete enactment. Alexandria *enacts* (for us) – that's it. (DML, 345-7)

Justine is the embodiment of Alexandria, of the sensual, feverish, neurotic aspect of the city, of Alexandria as Cleopatra Incarnate (other mythic courtesans lie behind Justine: Salomé, Lais, Charis, and figures such as Judith who beheaded Holofernes).

But the other spirit of the city is C.P. Cavafy, 'one of Alexandria's strangest figures' (Pinchin, 5), '*the genius loci*' of the city (R. Liddell, 210), who is called by Durrell 'the old poet of the city' in *Justine*. Cavafy, E.M. Forster says, is 'the great Greek poet who so poignantly conveys the civilization of his chosen city' (*Alexandria*, xxiii). Edmund Keeley writes:

---

46 Countering this view is the Groddeckian precept of the Rankian psychologist in *The Dark Labyrinth*, who states: 'the artist does not invent or discover; rather does he, by making himself receptive, be discovered or re-created'. (DL, 45) Again, Groddeck's 'It' speaks through the individual, just as Alexandria expresses itself through the characters of the *Quartet*.

Aware of the poet's point of view, I find it difficult to move through the streets of today's Alexandria without feeling the presence of Cavafy's ghost, especially the threat of its mockery. (ib, 3)

The Cavafian nostalgia of the *Quartet* is to be found on every page, sometimes wistful, sometimes bitter, sometimes 'tragic', sometimes humorous. Memory itself becomes the 'school of love' for the young lover-poet. Towards the end of *Justine* the memory of 'particular rooms' in one which makes love, or particular café tables, the site of romantic liaisons, or kisses, becomes a 'school' to the 'student of love' (J, 201).

It's inevitable that Durrell would use C.P. Cavafy in a novel set in Alexandria. Balthazar is a version of Cavafy, he has many of the poet's characteristics, and visits the poet in his rooms. Cavafy's poems appear at the back of *Justine*, two of Cavafy's most famous poems: 'The City' and 'The God Abandons Antony'. For Durrell, Cavafy is one of the most sublime melders of the twin polarities of Alexandrian (therefore Western) life, the extreme asceticism and extreme sensuality, the poles of ecstasy and excrement, spirit and matter. In *Justine*, Balthazar, the most Cavafian of Durrell's creations, explains why Cavafy is of such importance:

> His exquisite balance of irony and tenderness would have put him among the saints had he been a religious man. He was by divine choice only a poet and often unhappy but with him one had the feeling that he was catching every minute as it flew and turning it upside down to expose its happy side. He was really using himself up, his inner self, in living. (J, 82-83)

In Cavafy's art, one finds the major Durrellian themes united by an extraordinary talent: art, religion, eroticism and memory/ time. In Cavafy's poems, eroticism and art, spirituality and degradation merge in an ironic fashion, wholly in tune with Durrell's own hyper self-conscious sensibility. Cavafy is the poet Durrell might like to be, for Cavafy understands the primacy of the imagination and art. Cavafy, too, stylishly integrates Durrell's love of all things Greek, Egyptian, English and French; Cavafy is the multi-lingual, cosmopolitan poet, also at home everywhere and nowhere, but at home only in Alexandria, the beloved city. Cavafy's poetic stance is the model for Durrell's new sense of exile, at its most piquant in the poem 'The City', one of Cavafy's great poems, here rendered by Durrell:

You tell yourself: I'll be gone
To some other land, some other sea,
To a city lovelier far than this
Could ever have been or hoped to be –
Where every step now tightens the noose:
A heart in a body buried and out of use:
How long, how long must I be here
Confined among these dreary purlieus
Of the common mind? (J, 221)

The two key poems of Cavafy's which relate to the themes of the
Quartet are 'The City' and 'In the Evening'. The following three poems,
like so many of Cavafy's poems, also go to the heart of the *Quartet*. In
'One Night', Cavafy writes:

now as I write, after so many years,
in my lonely house, I'm drunk with passion again. (1983, 41)

This is precisely the psychic space in which Darley writes, on his lonely
island in the Mediterranean, recreating the characters of 1930s Alexandria.
It is also the basic situation of poets everywhere, from Sappho and the
anonymous poets of the *Greek Anthology* onwards.

In 'Understanding', Cavafy writes of the shaping structure of love:

In the loose living of my early years
the impulses of my poetry were shaped,
the boundaries of my art were plotted. (1983, 60)

Here Cavafy's narrator acknowledges how the trajectory and structure of
his whole life after youth was formed in the (sensual) experiences of his
youth. The erotic attachments of teenage and his twenties become his food
and foundation of his later, mature years. It is to the years of late teenage
and early 20s that Cavafy's narrators return, time after time.

In 'Half an Hour' Cavafy describes the shamanic power of the artist:

I never had you nor, I suppose, will ever have you.
A few words, an approach,
as in the bar yesterday - nothing more.
It's sad, I admit. but we who serve Art,
sometimes with the mind's intensity
can create pleasure that seems almost physical –
but of course only for a short time. (1983, 149)

Robert Liddell, in his biography of Cavafy, writes:

When I returned a few months later to live and work in Alexandria, Cavafy seemed the *genius loci*... That same spring, walking between the splendid herbaceous borders of Nimr Pacha at Meadi, Sir Walter Smart had said to me: 'If you're going to write an Alexandrian novel, it must centre round Cavafy.' (210-1)

These days, you can go on literary pilgrimages in Alexandria not only to find the locations of Cleopatra's fabulous temple, or the Great Library, or the Gates of the Moon, or Alexander's tomb, but also places where C.P. Cavafy, E.M. Forster and others lived. Durrell himself has become another mythical Alexandria figure. You can find the tower Durrell built over the Italian garden at 19 Maahmoud Street, or Cavafy's flat, now the Cavafy Museum, or the café where characters from *The Alexandria Quartet* used to meet – Pastroudis. Already Durrell's *The Alexandria Quartet* has become integrated into the poetic-mythic fabric of modern day Alexandria.

The 'real' Alexandria, then, exists as an artistic/ cultural creation.[47] It is not the 'actual' city in North Africa but the literary edifice created by Durrell, Cavafy, Forster, Mahfouz and other writers. Edmund Keeley writes:

The surface of Alexandria is now Arabic once again – Arabic and little else – and the mythical city beyond it is visible only to the inner eye of an Egyptian poet, one who can see the vital imaginative resources that remain hidden from those confined to a European perspective. but if the surface one sees today is unrecognizable to someone brought up on the images created by Cavafy, Forster, and the other literary "Alexandrias", this merely serves to reinforce the sense that the literal Alexandria is not the one that has counted most for the world of letters. The mystery of modern Alexandria seems to be not in what it actually is or was at any given moment but in its power to stimulate – as perhaps no other city in this century – the creation of poetic cities cast in its image, cities that imitate it as it can be, or even ought to be, in its essence. (ib, 5-6)

Durrell's Alexandria is thus one those mythical cities of imagination, one of those 'cities of the interior', as Anaïs Nin called them, which are found

---

47 Jane Pinchin glosses Durrell's assertion that '[o]nly the city is real' with Vladimir Nabokov's remark that 'real' is the only word that requires quotation marks. The quotation marks around 'real' chime with the postmodern critiques of society of Jean Baudrillard, Fredric Jameson, Umberto Eco, Pierre Bordieu, Jacques Derrida *et al*, with their talk of the 'hyperspace' and simulation of global media.

in much of literature. Michael Moorcock has his own version of a mythical London, as has Iain Sinclair, William Shakespeare, Charles Dickens, Peter Ackroyd, Salman Rushdie – even Spike Milligan's the Goons created their version of London. Henry Miller has his beloved Paris, while Woody Allen joyously mythicizes New York in his movies. Anaïs Nin's own mythical city was the ever-exotic Fez, one of the few cities that can vie with Cairo for extraordinary scenes and sensual overload.

People often confuse cities as they appear in fiction with real cities. Go to Alexandria now and you find only fragments of Durrell's or Cavafy's Alexandria. People go to Thomas Hardy's Wessex and expect to be moved by, say, Tess's Cottage, or Michael Henchard's house (now a bank) in Dorchester. But Hardy's Wessex, like André Gide's North Africa, Bertie Lawrence's Tuscany, V.S. Naipaul's India or Graham Greene's Brighton, is a literary, creative invention. Hardy's Wessex takes the county of Dorset and its environs as a point of departure merely: the rest is invention. In a similar fashion, the Oriental flavour of *The Arabian Nights,* with its labyrinthine bazaars, was based not on Baghdad, but Cairo. Go to Cairo today and the *souks* and casbahs are still astonishing, whereas Alexandria's historic past is disappointing, lost and fragmented in the modern city.

Lawrence Durrell's *Quartet* is thus also an exploration of the Arabic world, and its relationship with and contrast to the Western (European) world. In contrasting Islam and Europe Durrell's references can be seen in the politically correct post-colonial world as racist and insensitive. Durrell does not reserve his scepticism just for Arabs or Jews, though: the French, the Germans, the Italians, the Greeks, and most obviously the English all receive a share of vehemence and bile.

As landscapes, Durrell explores the contrasts between England and Egypt, how the social and personal space of Europe and Arabia are organized along different lines: how the Arabic/ Egyptian way of life is lived crowded-in together, with few private spaces,[48] not in separate suburban homes as in England; the Arabic smellscape is rich and intoxicating, with its incense, live animals, leather, spaces, while the European city is dominated by traffic fumes and air fresheners; the Arab *souk* is a maze of passageways, while the British and French town is a po-faced plastic High Street. Durrell's Arabia is an investigation of contrasts and differences, it is a world constructed on different cultural foundations from the 'air conditioned

48 S. Bianca: "Traditional Muslim cities and Western planning ideology: an outline of structural conflict", in Serageldin 1982, 40; E. Hall: *The Hidden Dimension*, Bodley Head 1969

nightmare' (Henry Miller's phrase) of the West. Miller's title for his voyage around American culture describes the mechanized, saccharine sterility of the West.

Durrell's Alexandria is thus to be found not in the North African city, not in the text or words of *The Alexandria Quartet*, but in the interface between the reader and the text. In short, in the reader's mind. This is where mythical cities live, in the fantasizing brain. As Michael Haag writes in his Egypt guidebook:

> A Roman theatre, Pompey's Pillar, the catacombs at Kom el Shogafa; these and a medieval fortress squatting on the foundations of the Pharos lighthouse are the principal but paltry remains of Alexandria's resplendent past. Some will see nothing in her. Others will voyage through the phantom city and listen to her voices and her music. (418)

Durrell's Alexandria is a ghost, which floats on the breath of long-buried glories. Alexandria relies on stories, comments, myths, historians' accounts, essays, intimations and shadowy figures for its resplendence. It is a city founded on hearsay, on narratives and inventions. Words and legends keep Alexandria buoyant. Without language and artistic invention, Alexandria, like any other mythical city – Carthage, Babylon, Atlantis, Antioch – would fade away to nothing.

> What one might call the Alexandrian mode is first of all to search for the hidden metaphoric possibilities, the mysterious invisible processions, of the reality one sees in the literal city outside one's window. (Edmund Keeley, 6)

Durrell introduces Alexandria early on in *Justine* as the archetypal exotic landscape, full of dust, flies, beggars, decay and debauchery:

> Capitally, what is this city of ours? What is resumed in the word Alexandria? In a flash my mind's eye shows me a thousand dust-tormented streets. Flies and beggars own it today – and those who enjoy an intermediate existence between either. Five races, five languages, a dozen creeds; five fleets turning through their greasy reflections behind the harbour bar. But there are more than five sexes and only demotic Greek seems to distinguish between them. The sexual provender which lies to hand is staggering in its variety and profusion. (J, 11-12)

Here we see Durrell setting up his landscape of the Book of the Dead: he mentions the notion of Alexandria as a capital, a world (mythic) centre; he mentions the archetypal scenes of the Orient (flies, beggars, dust); he notes the syncretism of the races and creeds; politics (in the 'five fleets'); decay ('greasy reflections'); and of course, sex. Also, how sexuality relates to language, how language tries to define sexual possibilities.

Lawrence Durrell's Egypt – chiefly Alexandria, Cairo and (excursions into) the desert – is a torment of conflicting desires, histories, politics and personalities. In *The Alexandria Quartet* we veer from extreme to extreme, from heat and dust to rain and mud; from exotic pantomime-like parties where the rich and famous cavort in black dominos, to camels being sliced up while still alive. In amongst the opulence there is brutality: a famous example is the death by a hat-pin being driven into the brain at the party (which is also the manner of the murder at the end of Paul Bowles' *Let It Come Down*).

As with Paul Bowles' fictions – *The Sheltering Sky, Let It Come Down, The Spider's House* – violence is sudden and overwhelming when it occurs. The violence is seen as the natural outcome of the 'spirit of place', where the inhabitants are so profoundly bored, 'bored to death', to use a common phrase. The weariness of North Africa is so intense it produces outbreaks of violence, like a thunderstorm suddenly erupting. In the fictions of André Gide, Paul Bowles and Durrell set in North Africa, violence is an occasional but inevitable outburst in a weary life.

Durrell's Egypt reproduces the traveller's impressions of a Third World environment: the dust, poverty, slums and flies. Egypt is summarized in *Balthazar* as a series of symbols, thus: 'minarets, pigeons, statues, ships, coins, camels and palms'. And one sentence sums up Egypt: '[a] woman counting money on a glass table, an old man feeding a dog, an Arab in a red flowerpot drawing a curtain.' (J, 189-190) This extract from the beginning of *Justine* is typical of *The Alexandria Quartet*, and of so much of European fiction set in Africa, India, South America or other non-Western landscapes:

> Streets that run back from the docks with their tattered rotten super-cargo of houses, breathing into each others' mouths, keeling over. Shuttered balconies swarming with rats, and old women whose hair is full of the blood of ticks. Peeling walls leaning drunkenly to east and west of their true centre of gravity. The black ribbon of flies attaching itself to the lips and eyes of the children – the moist beads of summer flies everywhere; the very weight of their bodies snapping off ancient flypapers hanging in the violet doors of booths and cafés. The smell of sweat-lathered Berberinis, like that of some decomposing stair-carpet. And then

the street noises: shriek and clang of the water-bearing Saidi, dashing his metal cups together as an advertisement... (21)

And so it goes on. Periodically throughout his fiction, Durrell throws in these descriptions, sometimes lengthy, of particular places. Durrell loves 'set-pieces', extended sequences such as the carnival in *Justine*, the duck-shoot in *Mountolive*, the bathing and hand-cutting in *Clea*, Mountolive in the child brothel, Lord Galen's 'spree' in *The Avignon Quintet*, Caradoc's Acropolis lecture in *Tunc*, the exploration of the labyrinth in *The Dark Labyrinth*, and so on. These are the sequences that critics seem to love or hate. Henry Miller, naturally, loves the bits where he goes wild, where Durrell lets himself go, and it is most often in a set-piece in an exotic location that he does this. Miller wrote to Durrell in November 1958 thus:

> Am half-way through [*Mountolive*] now and write to tell you how very very good it is – in every respect. Am always amazed by the way you digest the countries you've lived in. A vast, penetrative knowledge rendered in poetic fashion, even the mud, the sores, the flies! (The slaughter of the camels, which I read a while ago, is simply tremendous.) (DML, 335)

The times when a character returns to Alexandria is often the signal for landscape lyricism. When Mountolive goes to Alex on that fateful night when he meets a vastly changed Leila and ends up in a child brothel, he arrives during a storm. To presage Mountolive's crucifixion, the narrator keeps emphasizing the fact that it's winter, it's stormy, the clouds are 'blood-stained' (Mt, 248). In the stormlight, the city becomes spectral, like a fairy tale landscape with its minarets and mosques, brick buildings, dust, surrounding desert, liners groaning like animals in the harbour (M, 248-9). The two set-pieces at the end of *Mountolive* – Narouz' death and Mount-olive's descent into hell – both involve lengthy evocations of the 'primitive' or 'native' aspects of Egypt and Alexandria. Mountolive ventures into the Arab quarter got up like a Syrian sheikh in flowerpot hat and shades. Durrell trots out the usual descriptions of the seedier side of Egypt: the dust, cafés, incense, card players, narguilehs, stenches, markets, and the inevitable pornography and prostitution.

When Darley returns to Alexandria, at the start of *Clea*, his homecoming is described in terms of artifice. The narrator emphasizes that the images of wartorn Alexandria which Darley sees from the boat as he arrives by sea by night are theatrical, cinematic, painterly. Allusions are constantly made to cinema, theatre and painting. Durrell doesn't simply write 'like a painter', he uses painting metaphors all the time, referring, for instance, to a sky looking like a painter has smashed his colourbox against it. And the chief protagonist of *Clea*, after Darley, is a painter (Clea).

The set-piece where Darley in the boat sees Alexandria in an air bombardment is a typical example of Durrell's literary, self-conscious style of description. It is a suitably 'dramatic' way of reviving Alexandria for the last time in the *Quartet*. To emphasize the unreality and noise of wartime Alexandria, Durrell contrasts it with the other key landscape of his life, island Greece. Darley is shown lying 'on a flat rock above the sea, eating an orange' (12). This Hellenic, Arcadian calm is shattered, in the best literary tradition, by the horror of war. It is not a gut-wrenching, nauseous horror, however. Durrell's narrators do not rub the reader's nose in the slime. Instead, the horror is highly stylized, as in all Durrell's work, and the aerial bombardment becomes for Darley a firework display on a colossal scale:

> A dense stream of coloured rockets now began to mount from the haze among the battleships, emptying on the sky their brilliant clusters of stars and diamonds and smashed pearl snuff-boxes with a marvellous prodigality. (C, 21)

The violence and pain of war is replaced by an insistence on the unreality and vividness of it. Darley's psychic dislocation from the 'real world' is so great that he sees the attack on Alexandria as a series of marvellous effects, created solely for him to witness. The adjectives in the first seventy or so pages of *Clea* emphasize light and brilliance. The word 'brilliant' is employed a good deal. It occurs three times in one sentence – Durrell the craftsman is not usually this slipshod. Indeed, Durrell emphasizes the radiance of Alexandria continually in *Clea*. It is the brightest book of the *Quartet*, and of all his novels. In the three-'brilliant' sentence we find the phrase 'the warm gold of oranges'. This phrase uses three 'hot' words. The image of oranges might be thought enough, but the narrator calls them not only 'gold' but 'warm', to really highlight the glow. Another sequence, the shooting of Fosca, is depicted in a visual way 'like some majestic seascape by a great master' (Cl, 180). When the dead pregnant woman is being brought back to the shore, the narrator switches from painterly and cinematic modes to aural ones: the click of Balthazar's tongue, heels on the street, voices barking orders, etc (Cl, 182).

Alexandria provides Durrell with much 'local colour' as it's called, which he duly describes. As Durrell describes the squalor he inevitably romanticizes it, just as Shakespeare romanticized the 'primitives' in *The Tempest*.[49] Durrell treats the 'natives' of Egypt in a patronizing, colonial manner, which seems to be unavoidable. Shakespeare did it, Dickens did it, Greene did it, Huxley did it, Lawrence did it.

The particular spaces of *The Alexandria Quartet* offer a landscape of extremes, where Durrell portrays faded elegance in the opulent rooms of Nessim, contrasting it with the stylized poverty of the Turkish quarter of Alexandria. Whether Durrell is describing opulence or squalor, stylization is uppermost. The spatial aspects of Durrell's Alexandria function to describe the main themes and states of consciousness of the tetralogy. The connections between the tiny boxroom of Pombal's flat, where Darley lives and makes love to Melissa ('those sun-tormented afternoons', J, 47) are the Egyptian equivalents of those squalid rooms in *The Black Book*. Scobie's rooms are similarly horrible. But it is such seemingly tiny spaces, such as Clea's studio near Cavafy's old apartment, that the creative people in the *Quartet* flourish. The characters who have huge, endless space, such as Justine and Nessim, are stunted, creatively. Justine has endless rooms through which she can prowl, but she too returns to the more intimate enclosure of her bedroom with its totem skull towards which she addresses her feelings. Durrell spends much time describing Nessim's 'Summer Palace' for Justine: here the combination of austerity and extravagance neatly summarizes Nessim's state of mind.

---

49 On Shakespeare and colonialism, see O. Mannoni: *Prospero and Caliban: The Psychology of Colonization*, Praeger, New York 1964; Paul Brown in Jonathan Dollimore & Alan Sinfield, eds: *Political Shakespeare*, Manchester University Press 1985; Leslie Fielder: *The Stranger in Shakespeare*, Croom Helm 1973; Thomas Carteli in Jean E. Howard & M.F. O'Connor, eds: *Shakespeare Reproduced: The Text in History and Ideology*, Methuen 1987, 99-115; Francis Barker & Peter Hulme in John Drakakis, ed: *Alternative Shakespeares,* Routledge 1985, 191-205; Charles Frey: "*The Tempest* and the New World", *Shakespeare Quarterly*, 30, 1979, 29-41;

7

From Desire to Revulsion:
Love in Durrell's Fiction

Love is the time and space in which "I" assumes the right to be extraordinary.

Julia Kristeva[1]

Love is very much Lawrence Durrell's major theme. It dominates his major fictions, from *The Black Book* through *The Alexandria Quartet* to *The Revolt of Aphrodite* and *The Avignon Quintet*. Portentously at the beginning of the second volume of *The Alexandria Quartet*, in an author's note (always a bad idea), Durrell announces: '[t]he central topic of the book is an investigation of modern love.' (B, 7)[2] For critics, Durrell's books are not about 'modern love',[3] but, rather, 'Narcissism and desire. Sterile, they are talking about its perversity, its sadness, its anecdotage, its variety, its passing.'[4]

1 Kristeva: "In Praise of Love", in 1987, 5
2 Significantly, the stated intention of the *Quartet*, often quoted by critics ('an investigation of modern love', from the preface to *Balthazar*) originally ran, in the first draft, 'my topic is an investigation of love; the bisexual psyche'. (Ill, 42, 19, 8)
3 Lionel Trilling, "Lawrence Durrell: Two Reviews", in W, 52
4 V.S. Prichett, 1960, 223

Durrell speaks often about love, but nearly always in a sarcastic, ironic, self-aware fashion. He writes as the Elizabethans did about love: he loves love, but keeps a distance from it; he's in love with love, like St Bernard and other Catholic saints, but he knows about the bitterness and dejection love can bring; he desires love but knows the paradoxes and problems that love can produce.

Durrell's view of love is distinctly European, white, male, bourgeois, patriarchal, intellectual, as found in the courtly love poets (Giraut de Borneil, Bernart de Ventadour, Arnaut Daniel); Dante Alighieri in the intense, autobiographical and visionary *Vita Nuova*, where he wrote so passionately of his beloved, Beatrice Portinari, whom he later deified in *The Divine Comedy*; in Francesco Petrarch in the *Canzoniere*, that elegant series of *cansos* and sonnets to the love object, Laura de Sade (whom Durrell alludes to in *The Avignon Quintet* a few times); in the Elizabethan love poets, whom Durrell loved (Thomas Campion, William Shakespeare, Samuel Daniel, Sir Philip Sidney, edmund Spenser); in the Romantics (John Keats, Victor Hugo, William Wordsworth, Johann Wolfgang von Goethe); and in the Symbolists, in particular the debauched, decadent eroticism of Charles Baudelaire, Arthur Rimbaud and Paul Verlaine.[5]

This is Durrell's ancestry, and the philosophers he invokes are often thinkers who have written much of love: Plato, de Sade, Goethe, Freud, de Rougemont. Durrell's metaphysics of love is firmly based on the European tradition of de Sade, Stendhal and Freud. Stendhal (Henry-Marie Beyle) Durrell invokes, often indirectly: he mentions Stendhalian crystalization in *The Avignon Quintet*. Stendhal's *De l'Amour* is a key text in Durrell's metaphysics of love. Sutcliffe muses, in Venice, about Sabine: 'It was the old Stendhalian crystallisation all right' (M, 186).

The Marquis de Sade is used throughout *The Alexandria Quartet* as a reference point. For Pursewarden, who, apart from the Sutcliffe-Blanford figure, is Durrell's major philosophical mouthpiece, reckons de Sade simply took human love to logical extremes. For Pursewarden, de Sade is a philosopher of love, who plays out the real, fundamental desires of people. In *The Alexandria Quartet*, Durrell often speaks of 'human love', as if he could be talking of any other kind of love. Love between trees and clouds perhaps? Love between killer whales? It's odd that Durrell keeps

5 The æsthetic theory of the *Quartet* derives from Decadence and *fin de siècle* culture – *À Rebours* is one of the novels cited in the *Quartet* (J.R. Nichols: "The Paradise of Bitter Fruit: "Lawrence Durrell's *Alexandria Quartet*", Cartwright, 227)

emphasizing the phrase *human* love, as if he's embarked on some anthropological or natural history exploration (which indeed he is). The epigraphs for the four novels of *The Alexandria Quartet* include Freud and de Sade. Durrell is like other Romantic and symbolist writers (Byron, Shelley, Novalis, Rimbaud, Verlaine) in that the Sadeian ethic of going to extremes is central: thus, for Durrell, love is an extreme state, as in de Sade's work. Love is, Darley says in *Justine*,

> an absolute which takes all or forfeits all. The other feelings, compassion, tenderness and so on, exist only on the periphery and belong to the constructions of society and habit. But she herself - austere and merciless Aphrodite - is a pagan. It is not our brains or instincts which she picks - but our very bones. (J, 93)

Durrell regards love in the typical Western manner: it is a mania, a self-deluding madness, a psychosis where boundaries between self and others, between self and world, breaks down. Sigmund Freud is very much a central reference point in Durrell's *œuvre*. The main discussion in *Constance* is about psychoanalysis, and how psychoanalysis compares with yoga as a life system.

From his first fictions of the 1930s (especially *The Black Book*) Durrell explored Freud's view of love. Psychoanalysis becomes for Durrell a way in to the exploration of love, of love seen as childish dependency, of the oral, anal and genital stages, of love as investment. One of the best lines of *The Avignon Quintet* is Affad's in *Constance*: 'I love you! I invest!' (C, 303) Durrell makes fun of Freud and his accomplices, Jung and Georg Groddeck, Otto Rank and Alfred Adler. Constance is deeply into psychoanalysis, while Sutcliffe criticizes it bitterly, as he hangs around Vienna and Geneva while Pia is under-going therapy. For Durrell, psychoanalysis is both to be welcomed and criticized, to be exalted as a marvellous breakthrough, and laughed at for being so simplistic in its view of personality and desire.

William Shakespeare appears as a reference point in Lawrence Durrell's ethics of love. The complex love triangle in Shakespeare's *Sonnets* is alluded to, particularly concerning the incestuous relations between Piers, Bruce and Sylvie. 'Ah, the sweet mooncalf of the dark lady of the soblets!' writes Sutcliffe during one of his rambling notebook sessions (M, 232). The scenario of the *Sonnets* - the complex homoerotic love triangle - forms a background to Durrell's trinities of love in *The Alexandria Quartet* and *The Avignon Quintet*. This is pure drama for Durrell, this complex entanglement of relationships. Durrell mentions in *The Avignon Quintet* that the situation described in the *Sonnets* would have made Shakespeare's best play. The *Sonnets*, though they contain the basic tensions of rivalry in erotic love, do not have the dimensions of royalty, power politics and history which Shakespeares loved to put into his plays.

The Elizabethan mentality is very much in tune with Durrell's, or vice versa. Like Thomas Campion, Robert Herrick, Philip Sidney, Edmund Spenser, Michael Drayton and Shakespeare, Durrell loves love, loves the games, ecstasies and pains. Like the Elizabethans, Durrell writes of love in an ironic, knowing, self-conscious fashion.[6] Like the Elizabethans, Durrell makes word games, witticisms, puns and bawdy allusions to love. Like the Elizabethans, Durrell exalts heterosexual love in an intellectual yet also erotic fashion. The Platonic, philosophic, ideal and spiritual aspects of love fascinate Durrell, as they fascinated the Provençal troubadours, the German *Minnesängers*, the *jongleurs* and minstrels of courtly love, and the Italian *stilnovisti*. Yet Durrell loves the bawdiness of love, he loves to discuss the fleshly fundamentals of love, and there is much talk in *The Avignon Quintet* of pricks, cunts, arses, and so on, but always couched in word games and convoluted conversations, always glossed by the ever-ironic Sutcliffe and Blanford. There is much talk of genitals in Shakespeare's work, but always written in brilliant word games, or saved from idiocy by jokes, humour, and distantiation devices. But, as with Shakespeare and the Elizabethan poets, Durrell believes in love, and makes it central to his life-philosophy. For all he makes fun of it, Durrell exalts love.

> ...how long since Petrarch sighed and sobbed his way into old age, verse after dry verse like the beat of a metronome in the shrinking skull. And yet I believe in great attachments, in the stabbing recognition that assailed him as it assailed Dante. Freud can keep his mouth shut firmly on his cigar. The good poet needs an unripe girl as a Muse. (M, 208-9)

Elsewhere Durrell is more cynical about the notion of 'the couple': '[i]t is stupid to believe in the couple and enjoy marriage as a state of things which enables me to be happy and work' (DML, 483). The dream of living in a couple lies behind much of Durrell's discourse: against all the odds, his narrators still believe in the couple. Whether he sees lovers as indulging in

6 In *Balthazar* Durrell/ Darley puts the word love into quotation marks, as it should always be in Durrell's work. He/ 'he' writes of '[m]y 'love' for her, Melissa's 'love' for me, Nessim's 'love' for her, her 'love' for Pursewarden' (B, 109)

childish narcissism, seeing their desires reflected in the other, or whether the lovers are the supreme example of a spiritual, alchemical relationship, it doesn't matter. The important thing, for Durrell's narrators, is that there is always, somewhere on Earth, the possibility that two lovers may unite.[7] Without this potential for loving kindness, Durrell reckons, life would be severely impoverished. In her essay on *Romeo and Juliet*, Julia Kristeva writes:

> If desire is fickle, thirsting for novelty, unstable by definition, what is it that leads love to dream of an eternal couple? Why faithfulness, the wish for a durable harmony, why in short a marriage of love - not as necessity in a given society but as desire, as libidinal necessity?[8]

The problem is that love and the couple is always a problem, is always fraught with problems. Maybe it's because, as Sigmund Freud suggests, in the narcissism of love, hatred is deeper and more ancient than love.[9] Certainly in Durrell's fiction, as in most fiction and art, bourgeois romantic love is presented as a struggle, where the lovers are in conflict with the social order (*The Rainbow*), with parents (in *Romeo and Juliet*), with neighbours (*Jude the Obscure*), with education and background (*Wuthering Heights*), etc. 'As soon as an *other* appears different from myself, it becomes alien, repelled, repugnant, abject - hated', writes Julia Kristeva. [10]

In Durrell's novels we see so clearly the simultaneous desire and revulsion - in the love affair of Leila and Mountolive, for instance, where the œdipal tension is in conflict with the erotic interplay of lovers.[11] Mountolive's two lovers, Leila and Liza, are both women with radically altered faces: Leila's beauty was ravaged by smallpox; Liza is blind. These are two version of the face of the Medusa, that image of the Terrible Mother which, as Freud noted, haunted Leonardo da Vinci throughout his life. For Freud, Leonardo was forever replaying the encounter with the castrating mother, the murderess Medusa. Durrell's ambassador, a seemingly macho, authority figure, Mountolive, has to learn to deal with

---

7 But also one should remember, as Shakespeare in the *Sonnets* knew well, that desire kills. 'Above all, one should not make a mythology out of one's longing.' (*Tunc*, 270)
8 Kristeva: "Romeo and Juliet: Love-Hatred in the Couple", in 1987, 225
9 Freud: "Drives and their vicissitudes", *Papers on Metapsychology*, 1915
10 Kristeva, 1987, 22, also 1982
11 Jane Lagoudis Pinchin, 1981, 34

his two lovers as a child relates to a mother. Leila and Liza, though, are, like Justine, Melissa and Clea, incarnations of the primal Mother of all, whose her body is the site of so many conflicting feelings. She is both the giver and taker of life, the desired and the loathed object of desire.

> Her replete body, the receptacle and guarantor of demands [writes Julia Kristeva] takes the place of all narcissistic, hence imaginary, effects and gratifications; she is, in other words, the phallus.[12]

The 'phallic Mother', site of childhood bliss, site of childhood anxiety, has to be integrated, otherwise the consequences may be dire.

Desire and revulsion. As Justine says to Arnauti in *Mœurs*: '"Quick., *Engorge-moi*. From desire to revulsion – let's get it over"', a phrase which encapsulates Durrell's philosophy of love (J, 62). The erotic attraction of Justine and Darley is presented by Darley as the uniting of opposite temperaments, whereas in fact, as Darley grows to realize, as all Durrell's lovers grow to realize, they are very similar. Mountolive recoils from Leila, but then becomes attracted.

The lover, if love is going to work at all, has to acknowledge the individuality and subjectivity of other people. Though the ecstasy of love may be Freudian narcissism, it only fulfils if the other is acknowledged. The ego is not alone: there *are* other people in the world! Most fiction and art demonstrates the anxieties love produces when the self or ego realizes it is not the centre of the world. Erotic, romantic love is more 'mature', emotionally, because, in psychological terms, it involves another person. In art, love becomes a means of adaption and growth. Successful lovers grow to grapple with anxiety and frustration. They learn from frustration and disappointment, compromise and hatred. Unsuccessful lovers (Romeo and Juliet, Giovanni in John Ford's Jacobean tragedy *'Tis Pity She's a Whore*, Jude Fawley and Sue Bridehead in Thomas Hardy's novel) have not learnt to grow beyond or to incorporate frustration, anxiety and denial.

Lovers in Durrelland have to match their idealizations against actualities: Darley, for example, thinks, arrogantly, that Pursewarden gives him five hundred pounds to spend on Melissa because 'he [Pursewarden] loved, not her, but my love for her.' (J, 102) What Darley doesn't know at this point is that Pursewarden has poked Melissa, just as he pokes all the other women Darley is involved with. Pursewarden simply gets there first, or 'does it better' than Darley. Darley thinks he's got things sorted out, in his

---

12 Kristeva: *Revolution in Poetic Language*, in Kristeva, 1986, 101

mind, but circumstances prove him wrong, time after time. Darley thinks Justine loves him. Balthazar puts him right, pointing some of Darley's errors: '[t]hat Justine "loved" you. She "loved", if anyone, Pursewarden. "What does that mean"? She was forced to use you as a decoy in order to protect him from the jealousy of Nessim' (B, 18).

Durrell's lovers, like most lovers in fiction, manifest the usual states of love that are familiar from any Western art: paranoia and faith, lust and repulsion, idealism and cynicism, dependency and isolation. In Durrell's lovers we see the typical crises of desiring to 'merge' with the other, and the desire to remain inviolate, intact and individual. Durrell's view of love is thoroughly Freudian, and can be reduced to the Freudian notions of oral/ anal/ genital pleasure, œdipal tension, narcissism, and so on. Love in Durrell's cosmos is eternally disruptive, always subverting the status quo, with its elements of œdipal rebellion, socio-sexual taboos and orgasmic pleasure.

Lost in the epiphany of their emotional subjectivity, Durrell's lovers simultaneously are acutely conscious of the idiocy, the childishness, the insanity of the whole enterprise. Loving love, they also know that love is a madness, a regression to an earlier stage of psychosexual development. In Durrelland, lovers are simultaneously naive and worldly-wise, simultaneously childish and streetwise. Think of Justine, Pursewarden, Affad, Julian and Benedicta. They regard themselves as 'grown-up', savvy, knowing, in control. Yet they all act childishly, petulantly, naively. Pursewarden, all super-cyncial literary persona, well-travelled, seemingly wordly-wise, commits suicide over seeing his childhood incestuous love turn sour (even though other reasons given include honour, duty, loyalty, art and, *lawks-a-mercy!*, Empire).

The most ironic and self-conscious of Durrell's characters, superior, arrogant, nonchalant, turn out to be the most obsessive, and childish. Much of the emotional life in Durrell's fiction is lived in a state of potential. In Durrell's art, for instance, there are many permutations of sexual relation-ships possible – and the mature people do not limit themselves to one view of sexual possibility. Constance knows, for example, that women consider a number of 'sexual possibilities, several choices which circumstances might put her way' (C, 82).

In Durrelland, love seems on the outside to be a case of people meeting who have 'seen it all, done it all' before. When Justine and Darley meet, they are both tired and cynical. Darley is a dejected, disaffected, alienated youngish school teacher in a shabby raincoat. He is boorish, indifferent, embarrassed when he first meets her. Typically, it is the spirit of Alexandria, C.P. Cavafy, who unites Darley and Justine: the three Durrellian themes of love, art and landscape are united in this odd meeting. Yet, exhausted and fed up and indifferent and worldly-wise as they are, both Justine and Darley act stupidly, selfishly, childishly.

Durrell's lovers, even as they decay into hatred and revulsion, talk a lot about their predicament. The problem with so much talk of love, as Justine recognizes, is that it destroys the spontaneity of love (Darley treasures spontaneity).[13] Darley, exasperated with Justine's relentless analyzing of love, wants to say, '"You are exhausting our lives before we have a chance to live them".' (J, 118) Justine and Darley discuss love more than they make love. Although Durrell ensures that they have one or two moments of sensuality – Darley burying his face in Justine's hair, for instance – most of their times together are filled with meta-love, talk of love, a metadiscourse of love. Darley and Clea superstitiously avoid using the word 'love' when they start their affair in *Clea*.

For Durrell's narrators, love is always *narrated*. That is, love is not described in the present, as it's happening, but in the past. Love has already happened, and like all poets and writers, Durrell's narrators write of love nostalgically. They are not kissing and loving at the time of writing; if they were, they would not write. Writing of love comes out of lack, out of not being in love anymore. The desire to keep writing is (as Blanford knows) like an itch that never goes away. But, as Sutcliffe rumly remarks, '"if you can't love it's your only alibi"' (S, 136). It's a thought guaranteed to unsettle Blanford, who regards himself as a lover as well as a writer. Sutcliffe's view is spot on, though: if you can't love, then write your way out of your predicament. Love exists in a nostalgic past or in a never to be attained future. 'The *meeting*, then, mixing pleasure and promise or hopes, remains in a sort of future perfect', writes Kristeva.[14]

It is precisely this sort of 'future perfect' that is evoked towards the end of *Constance,* where the two lovers prepare to part: Affad must return to Egypt to confront his Gnostic brotherhood. Constance is thrown into an emotional limbo, like Connie Chatterley, and is unsure about her future. In the confusion, though, Constance acknowledges that their new, Oriental love offers a different sort of interiority and union, which would last

13 Lawrence Thorton: "Narcissism and Selfishness in the *Alexandria Quartet*", *Deus Loci*, 1, no.4, June 1978, 18
14 Kristeva: "In Praise of Love", in 1987, 6

beyond their impending separation. In 'rendering the orgasm conscious', Affad and Constance extend love, as Blanford realizes (C, 359).

Writing of love is thus always nostalgia, a recreation of past experiences, an exercise in memory, as C.P. Cavafy, king of nostalgic eroticism, knew well. Durrell, essentially a Cavafian writer,[15] speaks nostalgically of love. There are moments in the *Quartet* where Durrell directly develops scenes out of Cavafy's poetry, as when Cavafy's beautiful poem 'In the Evening' is recited, and the action of the poem – going out onto the balcony – is reflected in Durrell's narrative.

> I picked up a letter again,
> read it over and over till the light faded.
>
> Then, sad, I went out on to the balcony,
> went out to change my thoughts at least by seeing
> something of this city I love,
> a little movement in the streets, in the shops. (1983, 53)

In 'The Anecdotes' Durrell redefines nostalgia as 'homing pain':

> *Nostos* home: *algos* pain: nostalgia...
> The homing pain for such as are attached...[16]

But perhaps the most poignant passage of nostalgia in *The Alexandria Quartet* occurs early on, when Darley thinks back to when he lay with Melissa: this passage contains all the main themes of Durrell's art, the fusion of art/ love/ religion/ memory, the spirit of place, the contrast of the exotic (the muezzin, Egypt, Alexandria) and the ordinary (the shabby room, ordinary love), and the controlling/ shaping drive of the artist, recalling and reworking his memory:

> ....I recover another such memory, lying beside a sleeping woman in a cheap room near the mosque. In that early spring dawn, with its dense dew, sketched upon the silence which engulfs a whole city before the birds awaken it, I caught the sweet voice of the blind *muezzin* from the mosque reciting the *Ebed* – a voice hanging like a hair in the palm-cooled upper airs of Alexandria. 'I praise the perfection of God, the Forever

15 Cavafy's mythopoeia of bringing the Hellenic past alive has an advantage over Yeats' Irish/ Celtic legends and T.S. Eliot's use of anthropology and religion in *The Waste Land* because it is a homogeneous group of material, which is familiar and still alive. (C.M. Bowra: *The Creative Experiment*, Macmillan, 1949, 33)
16 'The Anecdotes', II: 'In Cairo', CP, 203

existing' (this repeated thrice, ever more slowly, in a high sweet register). 'The perfection of God, the Desired, the Existing, the single, the supreme' ...The great prayer wound its way into my sleepy consciousness like a serpent, coil after shining coil of words – the voice of the *muezzin* sinking from register to register of gravity – until the whole morning seemed dense with its marvellous healing powers, the intimation of a grace undeserved and unexpected, impregnating that shabby room where Melissa lay, breathing as lightly as a gull, rocked upon the ocean splendours of a language she would never know. (J, 22)

Writing is a 'vertigo of words', and in writing of love the vertigo becomes simultaneously ecstatic and horrible. ('It is idle to go over all this in a medium as unstable as words', says Arnauti [J, 62]). Julia Kristeva writes:

Vertigo of identity, vertigo of words: love, of the individual, is that sudden revelation, that irremediable cataclysm, of which one speaks only *after the fact*. Under its sway, one does not speak *of*.[17]

Durrell's descriptions of love are precisely that – descriptions, using metaphor, poetic imagery, all the techniques and tactics of linguistic creation. 'The language of love is impossible, inadequate, immediately allusive when one would like it to be most straightforward; it is a flight of metaphors – it is literature', writes Julia Kristeva (1987, 1).

Knowing that love itself is beyond description, the poet's writing of love can only ever be writing of love, nothing more. Except writing *can* be more than writing. Writing can be love itself. The very act of writing can be a cultural *jouissance* which is like love itself. ('It was never in the *lover* that I really met her but in the *writer*', remarks Arnauti [J, 63]).

The French feminists – Julia Kristeva, Luce Irigaray, Hélène Cixous – speak of the *jouissance* of a text, the orgasmic nature of writing. The 'flight of metaphors' may become love itself. Discussing Baudelaire, Julia Kristeva says that in the 'incandescence of Romantic metaphoricalness', which is certainly Durrell's way of writing, 'metaphor becomes antithetical, as if to blur all reference, and ends up as synæsthesia, as if to open up the Word to the passion of the body itself, as it is.'[18] Unable to be in love, the poet may then write of love and literally re-create love, make love anew.

Writing, Kristeva suggests, may be 'synonymous with the amatory

17 Kristeva: "In Praise of Love", in 1987, 3
18 Kristeva: "Throes of Love: The Field of the Metaphor", in 1987, 277-8

condition'.[19] Love poetry may prolong love by writing of love. Darley, on his Greek island, is doing this throughout *The Alexandria Quartet.* He is prolonging love, revisiting love, analyzing love. And the key structure of *The Alexandria Quartet* is emotional, not to do with Einsteinian or post-Bergsonian/ Proustian notions of time and space, but with the importance of love and memory:

> What I most need to do [writes Darley] is to record experiences, not in the order in which they took place - for that is history - but in the order in which they first became significant for me. (J, 102)

This is how *The Alexandria Quartet* proceeds: from the crucial romance Darley has with Justine, through the revisions of his emotional past due to Balthazar's 'interlinear', to the apotheosis of his relationship with Clea. The emotional structure of the *Quartet* is also put forward by Arnauti, but in a different way. An interesting form of the modern novel, Arnauti suggests, would be to do away with the plot in the first few lines, so that 'we might dispense with the narrative articulation'. What follows would be freed from the burden of form. *I would set my own book free to dream.'* (J, 66) This is the form the first two novels of the *Quartet* take: they are fragmentary, constructed from bits and pieces, an insight here, an extract from a diary or notebook there. The fragmentary structure of the *Quartet,* or at least of *Justine* and *Balthazar,* reflects the way they were written - in stages, over the years. Sometimes Durrell wrote before dawn, before he went to teach on his Greek island. Durrell planned the work for years, and it was a long while before he had the space and time in which to write it.

For Darley, in Cavafian mode, memories, one's past life, are never lost. Mircea Eliade speaks of the continuity of one's life which re-emerges when one revisits places of one's earlier life:

> It is a comforting experience: you feel you haven't lost all that time, wasted your life. Everything is still there... (1984, 186)

This is Durrell's stance, that 'nothing is lost', so that past experiences are the very material which the writer uses in her/ his art. For Durrell, as for Eliade, one meets one's former selves as one travels in time and space. Eliade wrote of 'reactivating' former experiences when travelling. It is a

---

19 Kristeva: "Événement et revelation", *L'Infini,* no. 5, Winter 1984, 5

kind of temporal narcissism:

> ...the fact that, when visiting Venice, for example, I am reliving that time of my first trips to Venice. one rediscovers the whole past in space: a street, a church, a tree. Suddenly time past has been regained. That is one of the things that make travelling such an enrichment of the self, of one's own experience. One finds oneself again, one can communicate with the person one was fifteen, twenty, years before. One meets him, one meets oneself, one meets one's time, on's historical moment, of twenty years ago. (1984, 101)

This is precisely the state of Durrell's protagonists, most obviously in *The Alexandria Quartet*, but also in the other fictions. Writing of his first meetings with Justine, Darley says:

> These are the moments which possess the writer and live on perpetually. One can return to them time and time again in memory, or use them as a fund upon which to build the part of one's life which is writing. One can debauch them with words, but one cannot spoil them. (J, 22)

For the Cavafian, Gidean writer, life is not complete until it has been written about; this is the mania of the artist, the debasement before the idol of Art, the slavish reliance on art to make life meaningful. If Darley is a prey to such philosophy, Jacob Arnauti is much further into it. For Arnauti, '[l]ife, the raw material, is only lived in *potential* until the artist deploys it in his work.' (J, 66)

Writing simultaneously creates and destroys meaning, creates it and alters it. Durrell's postmodernism tendency is to comment upon his texts as he's creating them. D.H. Lawrence, arch modernist, also did this, interrupting his narratives to address the 'reader' with a comment or two. In D.H. Lawrence or Thomas Hardy or Leo Tolstoy, these authorial commentaries destroy the diegesis of the traditional novel. In postmodern texts, such metafiction is integrated with the narrative or plot.

> Literature appears to me as the privileged place where meaning is elaborated and destroyed, where it slips away when one might think that it is being renewed [writes Julia Kristeva]. (1987, 279)

Lawrence Durrell's narrators, like any narrator of any fiction, have '[t]he mania to perpetuate, to record, to photograph everything!' (*Balthazar*, 22) Elsewhere, Durrell remarks that all those people who keep diaries are really writers. Perhaps if life isn't rich enough as it is, then it needs to be embellished and mythicized by writing about it. Literature has long undertaken this mythicization function: television does it these days, where people don't think something is 'real' until it has been caught on video tape or digitally. Go to any wedding and you'll see half the congregation wielding cameras. Durrell's narrators are scientists, reviving the corpse, Frankenstein-like, of their former selves, their former loves:

> I had set myself [writes Darley] the task of trying to recover them [his friends] in memory, allot to each his or her position in my time. Selfishly. And with that writing complete, I felt that I had turned a key upon the doll's house of our actions. Indeed, I saw my lovers and friends no longer as living people but as coloured transfers of the mind; inhabiting my papers now, no longer the city, like tapestry figures. It was difficult to concede to them any more common reality than to the words I had used about them. (B, 12)

For the writer, people become 'paper recreations', or 'figments', to use Samuel Beckett's phrase from his late fiction (*Company, Ill Seen Ill Said*). Darley recognizes that characters in texts are functions or effects of the text, not 'flesh and blood' or 'real' people. As Darley remarks of Pursewarden's death: '[n]or, for the purposes of this writing, has he ceased to exist; he has simply stepped into the quicksilver of a mirror as we all must' (J, 104). In another place, Darley wonders if he lacks 'a belief in the true authenticity of people in order to successfully portray them' (J, 173).

It is a charge that is often brought against Lawrence Durrell: that his characters are too flimsy, or too cynically crafted, so that some critics regard Durrell as not really liking people (the biography of authors often upsets humanist critics, who like to believe in the basic goodness of authors as people). Darley is merely stating the artist's view of the relation between 'reality' and æsthetic 'illusion'. Which is 'real'? Both, and more. Both are 'real' in the sense that both are 'believable'. For images and fictions, like adverts, simply have to be 'believable', not necessarily 'true' in the empirical, scientific sense. The notion of 'truth' and subjective viewpoint is explored throughout Durrell's art.

One of the central themes of *The Alexandria Quartet* is: which viewpoint is the 'true' one? The answer is: every viewpoint has its own 'truth', and its own uses. Pursewarden's point that stepping two paces East or West and the picture is changed (B, 12) is central to Durrell's notion of the multiple viewpoint, the multiple ego or persona, the multiple narrative, the 'palimpsest' view of reality. In *The Alexandria Quartet*, there is Darley's narration, followed by Arnauti's diary of Justine, followed by the diaries of Justine, then Balthazar's Interlinear, then various characters recounting events and viewpoints, then the letters, between Leila, Mountolive, Pursewarden, Darley, Clea and others, all of which alter the readings.[20] In Durrell's world, there is no 'final' view of love, no rock solid third person narration upon which to base a theory of love.

The metadiscourse of love in Durrell's fiction engenders melancholy and solitude. These two words sum up the situation of the Durrellian lover, including the central narrator of *The Alexandria Quartet* – Darley on his island wallows in melancholy and solitude. The lack or void at the centre of his life, which he tries to fill with writing, is the outcome of his desire for love. The meta-texts of love become founded on emptiness or lack.

"You have been lonely here" said Balthazar.
"But splendidly, desirably lonely."
"Yes, I envy you. But truthfully." (B, 17)

Durrell once said that his life has been 'tremendously lonely'; he'd moved around a lot, with his work, and hadn't found it easy to find suitable friends. He lacked what he called a 'hearth', a real home. He suffered bouts of depression. His daughter Sappho's death by suicide in 1985 had deeply depressed Durrell.

Typically, and fatuously, Darley says his 'most solitary moments' are 'those of coitus' (J, 169). Durrell's characters often prefer their solitude and melancholy to company and pretending to enjoy oneself. In Durrelland, being alone is crucial: first time lovers often part so they can be alone with their new feelings of love. Discussing Georges Bataille's *My Mother*, Julia Kristeva makes remarks which apply to *The Alexandria Quartet*, and to the fundamental sense of solitude at the heart of Durrell's fiction:

Erotic fantasy merges with philosophical meditation in order to reach the focus where the sublime and the abject, making up the pedestal of love, come together in the "flash." ...The contemporary narrative (from Joyce to Bataille) has a posttheological aim: to communicate the amorous flash. The one in which the "I" reaches the paranoid dimensions of the sublime divinity while remaining close to abject collapse, disgust with the self. Or, quite simply, to its moderate version know as solitude.[21]

---

20 J. Unterecker, 1964, 39.
21 Kristeva: "Bataille and the Sun, or the Guilty Text", in 1987, 368

If art comes out of the 'crises of subjectivity' (1984, 131-2), as Kristeva suggests, and any number of artists' work could be cited to support her theory, then melancholy and solitude is inevitable. Melancholy is indeed the natural state of many poets and writers – especially love poets (think of Francesco Petrarch, Bernard de Ventadour, Giraut de Borneil, Emily Brontë, Emily Dickinson, William Shakespeare, Louise Labé, etc). The artist writes of love to bring back love. Metaphor becomes the mechanism by which love is reactivated, metaphor becomes 'the point at which ideal and affect come together in language'.[22] So important is writing and making art for some artists, that they are not really 'alive' unless they are making art. Many is the writer who does not feel a day has been spent well unless it has involved some writing. Writers often speak of feeling uneasy (or guilty) if they have not been writing. Durrell's characters are often scribbling. Writing not only enlarges life, it is central to the life of some writers. André Gide wrote copiously in his journal, as Durrell's characters do. For Gide, his life needed to be mythicized in literature.

> It is, very simply, through the work and the play of signs, a crisis of subjectivity which is the basis for all creation [writes Julia Kristeva], one which takes as its every precondition the possibility of survival. I would even say that signs are what produce a body, that – and the artist knows it well – if he doesn't work, if he doesn't produce his music or his page or his sculpture, he would be, quite simply, ill or not alive. (1984, 131-2)

Lawrence Durrell's metaphors, particularly in the realm of writing about love, are one of the most striking aspects of his art. For instance, when Darley realizes that Nessim had been spying on him and Justine lying on the beach through the telescope, Durrell uses a image of surprise that is not fantastical, but it's certainly scary:

> It was as if, all of a sudden, in a dark but familiar room one believed was empty a hand had suddenly reached out and placed itself on one's shoulder. (J, 150)

This is the primal scene of horror fiction: thinking one is alone, but one is not. It's a moment much explored in horror films: the protagonist wandering around the empty house. Another powerful metaphor, which unites Durrell's passions for emotion and science, for the everyday and the

---

22 John Lechte: "Art, Love and Melancholy in the Work of Julia Kristeva", in Fletcher, 1990, 24

extraordinary, is when the narrator of *Justine* discusses the Nessim-Justine affair:

> Their common life was like some cable buried in the sand which, in some inexplicable way, at a point impossible to discover, had snapped, plunging them both into an unaccustomed and impenetrable darkness. (J, 170)

In Durrell's art, depictions of love are always self-conscious, always aware of being attempts at describing the indescribable. He rarely depicts the 'love act' itself, that is, heterosexual intercourse. But sex is the central event upon which his whole metaphysics of love is based. Knowing the difficulty, nay impossibility of representing sex, Durrell instead resorts to metaphor, allusion, hints, and 'before' and 'after' scenes. The Justine-Darley romance is depicted in this fashion: they lie on the bed or beach moments before or after sex. When Nessim and Melissa spend all night together, the lead-up to their lovemaking is described in detail, but the actual fucking is left out. Centred in the European literary tradition which has, from Ovid to Cavafy, attempted to write about lovemaking, Durrell remains distanced and self-conscious in sexual writing. Knowing the problems arising from writing a full frontal depiction of sexual encounters *à la Lady Chatterley's Lover*, Durrell concentrates on displacing the force of sensuality into other areas. Hence the metaphor, which in Durrell's writing, as in the art of Baudelaire and Rimbaud, is pushed to extremes.

Lawrence Durrell and Lou Andreas-Salomé

Lou Andreas-Salomé (1861-1937) is another reference point in Lawrence Durrell's metaphysics of love. She represents the fully achieved, highly intellectual, sensual European woman. As a woman she was formidable, and something of Andreas-Salomé's character lies behind, in particular, Constance. Andreas-Salomé's effect on Rainer Maria Rilke, perhaps the greatest poet of modern times after Rimbaud, was massive. His experience of her was bound up with his time in Russia, his child-like notions of motherhood, his love of the Madonnas of Italian Renaissance painting, and his creative hunger. The effect on Rilke was deep and long-lasting. He wrote many passionate letters to her, which chime with Durrell's philosophy and descriptions of love in *The Avignon Quintet*. What Rilke says here is very similar to what Durrell's lovers say to each other:

> You were the right door through which I entered into the open [Rilke wrote to Lou Andreas-Salomé]. You can explain to me what I do not understand, you can tell me what I should do; you know what I must, and what I need not fear… I am in you![23]

Blanford says to Livia, or thinks of her: she made me realize I was a writer; later, Constance will 'try to write' Blanford's book for him; Affad helps Constance realize her 'full femininity'; Constance brings Blanford back to life, too. Rilke's words to Andreas-Salomé – 'you can explain to me what I do not understand, you can tell me what I should do' – could be said by Blanford to Constance, or Constance to Affad, or Justine to Pursewarden, or Felix to Benedicta. Throughout Durrell's fictions people realize things with their lover's help. When Rilke writes:

> The transforming experience which then seized me at a hundred places at once, emanated from the great reality of your being. I had never before, in my groping hesitancy, felt life so much, believed in the present, and recognized the future so much. You were the opposite of all doubt and witness to the fact that everything you touch, reach and see *exists*.[24]

You make me see! You make me live! How often, in more subdued ways, though, Durrell's men have said this to their beloveds. It is the familiar cry of the Muse-intoxicated poet, the projection of the Jungian *anima* or 'inner woman', familiar from a thousand courtly love poets, *dolce stil novo* lyrics and Elizabethan sonnets (in Durrell's fiction, the Muse is called by secret code names, as in most poetry: the names Laura and Beatrice are *senechals*, names which indicate the *donna* or lady without revealing her identity. Durrell uses Minerva, Marina (in 'Blue Light at Dusk', CVG, 171), and Melissa.) Somehow, love makes life fresher, richer, deeper. The beloved, the woman, is the key to this reawakening, male poets think. 'The woman makes things happen', as Durrell puts it.

For the Muse-poet (and Darley, Felix, Blanford, Sutcliffe, Bruce, Sam,

23 Rilke & Andreas-Salomé: *Briefwechsel*,ed Ernst Pfeiffer, Insel Verlag, Wiesbaden 1952, 250, 48; *Briefe 1907-1914*, Insel Verlag, Leipzig 1939, 22
24 Rilke to Lou Andreas-Salomé, November 1903, *Briefewechsel*, 119

Death Gregory and Pursewarden are very much Muse-poets in their own way) the woman 'makes' them. They realize themselves through the woman and through love. The heretical courtly love poets, the sonneteers and *stilnovisti*, and later, Dante and Petrarch are important for Durrell because they regarded love as a religion, they acknowledged the sacrality of love. This was apparent in the erotic sacrality of *The Song of Songs*, but Christianity suppressed eroticism. The twelfth century poets re-eroticized poetry, and gave it a spiritual slant. In the troubadours, adulterous love became part of a heresy which exalted human love above Godly religion, and Durrell used this historical/ psychological background in his *Quintet*.[25]

For Rilke, Lou Andreas-Salomé redefined his views of love (as Constance does to Blanford, Clea to Darley, etc). Her intellectual powers astonished Rilke: '[s]he moves fearlessly midst the most burning mystery'.[26] What Wolf Lappmann says of the Rilke-Lou Andreas-Salomé romance could equally well apply to the central romances of Durrell's two major fictions, *The Avignon Quintet* and *The Alexandria Quartet*:

> This love, transformed through the years into a deep friendship, was an unexpected boon that would live on as a permanent feature of Rilke's inner landscape.[27]

This is the creative togetherness that Clea and Darley and Blanford and Constance are aiming for. For Lou Andreas-Salomé, her relationship with Rilke was an exquisite time when 'body and soul [were] indivisibly one', verily the ideal unity of Plato.[28] For Andreas-Salomé, she achieved with Rilke a 'kneeling-together', not sex but a supra-sexual sacrament, a holy love. Later, she distanced herself from Rilke.

Rilke, though, was smitten, absolutely. His letters to Andreas-Salomé are his most rapturous writing. André Gide's letters to his wife were also his best work (Gide thought), and Durrell's Pursewarden felt the same about his letters to his sister. One imagines that there may be somewhere some letters of Durrell's to his lovers. The ones to his daughter Sappho have

25 see James Nichols: "The Risen Angels in Durrell's Fallen Women", in OMG, 180

26 Rilke: *Furstin Marie von Thurm und Taxis-Hohenlohe: Erinnerungen an Rainer Maria Rilke*, R. Oldenbourg, Berlin, 1937, 303f

27 Lappmann: *Rilke: A Life*, tr. Russell M. Stochman, Fromm International Publishing Corporation, New York 1984, 79

28 Andreas-Salomé: *Lebensruckblick*, ed. Ernst Pfeiffer, Insel Verlag, Taschenbuch 54, Frankfurt 1974, 138

become notorious, in the light of the allegations of father-daughter incest.

Henry Miller published his letters to his lovers, or other people did, after his death. The same has happened with Anaïs Nin. Nin's letters and journals have been released gradually – the sexual antics of Miller and Nin in *Henry and June* came out, and, later, a book of revelations about Nin's incestuous relationship with her father,[29] which one critic summed up as 'all rather sad'.[30] Like Constance, Nin had affairs with psychoanalysts (Otto Rank, René Allendy). Happily Nin unburdens herself of her intimate feelings and thoughts. Somewhere, there must be letters of Durrell's which write similar things to this, Nin writing to Henry Miller:

> I have the same feeling when I read a book you have marked. (*Cahiers de Brigge* [Rilke's *The Notebooks of Malte Laura Brigge*].) I love the sharing. I feel with extraordinary vividness your presence, as if you were reading with me. I actually experience the sensation of my leaning over your shoulder and kissing your hair and neck while you are reading or writing.[31]

Durrell's lovers are wary about love, about laying themselves open to love, about baring their souls to others about love. They are so superstitious and cautious about saying the dreaded three words ('I love you', or more coolly, 'je t'aime') that they clam up. As Constance thinks of Affad '[w]ith him she might even dare to utter the words *"Je t'aime!"* (S, 155) Yet, the narrator of the *Quintet* says, it is precisely the experience of being so utterly in love that one utters the words 'I love you' that everyone is yearning for.

---

29 Anaïs Nin: *Unexpurgated Diary*, Peter Owen, 1993
30 Jan Dalley: "Her heart belonged to Daddy", *The Independent on Sunday*, 20 June 1993
31 Nin: *A Literature Passion*, 92

Love in *Mountolive* / Mountolive in Love

Mountolive is a novel of resignation and weariness. It is shot through with a strange combination of European *ennui* (as found in the work of Jean-Paul Sartre, Albert Camus' *The Outsider* and André Gide's *The Immoralist*) and an English apathy, the 'quiet desperation' that Pink Floyd sang of in *Dark Side of the Moon*. Lawrence Durrell carefully relates the journey of the central figure, David Mountolive, from an English suburban background to being the Ambassador in Egypt. It is a 'classic' story of the growth of a provincial soul, narrated in the manner of Stendhal or Émile Zola. There are the usual lessons to be learnt, which the narrator defines as 'to make love honestly and to reflect' (Mt, 30). There are scenes of archetypal Britain and archetypal Egypt: Trafalgar Square in the snow with Pursewarden dancing to celebrate William Blake's birthday (one can almost hear *Jerusalem* in the background). The car journey to Mountolive's mother's home in another snowbound landscape. There are scenes of Westminster and the Foreign Office which even have Big Ben chiming in the background just like Hollywood films of the 1930s which had London fog in them, or the 1960s British films with a red bus driving by. Durrell's England in the *Quartet* is the usual England of sterility and boredom. The terrifying blandness of Britain is highlighted by Pursewarden's tirades ('Look at it all. Home of the eccentric and the sexually disabled.' Mt, 76).

There are the usual despised British characters: the simpering diplomats' wives, the anally meticulous and loathesome Brigadier Maskelyne, the fawning, subservient aides (Errol), the blustering old diplomat (Sir Louis), the ineffectual, fluttering Darley who acts just like a character out of a sit com: his specs steam up when Justine or Melissa is mentioned (100).

In *Mountolive*, Durrell does the whole Englishman abroad bit, the whole white middle class Protestant meeting the other-worldliness, violence and sensuality of the Orient. These are tried and tested themes (in the work of Rudyard Kipling, T.E. Lawrence, etc), and Durrell does not offer anything particularly new. There are the usual sequences which show the clash of cultures – Mountolve's stiff upper lip, puritanical anti-sensuality, resignation, passivity and indecision against the unpredictable, difficult, childlike and bizarre Middle East with its inexplicable customs, beliefs, habits and psychology.

The British stiff upper lip confronts the split hare lip of the Near East. It is Narouz who provides much of the violence in the *Quartet*, and Narouz' hare lip is constantly referred to. It is Narouz who cuts off a chunk of the boy servant's ear, who beats up the Magzub, who kills bats for sport with his whip, etc. Durrell's narrators have always delighted in relating scenes of sudden, vicious violence, as when Memlik Pasha allegedly had two girls 'flogged to death before his eyes while a third was obliged' (Mt, 231); in the *Quintet* a woman is literally, physically hunted like an animal and killed by hounds. The violence of the Orient reaches a climax when Mountolive is symbolically broken by the child prostitutes, a scene that echoes the mænads tearing apart Dionysis.

Like *Justine*, *Mountolive* opens with a white middle class Englishman falling in love with a powerful woman from the Levant. Mountolive shares many characteristics with Darley, indeed Darley and Mountolive are variations on a personality that recurs throughout Durrell's work (from Death Gregory through Felix to Blanford). Similarly, Justine is a younger version of Leila, and so similar are they, they loathe each other when they meet.

The love affair between Mountolive and Leila is given the usual May-September, young/ old turns, but the most interesting aspect about it for Durrell is clearly that their love is experienced mostly through letters. Here the twin Durrellian themes of love and art are graphically explored. If love is largely fantasy and psychic projection, then why can't a love communicated through words and images be as 'authentic' as one experienced in the flesh? The problems do not begin when Leila and Mountolive send each other long letters, but when they plan to meet again after a lengthy period apart. Then 'real' life and the literary life have to be merged. When Mountolive plans to return to Egypt, it upsets Leila because she has created her version of him in her imagination for such a long time.

Mountolive is not a figment, though, as Durrell showed in *The Avignon Quintet*, figments are no less 'real' than 'real' people.[32] Leila becomes scared, and delays meeting Mountolive. The meeting might shatter her long cherished creations and musings. Life might spoil art, finally, because art improves on life, even though life remains infinitely more complex. In Durrell's erotic world, lovers make love to their reflection in a mirror distorted by their own desires and needs. The Leila-Mountolive romance is one of the central relationships of the *Quartet,* but even to write about love is not only difficult, it soon reaches the limits of lingual expression.

---

32 Expounding his Gnostic philosophy, Akkad (in *Monsieur)* says that by pretending and imagining things become real: '[o]ne must begin by pretending in order to end by realising'. (M, 144)

Just as Leila realizes that her love with Mountolive is best conducted in letters, so the narrator of the *Quartet* emphasizes the limitation of language.

> You cannot write more than a dozen love-letters without finding yourself gravelled for fresh matter. The richest of human experiences is also the most limited in its range of expression. Words kill love as they kill everything else. (Mt, 43)

The implication is: *shut up and kiss me*. Durrell gives the dictum of T.S. Eliot about the limits of expression (in *The Four Quartets*) an obsessive, extreme turn. He likens language to a murderer: yet, always, the paradox is that though words kill love, and everything, the poet keeps blabbing out more and more words. He can't shut up. He *won't* shut up. So Durrell's narrators go on and on about love. Over a series of four novels, then five novels.

Mountolive is not entirely a novel of Mountolive's spiritual growth. It involves two other male characters just as much: Nessim and Pursewarden. All three are entwined by the political plot. Nessim is set against Mountolive in the classic style of friends who become rivals, as in so many of William Shakespeare's plays. Durrell explores the familiar themes of the conflicts of duty between private and public, friendship and business. The perception of Darley, in *Justine* and *Balthazar,* is shown to be severely blinkered by personal needs and sexual desire. Darley, for instance, sees Nessim as a sexual rival who plans to do away with him. Darley is caught up in a melodrama of bourgeois adultery. In *Mountolive*, we see Nessim's side of the events, and how coldly politically ambitious he is. The pact between Justine and Nessim is not based on sexual lust, as Darley and others might think. Rather, it is a 'Faustian pact' of political power, the lust for which is so great it makes Nessim tremble.

It is this offer of the political machinations surrounding Palestine that finally arouses Justine. She wants to fuck his political ambition, 'his obsessions, his money, his death!' (Mt, 180). What she's after, the narrator claims, is 'power, politics and possessions' (Mt, 181), and her sexual charms are wielded to this end. Essentially, the Justine-Nessim relationship is the one D.H. Lawrence explored with Gudrun and Gerald in *Women in Love*. Like Gudrun and Gerald's sexual relationship, there is always a powerful sense of death and decay behind Justine and Nessim's affair. And when they finally fuck, after the Faustian bargain has been detailed, Nessim is portrayed as a Birkin character (soft, 'feminine' body) who is overwhelmed by Justine's ruthless lovemaking. In describing Justine and Nessim fucking, Durrell employs quintessential Lawrencean terms: 'the *plunge* of her *loins...* to *fecundate* his actions... *fructify* him...' (Mt, 184, my italics).

Four-dimensional Love

In *The Alexandria Quartet* Durrell used the epigraph from Sigmund Freud that suggested that love could be considered as occurring between four, not two, people. Four people are involved in love, in an erotic quaternity of relationships. The four people of Freudian love are also two people: the man who has the female element in him, and the woman who has the male component in her. This fascinates Durrell. The sexual complexity is of course good for drama, but Durrell also enjoys the numerical symbolism. In *The Avignon Quintet* he talks about the three orifices and the five Oriental 'skandas', five senses, five arts (Q, 139). The imagination is the key to the ability to inhabiting the five senses and three dimensions (Key, 5). The three is of the West, the Trinity, and five of the East (S, 43). The symbolism of numbers is used to organize sexual complexities.

In *The Avignon Quintet* the notion that sex does not simply involve two people is developed beyond *The Alexandria Quartet*. Thus, Constance sleeping with Affad affects Blanford, the Prince, Livia and Sutcliffe, among others. Sex acts do not occur in isolation, because there are part of an erotic continuum. Thus, Blanford moves from various anonymous women, such as the hop-picker in Kent, to Livia, through the nurse and the British officer of the Field Transport Corps, Anne Farnol, to Constance. Blanford's liaison with the Kent hop-picker is framed by a stereotypical vision of youth, with the woman worrying about being pregnant, and Blanford fearing venereal disease and getting anxious about contraception (C, 9). This is pure soap opera/ kitchen sink drama stuff, the subject of a million sit-coms and magazine articles. And, just like Constance Chatterley who proceeded sexually from an undergraduate through to Mellors (like Darley who goes from Melissa through Justine to Clea), Constance travels along the sexual chain from Sam to Affad, Schwartz and Blanford.

Lawrence Durrell   *199*

The eroticism in *The Avignon Quintet*, as in the equally complex *Alexandria Quartet,* spirals out from one couple. Take any couple in the *Quartet* or the *Quintet* and you can make sexual connections between all the other main characters. The central sexual content of *The Avignon Quintet* pivots around Constance. She moves from the relatively inconsequential and messy preliminary sexual encounters with various youths to the earthy, 'innocent' sexual relation with Sam. This is a relatively uncomplicated love affair. Sam and Constance love each other, and make love in a straight forward manner; archetypal heterosexuality. After Sam's death, Constance gets deep into psychoanalysis, and along comes Affad. He shakes up her notions of love and sexuality completely. With Affad, all Constance's former sexual relationships are brushed aside.

Constance appears as the central character of *The Avignon Quintet,* at the crux of most of the key emotional relationships, but Blanford is equally important: he is the demiurge-like writer and creator of much of the narrative (including the first novel, *Monsieur*). Blanford is the lover of Livia, future lover of Constance, and he has the key dialogues with Sutcliffe. The trajectories of Constance and Blanford mirror each other. Elsewhere, the characters are constructed as opposites and similarities: Affad, the Egyptian philosopher and banker, is murdered by an Egyptian psychotic. The murderer and victim are both dressed in drag – Affad in his lover's dressing gown, Mnemidis in a stolen nun's costume. The cross-dressing and sexual ambiguity of both Affad and Mnemidis (one an effete financier, the other a rapacious homosexual) indicates the shaky, ambivalent philosophies with which they are associated (Mnemnidis with psychoanalysis, Affad with Gnosticism).

In the murder, then, Durrell points out the similarities (and failures) of both psychoanalysis and Gnosticism, the Western and Eastern systems. Western science (psychoanalysis) is unable to control Eastern mysticism (Gnosticism), and Mnemidis escapes and murders. In a bizarre twist, then, the man in drag killing the sleeping man in drag offers a 'strange kind of surrogate suicide' for Affad, the one that he has secretly desired.[33] Affad's death offers another twisted parallel – with Blanford's near-death: Blanford goes out from Europe to Egypt, and nearly dies; Affad travels to wartorn Europe, and dies – by the hand of an Egyptian.

Constance is the strongest character in the *Quincunx*: she is the one who teaches and heals, who offers the way beyond the sin and guilt of

---

33 William L. Godshalk: "*Sebastian*: Searches and Failures", Mac 4, 54

Luther, Calvin, Puritanism, the Fall of Man and the laws and prohibitions of Judæo-Christianity. Durrell's women, and Constance is his richest portrayal of a woman, offer not only sacrifice, fearlessness, sensuality, non-conformism and energy, they 'deny nothing and thus encompass all'.[34]

Constance feels much remorse after Sam's death. Durrell describes Constance's after-death shocks in detail, her weeping and shock, her despairing feelings. Strangely, there is not much of this despair in Constance after Affad's death. Sam, after all, dies 'on active service', so to speak. He dies a heroic, if stupid, death. Yet it is an accident – killed by his own side during target practice. Affad's death is a bizarre mistake made by a psychopath who's aiming for Constance. Yet it is Sam's death that absorbs Constance. It's odd, but she starts up with Blanford very quickly after Affad's death. There is hardly any interlude, and certainly not much contemplation of Affad. The Egyptian æsthete is soon forgotten as Constance brings Blanford back to life, physiologically with her therapy and massage, and of course sexually. All the sexual magic being ignited between Constance and Affad is suddenly switched to Constance and Blanford in *Quinx*.

There is little acknowledgement of Affad in *Quinx*. Blanford is the final stage in the life story of Constance's developing sexuality, but Blanford (like Darley) does not equate to Mellors. He does not open Constance up sexually. It is Affad who does that. Yet, in *Quinx*, we learn that, all along, Livia had sexually desired her sister, Constance, not Hilary. In *The Alexandria Quartet* the secret sexual relation that is finally revealed is brother-sister incest between Pursewarden and his sister, as also between Julian and Benedicta in the *Tunc-Nunquam* double-decker. Originally, the two central characters of 'The Book of the Dead' (the *Quartet*), were twins (DML, 176). The sexual web in *The Avignon Quintet* keeps unfolding until it reaches sister-sister incest.

Incest occurs over the generations in Durrell's fiction. In the *Quartet*, for example, Leila regards Mountolive as an emotional displacement for her son, while Clea is seen as closer to her father than a wife (C, 234), a reference which recalls Anaïs Nin's incestuous relationship with her father (Nin was also Otto Rank's lover, briefly, the psychologist and author of books on incest, including *The Incest Motif in Poetry and Saga*). In the *Quintet*, there are two incestuous groups: the 'happy trinity of lovers' of Bruce, Sylvie and Piers, and the more complicated group of Hilary and

34 James Nichols: "Ah – the Wonder of My Body", in MacNiven, 1987, 455

Livia, Constance and Livia, Constance and Blanford, Blanford and Livia. The brother-sister incest of Piers and Sylvie is further complicated by the homosexual relationship between Bruce and Piers – the Bruce-Sylvie marriage is a cover for this homosexual love. In Durrell's fiction, incest sometimes ends in emotional stagnation, and sometimes death (for Livia and Pursewarden).[35]

Brother-sister incest may be seen in Durrell's fiction, at other times, as a means to transcendence and salvation, a magical rebirth through the sister (ib., 439). The sisters, whom Durrell's anxious men turn to (Pursewarden, Julian, Hilary, Piers), are idealized sometimes too much, so that they cannot carry the intensity of the brother's spiritual idealization.

At the heart of the Isis and Osiris allusions is the complex inter-relationships of Isis, Osiris, the son Horus and the rival, Set. Durrell uses this ancient, mythic grouping many times in his fiction – not only in Nessim-Narouz-Justine, but also in Mountolive-Pursewarden-Liza, Benedicta-Julian-Felix, Blanford-Livia-Hilary, Piers-Bruce-Sylvie, and so on. The emotions and situations of jealousy, hatred, desire, lust, murder, crime, incest, œdipal/ parental pressure, royalty, sovereignty, duty, need and honour are all there in the Isis-Osiris myth, and provide plenty of allusions and metaphors for Durrell's lovers.

In Durrelland, incest is a forming of an erotic-spiritual unity out of the double or couple. In the *Quintet*, 'two equals one within orgasm'.[36] In the *Quintet*, the unifier is the orgasm. In the sexual intercourse of traditional sex magic, a third being is created, the sum, and more, of the man and the woman. The third person is the 'Magickal Child' of alchemy, that is, their combined creativity. During ovulation the flesh-and-blood child is created; during menstruation, the 'Magickal Child' is created.[37] In sex magic rites, making the 'Magickal Child' comes out of the aura of orgasm, the 'afterglow', the moment of lucidity and waking dreaming in which one envisions the future. In *Quinx* Sabine calls love a 'future-maufacturing yoga with a child at stake in it' (Q, 169). The aim is to make love with a spiritual purpose, in order to have orgasms that will be a rich breeding ground for the child.

---

35 Sharon Spencer: "The Ambiguities of Incest in Lawrence Durrell's Heraldic Universe: A Rankian Interpretation", in MacNiven, 1987, 436-7
36 Corinne Alexandre-Garner: "The Triangle of Love, Incest and Writing", in OMG, 54
37 see Peter Redgrove: *The Black Goddess and the Sixth Sense,* Blooms-bury 1987; "Greening the Orgasm", *Resurgence* (150), Jan/Feb 1992, 30-3

In Durrelland, looking magically into the future, that is, creating children, either flesh-and-blood or magical, is problematic: his female characters are often 'mad', menstrually 'mad', that is, they have 'womb madness' or hysteria. As the act of writing simultaneously (and painfully) creates and destroys, so coition in Durrell's art is simultaneous creation and destruction. His women characters create and destroy their offspring, and the people around them.

The males, too, have difficult times of conception and pregnancy: they have to be careful how they 'deliver' themselves of their books, their art. Any number of authors have spoken of their books as 'children', and Durrell speaks of being 'big with book', as women are 'big with child'. It is quite understandable, therefore, that there should be so much ambiguity regarding children, who in Durrell's fiction are aborted, or autistic, or blind, or lost, or dead. One of the central agonies in Durrell's fiction concerns children – Justine, for instance, agonizing over the whereabouts of her lost child.

Incest is both feared and desired, and the fears and desires are very, primævally deep. Durrell trades on the energies released by the primal taboo. In the incestuous union the androgynous body is created. Androgyny is a form of wholeness, and features in Durrell's 'Tiresias' figures, such as Balthazar, Leila, Caradoc (who even has the 'dugs' of Tiresias, straight out of *The Waste Land*) and Scobie (who is an archetypal modern Tiresias, a gay crossdresser).[38] There are at least four Tiresias-like figures in the *Quartet*: Scobie and Balthazar are the obvious ones, both of them androgynous/ sexually ambivalent figures who oversee the erotic shenanigans. C.P. Cavafy, who lurks behind, is another Tiresias, and so is Pursewarden, and Leila. At times, the incestuous couple becomes an androgynous being: Pursewarden is Liza's 'eyes', while he sees with her heart. They have a 'creative' union. At the end of *The Avignon Quintet,* Constance regards Blanford's book as her own project:

> she felt, in fact, that the whole *œuvre* for which he was going to try was as much her work, her responsibility, as his – which was indeed the case. To celebrate the mystical marriage of four dimensions with five skandas so to speak. (Q, 198)

---

38 In his novel, Pursewarden has a character called Parr, 'the sensualist Tiresias', who, like Pursewarden himself, subsumes in himself 'the whole intellectual history of Europe from Rabelais to de Sade' (Mt, 149).

Incest is one model of psycho-sexual-spiritual unity, androgyny is another; and bisexuality yet another. Many of Durrell's characters are bisexual: and what Tiresias saw, two snakes copulating, was perhaps bisexuality.[39] In Durrelland, bisexuality may be fine in theory, but his bisexuals (Pia, Justine, Bruce, Piers, Benedicta) cause endless problems. However good it may look in theory, in practice it is disruptive. Durrell's fictions show a 'heteropatriarchal' world in which anything outside of the sexual norm is condemned, problematized, ambiguous, difficult.

A large part of *Constance* is taken up with the narrator explaining in depth the new sexual religion of Affad, and the characters explain it to each other. Up until this point, the sexual encounters have been pretty much normal – normal for Durrell, that is. For sex in Durrell's world is not 'normal', in the usual heterosexual sense. There are, for instance, many scenes set in brothels.

The brothel was the setting for much of Henry Miller's 1930s prose. Or, rather, the world became a brothel in the *Tropic* trilogy, *Tropic of Cancer, Black Spring* and *Tropic of Capricorn*. Prostitutes, often called 'whores' in Durrell's fiction, often slink into view. He has a poem called 'Elegy on the Closing of the French Brothels' which is 'For Henry Miller and George Katsimbalis', Durrell's Greek friend, the 'Colossus'. Though Durrell speaks warmly of prostitutes, sadly he often regards women sexually, often reduces them to their sexual component, often, like Sigmund Freud, emphasizes women's sexuality, ignoring other aspects. This happens a lot in Durrell's work, this Freudian reductionism.

There are many prostitutes in Durrell's fiction, wandering about half-naked, proposing to undergraduates, giving them the clap, as in Henry Miller's writing. In 'The Anecdotes' Durrell speaks of being 'with four peroxide whores/ Like doped marigolds growing upon this balcony' (CP, 205), while Conon states that '[t]hree women have slept with my books' ('Conon in Exile', CP, 107). The London sequences, evoked nostalgically at the beginning of *Livia*, mention VD in the typical Durrellian manner: '"with the memory of some whore in mind, and the ever present worry of a dose"' says Blanford (L, 31).

In Durrell's fiction, prostitutes are affable young women, always anonymous, always without faces or names or characters. They are given sketchy personalities, they are stereotypes. The other type of prostitute is – you

---

39 Nicole Loraux: "Ce que vit Tiresias", *L'Ecrit du temps*, 2, Minuit, Paris, 1982, 104f

guessed it – the old hag, the aging streetwalker. Presiding over the Durrell brothel is some plump old woman – Mrs Gilchrist in *The Avignon Quintet*. In *Livia*, Prince Hassad organizes one of his 'sprees'. Basically, the Prince invites a lot of dignitaries for a slap-up meal and a good fuck. Henry Miller said his idea of a great day was a good meal, a good talk, and a good fuck (DML, 179). Durrell's wife, Claude, noted 'how closely the food and fucking references march together' in Henry Miller's *Plexus* (DML, 300). This is what Durrell delivers in *The Avignon Quintet* – good food (he supplies the menu to the Prince's Pont du Gard do), good talk, from Sut and Blan, and good sex, from Affad and Constance.

> Ah, Larry, it isn't that life is so short, it's that it's everlasting [wrote Miller to Durrell]. Often, talking with you under the tent at Engances – especially over a vieux Marc – I wanted to say, "Stop talking – let's *talk*!"' (DML, 351)

Although women occupy the foreground of Lawrence Durrell's fiction, they are nearly always seen in relation to men, so that it is the male artist or writer who is Durrell's real concern in his fiction.[40] Justine is regarded by the characters in the *Quartet* as a whore, although a high class one. Pursewarden calls her a 'sexual turnstile', through which everyone must pass. Every character has something cruel to say about Justine: as the ambassadress of the spirit or *zeitgeist* of Alexandria, and the *Quartet*'s themes, she is often criticized. For instance, Darley says of her, in a moment of vicious misogynism:

> Whatever passed for thought in her was borrowed... she had picked out what was significant in books not by reading them but by listening to the matchless discourses of Balthazar, Arnauti, Pursewarden, upon them. She was a walking abstract of the writers and thinkers whom she had loved or admired – but what clever woman is more? (J, 179)

The misogynism of such passages in Durrell's work are rarely commented upon in Durrellian criticism, as if the critics politely turn a blind eye. This is a double sexism, not only from Durrell's character Darley, but also from Durrell himself, or rather, from his text. For Durrell confuses the levels of author, narrator and narrative, and forgets for a moment that all characters are 'writing effects' of texts. The idiot criticism of Justine as a 'walking abstract of the writers and thinkers whom she loved or admired'

---

40 Jane Lagoudis Pinchin: "Durrell's Fatal Cleopatra", OMG I, 27

thus applies to all fictional characters. Indeed, as a character, Justine is far 'rounder' and more 'believable', using the traditional judgements of literary humanist æsthetics, than, say, male characters such as Toto, Scobie and Pursewarden. Pursewarden, in particular, is more obviously an amalgam or 'walking abstract' of other writers' thoughts and work: Pursewarden, as critics tell us, is something of an amalgam of Henry Miller, D.H. Lawrence, Wyndham Lewis, Dylan Thomas, Roy Campbell and Lord Byron, among others. 41

Darley's remark about Justine, then, more typically applies to Purse-warden, who, as the main writer in the *Quartet* is the most 'fictional', the most 'abstract' of figments. *The Avignon Quintet* re-tackled the question of the 'reality' of the fictional author. Socrates existed only in Plato's mind, and Sigmund Freud in Carl Jung's, Sutcliffe reckoned (but then he would, S, 133).

There are more than one or two occasions in Durrell's fiction in which women are reduced by men to nothing more than a couple of holes. It sounds crude, but Durrell's men express this idea a few times. Women are for fucking, in this masculinist view. 'The whore is man's true darling', says Clea (*pace* Justine) in *Balthazar* (202). Justine sleeps with people for her 'true knight', one critic observes, as a prostitute sleeps with clients.42

Women are reduced to sex objects and prostitutes many times in Durrell's fiction. The most blatant case is when a robot version of Iolanthe is made, and there are the inevitable jokes about her being a 'love machine'. 43 The Faustian-Frankensteinian theme of creating a machine-made woman is such an easy target for a feminist attack, it is hardly worth attempting here. Suffice to say that Durrell's *Revolt of Aphrodite* exhibits a barely concealed misogynism at many points. Iolanthe is a modern-day Love Goddess, that is, a movie star in the Marilyn Monroe/ Sophia Loren mould (Durrell wrote film script for Loren - *Judith*).44 Durrell had already explored the theme in *Justine*. Twenty pages into the *Quartet* Capodistra tells of his father who had a 'perfect' rubber woman made, which travelled

---

41 G. Fraser, 1968, 152.
42 Jane Lagoudis Pinchin, ib., 27
43 Women reduced to dolls occur more often in Durrell's work than in most writers. For example, around with an inflatable doll; the wife of Rumanades (in *Panic Spring*) ends up as a mummy.
44 Durrell has a writing credit for *Judith*, had a film made from *Justine*, and his *Antrobus* stories were used for some TV adaptions in 1967 and 1968, entitled *Stiff Upper Lip*. I haven't yet seen any of these Durrell adaptions, but would to see them.

around the world with him. In Durrell's fiction, women are both loved and loathed. It may be that women are loathed because they bring such a deep consciousness of being alive: 'the woman's body... reminds men of their own mortality.'[45]

Women perhaps disturb men partly because they make men aware of the human condition in such a vivid, focused fashion. Men are jealous of women because of their power, while realizing that they themselves give them that power because of the relationship between the sexes. For Durrell's characters, women enrich life - they make it deeper, psychically. As Arnauti says of Justine: 'with her one felt all around the companionship of shadows which invaded life and filled it with a new resonance.' (J, 64)

In Durrell's work, love is simultaneously a sin and a sacrament, simultaneously sacrifice and selfishness, ecstasy and pain. Women, in particular, are the means by which males fall from grace and are redeemed. In Durrell's art, love is a Fall, a sin yet also a restoration and transcendence.[46] Women make men 'fall' into flesh, and deliver them of it through love. In Durrell's writing, as in so much of literature (certainly in the work of James Joyce, Norman Mailer, Henry Miller, D.H. Lawrence, Virginia Woolf, Philip Roth, John Carey, etc) women and men are at odds with each other. The connection between men and women in fiction is always fraught with conflict. Luce Irigaray suggests a fundamental *difference* between the sexes: '[m]an and woman, woman and man are therefore always meeting as though for the first time since they cannot stand in for one another. I shall never take the place of a man, never will a man take mine.'[47] A politics of sexual union between men and women has still not been created, Irigaray suggests, because there is no continuity between the spiritual and material, the sacred and the sexual aspects of life.

> A sexual or carnal ethics would demand that both angel and body be found together. This is a world that must be constructed or reconstructed. A genesis of love between the sexes has yet to come about, in either the smallest or largest sense, or in the most intimate or political guise. (Irigaray, in ib., 127)

For Irigaray, as for Rainer Maria Rilke, the angel is the emblem or manifestation of a fluid openness, the angel is the one who opens up life,

---

45 V. Burgin, op. cit., 116.
46 James Nichols: "The Risen Angels in Durrell's Fallen Women", in OMG, 180
47 Luce Irigaray: "Sexual Difference", in Moi, 1987, 124

who circulates between God and humanity. Durrell does not use the term 'angel', perhaps its connotations are too sweet for him. But, in the *Quartet*, he uses the word *dæmon*. It is the cultivation of the inner dæmon that must be undertaken, and heterosexual eroticism is the method by which transcendence is achieved.

With Rainer Maria Rilke and D.H. Lawrence, heterosexual lovemaking, centred on women, is the means by which the union of the angelic and the material is attained. Lucifer is a 'fallen angel', and in the Gnostic system, which is Durrell's own philosophy, the Luciferan materiality of life must be united with the spiritual, dæmonic side. Only by nourishing both – in extreme sensuality and extreme asceticism – will wholeness be achieved.

Women are continually eroticized in Durrell's work, because they are eroticized throughout Western culture. Thus, the main block for Clea in her work is sexual: she is a virgin, and needs to be 'deflowered'. Clea is so wrong about herself, thinking that 'my own blasted virginity was the root cause' of her artistic block (Cl, 92). How ridiculous (if taken literally).

In Durrell's art, virginity is not a desirable state, because in being a virgin, one is 'missing out' on something, that something being sex. The fully alive person in Durrell Land is the fully sexual person. Virginity is deemed as being not purity but sterility. To get creative Durrell's characters have to be wet with sex. It is the wet soul that is creative, in opposition to the belief of Heraclitus. People must dive into life, and get wet, dirty, smelly, oily, to be fully creative. In Durrell's reading, virginity is a sexless state, a joyless state. It is a hoarding of creative juices, literally ovaries and sperm. One has to 'spend' to create, to spill seed, creative juice, *soma*.

It's a familiar theme in William Shakespeare's plays, where people are 'barren' as people because they are non-active sexually, an essentially reductive view of humanity, and, further, deeply sexist. For instance, with Clea's virginity, it is a man who has to make good her sorry state. Not Justine: Clea may sleep with Justine, but lesbianism, in Durrell's work, is not whole, rounded, creative. Lesbians kiss 'insipidly', as Pursewarden puts it, while Sutcliffe grimly follows his lesbian wife and her lesbian lover around, aching to be a part of their love. In pornography, a typical scenario is a male watching two women writhing together. The man appears at the end of the scenario, complete with throbbing phallus, ready to 'complete' the sexual activities with penetration and intercourse. Only coition, with the penis inside the vagina, is 'true' sex. Any other kind is not quite full sex.

So Clea's creative blockage, because of her virginity, cannot be solved by Justine's lesbian love, but by Pursewarden's promise of heterosexual fucking (it's the doctor, Amaril, who eventually does the deed). It's the same with Durrell's treatment of other lesbians: as in pornography, they are not regarded as complete people, having complete sexual experiences. The phallus is required to make everything complete. Benedicta, Clea, Pia, these are incomplete people until they've been tupped by the phallus.

One imagines Durrell would enjoy the 'new' 'women's' or lesbian pornography of the 1970s and 1980s. Elizabeth Carola, who describes herself as a 'radical feminist lesbian', writes of magazines such as *On Our Backs, Bad Attitude, OW! – Outrageous Women: A Journal of Woman-to-Woman SM, Yellow Silk, The Power Exchange*:

> *On Our Backs*, in particular, is full of adverts for phalluses and endless verbiage about (and imagery of) extremely masculine 'Butches' introducing large objects – fists, bottles, phalluses – into the bodies of 'Femmes'... The harder core publications like *The Power Exchange* feature half page adverts for surgical scalpels for 'unparalleled cutting and piercing' interspersed with litanies of young women being violently fist fucked, whipped and pierced and, of course, gratefully licking their 'mistresses' boots in return.[48]

One feels Durrell would enjoy lesbian pornography with its catalogue of phallic and S/M sex acts. Lesbian or 'women's' pornography is still extremely controversial, and feminists are very divided about it.[49] Writers such as Pat Califa, Lisa Henderson and Sheila Jeffreys argue that sadomasochistic pornography operating inside lesbian practice can be enrich-

---

48 Elizabeth Carola: "Women, Erotica, Pornography: – Learning to Play the Game", in Chester, 169-171; see S. Jeffreys: "Butch and femme: now and then", *Gossip*, 5, 1987
49 See the essays in Sally Munt's book; A. Koedt: *Radical Feminism*, Quadrangle, New York 1973

ing.[50] For men it is clearly threatening, because it excludes them; it is made *by* women, *for* women: 'it is no longer for men alone to decide what is, or is not, exciting in pornography', as Linda Williams writes in her book *Hard Core*.[51]

This resentment of lesbian sexuality underpins Durrell's treatment of Pia, Livia, Sylvie, Benedicta, Justine and Constance. Durrell calls a group of lesbians a 'clitoris club'. Like D.H. Lawrence, Durrell is wary of lesbians. For Lawrence, the worst sort of women were 'cocksure' women. Women must not become cocksure! yells Lawrence. If a women becomes 'cocksure', says Lorenzo, 'she has missed her life altogether.'[52]

Like other stereotypical ambitious women, Justine sleeps her way to power. Sex for her is a way of getting her own way. She and Nessim are embarked upon secret political schemes, and sex plays a part in obtaining information and power. The model for Justine is Cleopatra, and Justine has some of the magnificence and magnetism of Cleopatra.[53] Or, rather, Durrell hopes that in alluding to Cleopatra, some of her glamour and power will rub off onto Justine.

Cleopatra fascinates Lawrence Durrell. She is a mythical figure, like Faust or Pythagoras, who embodies an important area of culture for Durrell. The combination of eroticism and political power in the Justine and Nessim relationship is essentially that of Antony and Cleopatra: they live on beyond

---

50 Pat Califa: "Feminism and Sadomasochism", *Heresies*, 12, 1981, *The Lesbian S/M Safety Manual*, Alyson, Boston 1990, and "Unravelling the Sexual Fringe: A Secret Side of Lesbian Sexuality", *The Advocate*, 27 December 1979; also: Lisa Henderson: "Lesbian Pornography: Cultural Transgression and Sexual Demystification", in Sally Munt, ed, 173-191; Sheila Jeffreys: "Sadomasochism: the erotic cult of fascism", in *Lesbian Ethics*, 2, 1, 65-82; M. Sulter: "Reviewing lesbian erotica", *Spare Rib*, no. 219, 1990-1, 42-4; see also, on sadomasochism: R.R. Linden et al, eds: *Against Sadomasochism*, Frog in the Well, East Palo Alto, California 1982; Justine Jones: "Why I liked screwing? Or, is heterosexual enjoyment based on sexual violence?", in Onlywomen, eds: *Love your Enemy?*, Onlywomen Press 1981; Katherine Davis et al, eds: *Coming to Power, Writings and Graphics on Lesbian S/M*, Alyson Publications, Boston 1983
51 Linda Williams: *Hard Core*: Power, *Pleasure, and the 'Frenzy of the Visible'*, Pandora, 1990, 264; see also Andrew Ross: "The Popularity of Pornography", in *No Respect: Intellectuals and Popular Culture*, Routledge 1989, 171-208
52 Lawrence: "Cocksure Women and Hensure Men", in *Selected Essays*, 34
53 Acté too is like the spirit of Alexandria, like Cleopatra and Justine (Friedman, 1970, 36)

the destructive phase of bourgeois heterosexual relationships. They are not murdered, they are survivors. Justine and Nessim act like lovers who have 'gone through the fire' – 'look, we have come through!' as D.H. Lawrence cried. Julia Kristeva wonders what would have happened if Shakespeare's lovers, Romeo and Juliet, had survived: they might not become a normal, weary married couple, perhaps:

> the married couple continues to be a passionate couple, but covering the entire gamut of sadomasochism that the two partners heralded in the yet relatively quiet version of the Shakespearean text. Each acting out both sexes in turn they thus create a foursome that feeds on itself through repeated aggression and merging, castration and gratification, resurrection and death.[54]

Justine and Nessim so clearly go through cycles of death and rebirth, or rather, sham death and sham resurrection. They practice a particular form of cruel 'loving death', 'love-in-death'. When it all goes wrong for Justine and Nessim, their socio-political failure is translated into an erotic failure. Durrell makes sure the contrast between before and after is marked: at the end of *Mountolive*, Nessim is seen as a wealthy, powerful personage, moving in the super circles of society, one of the most influential men in Alexandria. At the start of the fourth book, Nessim is reduced to an ambulance driver, dressed shabbily, with a missing eye and finger, loathed by his wife.

Justine, once the beautiful, seductive companion in Nessim's nefarious plans, is now a harridan, a hag, feeling bitter and remorseful. The glowing Antony and Cleopatra union of Justine and Nessim is crumpled to ashes, turned in upon itself. As Justine explains, when Nessim does not act, is not dynamic like Mark Antony, he is nothing. Without the political operation, there is no danger, no *frisson* in Justine's love for Nessim, so it withers (C, 50-51).

At the end of *The Alexandria Quartet*, however, the allusions to Antony and Cleopatra have shifted from Justine and Nessim to the lovers who replace them: Clea and Darley. During their summer of bliss when they spend days swimming and picnicing at the tiny island of Narouz', Clea wonders if it is Timonium, where Antony returned after his Actium (Cl, 196-7).

Melissa is also regarded as a whore, though she is a passive, humble,

---

54 Kristeva: "Romeo and Juliet: Love-Hatred in the Couple", in 1987, 217

dejected personality, the meek opposite of Justine's voracious, predatory activity. Like Justine, Melissa is bound sexually to a man, Cohen, who might be regarded as her pimp. Melissa has an odd, uncomfortable master-slave relation with Cohen. Darley has a strange relationship with Cohen, seeing him in the streets of Alexandria, and not saying anything. At one point he sits next to his sexual rival in a bar for an hour, but still says nothing. Justine too has someone who haunts her, another sexual master, the man who raped her, Capodistra. He is an aficionado of pornography and stylized 'perversity'.

The relations Darley has with Melissa and Justine are largely sexual, but not much more than that. The narrator emphasizes the sexual nature of Darley's relations with Justine and Melissa. Darley, for instance, when he meets Melissa for a lover's assignation on the streets, imagines her coming from some darkened room. He does not imagine her coming from a shop, or having her hair cut, but leaving some sex scene. Melissa sleeps with men for money or favours, while Justine sleeps with men for power and ambition, for favours of a political kind. Justine demands much more from men than Melissa, and is thus much more disappointed. She dominates Nessim, she is the Mother-Goddess to his child-god, the Isis who nurtures Osiris back to life, the Cleopatra who encircles Antony. 'Her love was like a skin in which he lay sewn like the infant Heracles' (*Justine*, 28).

One of the ways in which *The Alexandria Quartet* is connected to *The Avignon Quintet* is sexual: in a short passage in Affad's novel, *Sebastian*, he sleeps with Melissa. Via Melissa, a web of sexual relations is built up: Darley sleeps with Melissa who sleeps with Affad who sleeps with Constance who sleeps with Blanford.

Most of the main characters of both the tetralogy and the *Quintet* are connected sexually: Pursewarden, Melissa, Darley, Justine, Nessim, Clea, Affad, Blanford, Sam, Livia, Hilary. One could put all these names of sexual congress onto a chart. Perhaps Durrell did, like Piers' star map of the dead. It's the sort of thing Durrell would do.

The authentic, emotional contact of love is not found in Justine or Melissa, but in Clea.[55] Like Constance, Darley has to progress from person to person before he reaches authentic, deep love.[56] Justine and Melissa are

---

55 Clea is the character who comes closest to being a 'self-actualizing personality', the 'model of independence and naturalness' for Darley to aspire towards (Lisa Schwerdt: "Coming of Age in Alexandria: The Narrator", OMG, 217)
56 James Van Dyck Card, 1976, 80

stages in his sexual progress of the soul. For Darley, the endpoint is a creative, sexual unity, between a writer and a painter. For Justine, the end is a sexual relation with Nessim based on money, politics and power, a relationship of intrigue and double dealings, firmly sited in the political and economic worlds. It is clear which the narrator of *The Alexandria Quartet* regards as the higher, more important relationship: the sexual, creative, artistic one.

Another woman who has to act as a prostitute is Nancy Quiminal. She exchanges sexual favours, as they are called, with the Nazi in return for his release of a few people who've been rounded up for deportation and death. It is a bizarre form of prostitution, echoing Oscar Schindler in Thomas Keneally's *Schindler's Ark*.

For his epic spree, the Prince combs Provence for exquisite furniture and the best prostitutes in the realm. The men, in dinner dress, are offered a prostitute:

> ...the whole dining-room was flooded with light and the advancing cohort of guests gave a collective gasp of pleasure. To the right of each male guest there was to be a *naked lady of pleasure*! ...The men, as befitted their superior sex, sat on chairs with high gilded backs, like thrones; the girls upon velvet piano-stools. (L, 257)

This is as sexist as you can get. Whose is the voice that says that men are the 'superior sex' here? The narrator, perhaps, seeing the scene through the eyes of the people watching on the Pont du Gard. At this moment, Constance is watching through binoculars at the spree. Is this voice then Constance? If so, is she being ironic when she says, or the narrator says for her, that men are the 'superior sex'? But there seems to be no irony here. The scene is one of Durrell's grand set-pieces, which he loves to write, and it finishes off - of course - with fireworks. It is the fête itself which is humorous, but the narration is not humorous. One senses that the narrator is not being ironic when s/he describes, in detail, the set-up of the Prince's 'spree'.

Another brothel scene occurs when Lord Galen is ridiculed at length by giggling, anonymous prostitutes in Avignon. Irony here is meant to be uppermost, as Galen, a jew, is crucified against some bedposts. This scene is a replay of the one in *The Revolt of Aphrodite*, where the British clown Sipple is 'crucified' in a brothel in Athens. The Athens brothel, like the one in Avignon, is a rundown building set apart from the rest of the city. In

Durrell's brothel scenes, people make a special journey to the place, a journey which marks out the events in the brothel as quite distinct from the rest of the novel.

In another brothel sequence, again with the Prince, characters happily indulge in pædophilia. A group of young children swarm around the Prince. Blanford and Felix watch from a toilet window, transfixed. Durrell makes references to the theatrical nature of the scene, for it is framed by a door and a window. The brothel scene is also called a circus, and the freakshow nature of a circus is emphasized. Madame Riquiqui has in her brothel, for instance, a dwarf: 'a puzzled female dwarf with a hideously rouged face as if ready for the circus; she was clad in white organdie with a marriage veil' (L 147). All this sexual activity is related as if it's ordinary and everyday. Although 'normal', heterosexual eroticism is usurped and mocked – the dwarf wearing a wedding veil, for instance, mocks marriage – Durrell relates it all as if it nothing unusual.

Homosexuality is also a feature of Lawrence Durrell's fiction, though the homosexual 'act' between men is not described. On male homosexuality, Durrell is reticent in his descriptions. He cannot disguise his dislike, perhaps distrust, of gay men. His interpretation of gay men is essentially that of Sigmund Freud: 'his attitude towards women is characterized by a tremendous hatred which he dare not admit', Durrell writes in his last book (CVG, 75), a statement which shows how he off-loads his misogynism onto homosexuals. Durrell quotes Wilhelm Stekel, who states 'the truth is that he [the homosexual] is unable to love!' (CVG, 75), an idiotic statement, the sort Durrell loves, because of its forthrightness. Lesbians are described in more detail – 'fingering their sex' in the Venice sequence, for instance.

Male homosexual acts occur rarely. There is the bizarre oral sex in *Sebastian*, where the psychotic, Mnemidis, is telephoned by a magician who holds down his wife's head over his penis as he speaks to Mnemidis on the 'phone. This may be the strangest sexual event in Durrell's fiction. Later, Mnemidis seduces a youth on his escape from the clinic, dressed as a nun. Durrell clearly loves to describe odd sexual occurrences. But the heterosexual 'sex act', as Durrell calls it, is central to his fiction.

The homosexual relations of Bruce and Piers remains vague in *The Avignon Quintet*, like the homosexuality in Durrell's other books. Affad is at first thought a secret homosexual, but he turns out to be rampantly heterosexual. Scobie, by contrast, is a closet queen, a camp pirate with his rolling eye and idiot parrot. His end, being beaten up by sailors, is supremely stereotypical. Scobie, who becomes apostrophized by the locals as El Scob, a saint, is the typical man who dresses up as a woman, with all the trimmings, so to speak. Durrell's notions of homosexual identity do not depart from the mainstream.

Lawrence Durrell's views of lesbianism is altogether different. Generally, he is sceptical of lesbianism, and lesbianism is regarded, finally, as inferior, as a sexual experience. Lesbians are mocked, sometimes cruelly, and the digs Durrell makes against lesbianism are bitter, and seem to come from some place in 'Durrell' which has been hurt by lesbianism in the past. Sometimes the fulminations against lesbians are couched in Durrell's word games, such as this from *Quinx*: 'Tomboy with a clitoris like an ice-skate seeks rational employ' (Q, 138).

Somehow, Durrell has really go it in for lesbians, who receive the biggest dose of vitriol from his pen. Livia is called a 'Principal Boy' by Sutcliffe, a violent predator who wears 'Sadist Red' nail varnish and the fur of animals. 'Lean tomboy of the sexthrust, it was she who impregnated me with her despairing anodyne, phantasy sensuality.' (L, 14, 21) At times Durrell and his narrators seem to harbour deep grudges against lesbians. Durrell appears at times more vicious than D.H. Lawrence in the latter's loathing of 'bossy', independent women, or Ernest Hemingway's or Norman Mailer's misogynism.

What is it Durrell so dislikes about lesbianism and lesbians? It is surely something to do with the general, masculinist view of lesbianism as inferior sexuality. Lesbian sex, in the general, patriarchal view, is marked by the *lack* of the phallus. Hence, lesbian eroticism must always be 'deviant', because it departs from the patriarchal norms which exalt the phallus. Lesbianism must always be 'Other', sexually, and many feminists note that the otherness of lesbian sexuality is one of the reasons that men and their patriarchal institutions are very threatened by lesbianism.[57] Lesbians threaten patriarchy at its powerbase. Men cannot control lesbians: '[l]esbians, by loving women and not men, pose a direct threat to the very

57 Ti-Grace Atkinson: *Amazon Odyssey*, Links Books, New York 1974; Alice, Gordon, Debbie and Mary: "Separatism", in Sarah Lucia Hoagland & Julia Penelope, eds, 31-40; Adrienne Rich: "Towards a woman-centred university", in *On Lies, Secrets and Silence*, Novotny, New York 1979; Jill Johnston: *Lesbian Nation: The Feminist Solution*, Simon & Shuster, New York 1974; S. Rowbotham: *Beyond the Fragments: Feminism and the making of Socialism*, Merlin 1979

basis of male supremacy' write Alice, Gordon, Debbie and Mary.[58]

We can see this fear of lesbianism behind much of Durrell's discussion of lesbianism. Sutcliffe, for instance, feels distinctly left out and resentful as he shuffles along behind Pia and Trash on the Corniche in Geneva. What an ignoble turnaround, to be a manly male thrown overboard for a lesbian! Sutcliffe suffers deeply from this sexual humiliation.

Yet Sutcliffe's patriarchal power is reasserted when Trash comes to him to ask for permission to go on a grand tour of the world with Pia. In order to gain his permission, Trash appears to Sutcliffe naked under furs. They fuck. Sutcliffe agrees. An outcast male, he still retains a vestige of social power.

Livia is the key lesbian in Lawrence Durrell's fiction. Various characters try to psychoanalyze her: Blanford, Sutcliffe, Constance, Quatrefages and Felix. Livia is the stereotypical prostitute of Western art. She undervalues herself, she goes about unkempt and surly, yet she is fanatical – in particular about National Socialism, which turns out to be a grave mistake. Massive disillusionment follows. Livia of course commits suicide, as do so many people in Durrell's fiction. The reasons for suicide in Durrell's world are always ultimately personal and emotional, to do with love and betrayal. In Livia's case, it is not her disillusionment with Nazism that drives her to suicide, as at first might be apparent. It is, rather, the horror of seeing her brother (and lover) being beheaded.

Livia is depicted as otherness, as somewhat incomprehensible. People try hard to figure her out. Constance tries to psychoanalyze her, and Sutcliffe provides her with clues, gleaned from his experiences with Pia's lesbianism. The lesbian, argues Monique Wittig, 'is the only concept that I know of which is beyond the categories of sex (man and woman)'.[59] The otherness of Livia and Pia remains inexplicable to some of the characters in *The Avignon Quintet*. Blanford comes out of his love affair with Livia confused and troubled. He has not understood her 'heraldic sigil', as the Durrell of the 1930s would put it. Only later will he experience the inner unity and harmony of the heraldic universe with its 'love-in-time' (FWJ, 54).

In Durrell's fiction, lesbianism is disruptive and difficult. Durrell's view of lesbianism is that of patriarchy, where lesbianism questions the prevalence of patriarchal sex (heterosexuality) as the norm. In her excellent

58 Alice, Gordon, Debbie and Mary, op. cit., 31-40
59 Wittig: "One is not born a woman", in Hoagland, 446-7

essay "Compulsory Heterosexuality and Lesbian Existence", Adrienne Rich writes:

> for women heterosexuality may not be a 'preference' at all but something that has had to be imposed, managed, organized, propagandized, and maintained by force.

In Durrell's fiction women sometimes have to comply to patriarchal laws by force (the young mother who is hunted down like a wild animal in the *Quintet*, for example). We see Livia struggling to balance the imposition of heterosexuality upon her from outside (her enculturation) and her own private desires. The result is constant conflict and ambiguity in Livia, which the characters around her cannot assuage. Livia is the archetypal outsider. But not the bourgeois, intellectual, Bohemian 'outsider', like Blanford, like the 'outsiders' of male literature (Jude the Obscure, Des Esseintes, Paul Morel, Rosquentin, Meursault). Livia is a sexual outsider, a sexual misfit.

Livia's lesbianism, like Pia's and Sylvie's and Benedicta's and Justine's, is not revolutionary, as contemporary feminists might wish, because it is a lesbianism that keeps defining itself in terms of patriarchy. Elizabeth Mees reckons that 'lesbianism, as in hetero-relations, takes (its) place within the structure of the institution of heterosexuality. The lesbian is born of/in it.'[60] Durrell's women and lesbians are very much defined by patriarchal norms. There is no escape, it seems, from patriarchal heterosexuality. As Sheila Jeffreys wrote: '[e]very woman grows up in a heteropatriarchal world',[61] while Ann Barr Snitow writes:

> One of our culture's most intense myths, the ideal of an individual who is brave and complete in isolation, is for men only. Women are grounded, enmeshed in civilization, in social connection, in family and in love...[62]

In Durrell's fiction, we find lesbian sex being treated in the same way as in pornography. Durrell's descriptions of sex, as we have seen, are largely the same as those found in pornography. In mainstream pornography, lesbian eroticism is always controlled by a patriarchal force. Typically, in a

---

60 Elizabeth Mees, in Karla Jay & Joanna Glasgow: *Lesbian Text and Contexts: Radical Revisions*, New York University Press, New York 1990, 82

61 Sheila Jeffreys: "The Censoring of Revolutionary Feminism", in Chester, 139

62 Ann Snitow: "Mass Market Romance: Pornography for Women is Different", *Radical History Review*, no. 20, Spring/Summer 1979

soft porn scenario, two bisexual women cavort on a bed overseen by a male ('I've always wanted to see you with another woman', drools the boyfriend to his girlfriend; or, frequently, 'I got back from work an' saw 'em writhin' on the bed'). Towards the end of the soft core lesbian scene, the man makes love to both women. Why? Because they needed the phallus, they needed a man, a real *man*, to be fulfilled ('women need cock after all,' says the male in pornography, 'to satisfy 'em'). We find this theme occurring endlessly in pornography. The male presence (the phallus) is seen as necessary for the true satisfaction for women. In Durrell's world men watch women having sex - men look into rooms, in the classic voyeur scenario, and see women relaxing after sex.

Lawrence Durrell includes many aspects of sexual politics which come out of 'second wave' feminism, the sexual politics of the 1970s and 1980s. Durrell puts this 1970s and 1980s sexual politics into the war years, which is why at times *The Avignon Quintet* reads oddly. Fist-fucking, for instance, is mentioned a couple of times, though it wasn't a major part of Second World War culture. Constance reads a psychoanalytic paper on fist-fucking (C, 286), while Sutcliffe or Blanford mentions that lesbians make love with their arms in up to the elbow ('arms thrust to the elbow up/ Is how the modern hardies [harpies?] tup!' Q, 137).

These aspects of sexual politics are very much a part of the late 1970s and 1980s, the era when Robert Mapplethorpe shocked people by photographing someone being fist-fucked, when feminists such as Susan Griffin, Andrea Dworkin, Susan Brownmiller and Catherine MacKinnon attacked pornography in heated, incisive polemical books, when people marched and protested for gay and lesbian rights, when the French feminists, Hélène Cixous, Luce Irigaray, Monique Wittig and Julia Kristeva, were writing provocative texts.

You wouldn't think Durrell would be interested in feminism and sexual politics in the post-1968 era, but he's a clever, perceptive writer, and absorbs all manner of influences. Living in France he would not be immune to all sorts of cultural activity, not least French feminism, some of which is very radical. For instance, some of the French feminists say that 'woman' does not exist, except as a 'writing-effect' - that is, as a product of a cultural space, but not as an actuality. Mary Jacobus writes:

> The French insistence on *écriture féminine* - on woman as a writing-effect instead of an origin - asserts not the sexuality of the text but the textuality of sex. [...] The 'feminine', in this scheme, is to be located in

the gaps, the absences, the unsayable or unrepresentable of discourse and representation.63

The guru of the Surrealists, André Breton, said that 'existence is elsewhere'. French feminists say that 'woman' is elsewhere. 'She is indefinitely other in herself,' writes Luce Irigaray, maintaining that women

are already elsewhere than in the discursive machinery where you claim to take them by surprise. They have turned back within themselves, which does not mean the same thing as 'within yourself'. They do not experience the same interiority that you do and which perhaps you mistakenly presume they share.64

Julia Kristeva writes: '[i]n "woman" I see something that cannot be represented, something that is not said, something above and beyond nomenclatures and ideologies.'65 Other feminists echo this idea, that women cannot be fully represented in the traditional media of patriarchy. As Hélène Cixous writes:

It is at the level of sexual pleasure in my opinion that the difference makes itself most clearly apparent in as far as woman's libidinal economy is neither identifiable by a man nor referable to the masculine economy.66

This otherness of women provides an interesting gloss on Lawrence Durrell's notion of the fictional character. Sutcliffe has a vicarious, shifty existence, never quite sure how 'real' he is. Sutcliffe (like Pursewarden) is very much a 'writing effect', a fictional product of a piece of fiction, a fiction within a fiction. Durrell 'writes' (creates) Blanford who writes Sutcliffe and Sutcliffe writes his own fictions. Durrell creates Blanford who creates Sutcliffe who in turn creates fictional characters, one of them being Bloshford, a novelist Sutcliffe hates because he's successful ('Bloshford carried all before him, and had managed to buy a couple of Rollses!' [M, 178]). But Bloshford is Sutcliffe's parody of Blanford. So there are at least five, and more, layers to Durrell's fictional confection in *The Avignon Quintet*. This Chinese boxes self-quotation and parody is postmodern, a

---

63 Mary Jacobus: "Is There a Woman in This Text?", in *New Literary Criticism*, Autumn, 1982, 14, 1
64 Irigaray: *Ce sexe qui n'en est pas un*, Minuit, Paris 1977, 28-9
65 Kristeva: "La femme, ce n'est jamais ça", *Tel Quel*, Autumn 1974, in Marks, 135
66 Hélène Cixous: "Sorties", in Marks, 95

mise-en-âbyme firmly in tune with the cultural theory approach of French feminism.

Durrell's notion of love is so firmly bound up with notions of art and artifice that one cannot discuss love in Durrell's work without mentioning how it is represented in art. For Durrell, the two modes of experience and ideology, love and art, are inseparable. It is simply not possible to talk about love without discussing language and art. In Durrell's concept of love, the myth of Narcissus is prominent: that is, the self-reflexivity of love, the *mise-en-âbyme* of love, the auto-eroticism of love, love as a crystallizing mirror in the Stendhalian manner. 'Vision is exorcism' is one of Durrell's mottoes.[67]

In Plato's *Symposium*, love is of/ for the other, the other half of one's being. One searches for the completeness to be found in the beloved. The beloved thus becomes that missing fragment which rounds out the desiring self. In Neoplatonism, there is a shift towards a different kind of narcissism. In Plotinus' *Enneads*, one of the touchstones for Durrell's *Quartet*, love is God, but God is also Narcissus. In Plotinus's philosophy, the One is 'simultaneously the *loved one* and *love*; He is *love of himself*; for He is beautiful only by and in Himself.'[68] With Neoplatonism, a new kind of love is born, one founded on interiority and autoeroticism. Narcissus loves himself, he is both subject and object. His real object of desire is an image of himself – that is, representation, art. Julia Kristeva writes:

> He loves, he loves Himself – active and passive, subject and object... *The object of Narcissus is psychic space; it is representation itself, fantasy.* But he does not know it, and he dies. If he knew it he would be an intellectual, a creator of speculative fictions, an artist, writer, psychologist, psychoanalyst. He would be Plotinus or Freud.[69]

This is what happens in Durrell's fictions: characters become Nar-

---

67 Ray Morrison: "Memory and Light in Lawrence Durrell's *The Revolt of Aphrodite*" (in Matthews, 1979, 153). There are many gnomic, anecdotal and epigramatic notes and maxims on love scattered throughout *The Alexandria Quartet*, such as: '[i]t is quite possible to love those whom you most wound.' (B, 40) 'Love rejoices in self-torture.' (B, 171) The *Quartet* can be seen as Durrell's 'Book of Love', a wide-ranging treatise on love in the manner of Stendhal's *De l'Amour* or Denis de Rougemont's *L'Amour et l'Occident*.
68 Plotinus: *Enneads*, VI, 8, 15
69 Kristeva: "Narcissus: The New Insanity", in *Tales of Love*, 116

cissus,[70] the One, self-reflecting æsthetes: they become philosophers like Plotinus (Balthazar, Caradoc, Max), or they become psychologists like Sigmund Freud (Schwartz, Arnauti), or artists (Darley, Pursewarden, Blanford, Sutcliffe), or scientists (Sacrapant, Felix), or businessmen (Nessim, Julian, Galen).

Narcissus in Ovid's poem is in love with an image, a representation of the beloved (himself), much as the artist is. Although he kills himself for falling in love with a fake, Narcissus nevertheless goes about dealing with his idealism by fetishizing his own image. As Kristeva writes, 'instead of having to *create* what will enable him to equal his ideal – a work, or an idealized object to love – Narcissus will *fabricate* an *ersatz*.' (in ib., 126) This is what Durrell's 'great coven of real lovers' do, what lovers in literature do (a line from the poem 'Why Wait?' [CVG, 58]). They create the idealism from their projections.[71] Poets are in love with their self-created images.[72] They have to be: it's their 'truth'. Poets are 'fascinated by images on the one hand, in quest of truth on the other.' (ib., 131) Artists recognize their love of images even as they adore them.

The two things, representation and 'reality', are constantly used in a way that still confuses observers. Non-artists still get confused about the relation between illusion and the 'real' world. They still wonder whether Thomas Hardy's Wessex is a 'real' place or not; they still find it frustrating when Hardy did not 'keep to the original place'; they still find it annoying that Hardy changed the topography and history of Dorset and the surrounding counties.

It's desire that counts, not so much the object of desire. 'It's being obsessed that takes over', says film director Bette Gordon.[73] All the problems Darley, Felix, Constance, Livia, Death Gregory and other Durrellian lovers have with love and life stem from this ambiguous, paradoxical relation between self-made images and the 'real' world, which includes other people. Darley finds his conceptions about love and Alexandria and his past have been mostly misconceptions. Blanford finds

---

70 Some critics claim Durrell's heraldic love in the *Quartet* is not narcissistic (Ray Morrison: "Mirrors and the Heraldic Universe in Lawrence Durrell's *The Alexandria Quartet*", in MacNiven 1987, 507)

71 In *Monsieur* Sutcliffe realizes that the 'projection' process in love 'was in the long run an act of self-mutilation' (M, 111)

72 Elsewhere in *Monsieur*, Sutcliffe knows that all meetings are predetermined, that 'one hunts for the person one is anyway doomed to meet' (M, 198).

73 Gordon: "Look Back/ Talk Back", in Gibson, 1993, 91

out that much of his ideas on love have been delusions. The trouble is that the poet narcissitically believes her/ his creations, her/ his images.

8

From Western Sex
to Eastern Sex Magic

Writing about sex is an impossibility. Sex doesn't exist in writing, or does it? Writing is not kisses, caresses, orgasms. These occur elsewhere. Yet, for French feminists, some writing can be erotic, and orgasmic. French feminists speak of the *jouissance* of a text. The unrepresentable in art and pornography, according to some feminists, is women's eroticism, their *jouissance*, that 'explosive, blossoming, sane and inexhaustible *jouissance* of the woman', as Julia Kristeva describes it.[1]

Despite being 'unrepresentable', some French feminists have had a go at describing women's eroticism, most notably, and controversially, Luce Irigaray. Irigaray spoke in spatial terms of idealist feminism:

> We need both space and time. And perhaps we are living in an age when *time must re-deploy space*. Could this be the dawning of a new world? Immanence and transcendence are being recast, notably by that *threshold* which has never been examined in itself: the female sex. It is a threshold unto *mucosity*. Beyond the classic opposites of love and hate, liquid and ice lies this perpetually *half-open* threshold, consisting of *lips* that are strangers to dichotomy. ...their shape welcomes without

1 Kristeva: *About Chinese Women*, Marion Boyars 1977, 63

assimilating or reducing or devouring.[2]

Pornography has the problem of representing the unrepresentable. Pornography has developed over the years, becoming more and more 'explicit'. The term 'explicit' neatly describes the efforts of pornography to 'show' more and more. The thing is, what is there to 'show'? Mere genitals is not enough, although photography in pornography gets closer and closer, and the genitals are shown in ever more detailed images. The man ejaculates, the 'come shot' or 'money shot'. Ejaculation, like erection, is a clear sign of arousal and pleasure. Woman's *jouissance*, her orgasms, are not so immediately visible. Hence a tendency in contemporary pornography to show female 'ejaculation', a form of orgasm that shows women's pleasure.

This was the problem that Lawrence Durrell faced. One of Durrell's solutions was to omit the sexual words, to replace them with asterisks. Durrell likes the mocking nature of asterisks. His use of asterisks recalls those critics and newspapers who quote from D.H. Lawrence, Miller, *My Secret Life*, and other 'erotic' books inserting asterisks where 'appropriate'. The hypocrisy of asterisks, still prevalent in certain newspapers today, is that these same newspapers cultivate sensational, slanderous, 'sexy' news stories founded on the experiences the asterisks stand in for. Thus, the tabloids and Fleet Street rags trade on the f***, yet they maintain a slither of decorum and censorship by not printing the word fuck in full. It's so insulting! As if people don't know what f*** or f— means. You can't print s***, c***, f***, without people knowing what they are. And yet the tabloid newspapers print f*** because they think people will be offended! The hypocrisy is sublime.

Parodying the idiot use of asterisks, Durrell writes in *Constance*:

He had taken his ***** in quiet fingers and countered the web of tensions in her by his deep ***** and careful ***** while she for her part ***** and reaching into the wealth behind her groaned as she *****... How deeply he hurt her now with his ***** and his violent *****, each awkward spasm lifting itself into the centre of her *****, the flower and branch of all sex. (C, 281)

Here Durrell is of course parodying D.H. Lawrence. Lawrence wrote eloquently of women's orgasms in *Lady Chatterley's Lover*, in those now

---

2 Luce Irigaray: "La différence sexuelle", *Ethiope de la différence sexuelle*, Minuit, Paris, 1984, and in Toril Moi, ed: *French Feminist Thought*,128

famous passages of 'rippling, rippling, rippling', passages of orgasmic writing which so impressed Anaïs Nin:

> Rippling, rippling, rippling like a flapping overlapping of soft flames, soft as feathers, running to points of brilliance, exquisite, exquisite and melting her all molten inside. (138)

Lawrence aims to go all the way, as far as language will go. As always in Lawrence's fiction, there is a tension between wanting to show or describe sex, and the knowledge, only half-admitted, that this sort of writing is doomed to fail, and worse, it 'cheapens' sex, as he said pornography cheapened sex, made it 'dirty'.

Bertie Lawrence wants to show the transformative experience of great sex for Connie – that's why he uses tidal and oceanic imagery and metaphors. Durrell too wanted Constance in *The Avignon Quintet* to be swept away by the tidal energies of her new found orgasmic love with Affad. Pursewarden, Durrell's Lawrencean novelist, proposes a simultaneous exaltation of sex, a diving into sex, and a self-censorship, a Puritanical/ Protestant buttoning up. The '"secret of my novelist's trade"' Pursewarden informs Darley in a public toilet (where else?), '"is sex and plenty of it... Lashings of sex... but remember... *stay buttoned up tight...* You must stay buttoned up and suffering."' (J, 103) Clutching his dick in the urinal, Pursewarden espouses the paradox of the post-Lawrencean literary world: 'lashings of sex' set against Presbyterian restraint.

Certainly sex-obsessed is not too strong a term to apply to Lawrence Durrell's fiction.[3] Durrell's characters emphasize sex at every step of the way, for, in their view, '[n]othing except the act of physical love tells us this truth about one another' (B, 53). Durrell's reason for writing so much about sex (in the *Quartet* at last) is that there is so much of it about. In a letter to his mentor T.S. Eliot of 1946, when he was still shaping up his 'Big City Poem', Durrell wrote:

> I want to do a book involving the attitude of the near-Levant to sex – it's so passionate and natural and really wonderful... I don't want to accentuate anything. I am not proselytising with dark abdomens or anything. But the central dramas of life here come out of sex; and sex informs and warms everything. One is saturated and exhausted and bored to death with sex; consequently it is only here that one is ever *free* of

3 'For all the interest expressed in love and sex, the major concern of Durrell's fiction is with writing.' Jane Pinchin: "Durrell's Fatal Cleopatra", CE, 194

it... (SP, 83)

It turned out, though, that Durrell's depiction of sex in the *Quartet* was not 'passionate and natural' but full of neuroses and hang-ups and repressions and puritanical self-hatred. As Justine sighed early on in the tetralogy: '"from desire to revulsion, let's get it over with quick"'. Rather than being a representation of free, open, liberal sexuality (the purity and 'innocence' of ancient Greece), Durrell depicted sexuality that was often frenzied, vicious, uncaring and manically self-regarding (more 'modern', alienated Freudian Vienna or Paris than the 'natural' and 'passionate' Levant or Alexandria).

Up until *The Avignon Quintet,* Durrell was reticent about describing sexual experiences in detail. He would allude to sex a lot, but not describe it. In *The Alexandria Quartet,* Durrell depicts a couple hard at it in a brothel as a writhing mass of confused flesh and clothes, a lump of molten organic material such as Francis Bacon might have painted in one of his unfocused, smeared triptychs. Sex here is described as the 'whole portentous scrimmage', in which the participants are entangled like 'the victims of some terrible accident' (J, 164-5). The orgasm is shown as hands and toes curling. 'Sensitive' novelists are wary of writing 'sex scenes', because they know that what they write defines themselves. Yet sex is crucial to art, many artists say. As Gertrude Stein wrote: '[l]iterature – creative literature – unconnected with sex is inconceivable.'[4]

Knowing the centrality of sexual experience, Durrell only depicts it in full in *The Avignon Quintet.* Up until *The Avignon Quintet,* sex has been something invisible and indefinable. In *The Avignon Quintet,* in the orgasms of Constance and Affad, Durrell tries to describe the indescribable. The result can only be disappointing, for Durrell has high standards, like all good artists. Yet he has a go at describing sex, knowing the result will be disappointing.

The first time Constance and Affad make love is during her period, a significant time of the month in Tantric sex magic of the Left Hand Path. It is an allusion Durrell would know about, evoking the visionary lovemaking that can occur during menstruation, when the woman becomes 'witchy',

---

4 Stein, in "A Conversation", John Hyde Preston, *Atlantic Monthly*, CLVI, August 1935, 191

has the powers of witchcraft.[5] Durrell goes for the naturalistic, literary depiction of lovemaking, a tradition developed by D.H. Lawrence, James Joyce, Henry Miller and Anaïs Nin:

> "O God!" she groaned. "I'm bleeding. It's too soon." But the gradual strengthening of his embrace was accompanied not only by kisses, warm and shocking in their precision, but the excited whisper: "Bleed! Thank you, Constance. Bleed!" He was overwhelmed with gratitude for he realised that it was for him, this dark menstrual flow; and turning her slightly to depress her legs and pull her downwards towards him he entered her softly, circumspectly, disregarding her faint mewing protests, which soon subsided as she quietly opened herself to him, profoundly and completely, made herself the slave of his lust in a way that had never before happened to her. Where, she wondered, had she acquired the experience to react so absolutely? (C, 265)

Here, then, is Durrell's version of the total, transforming love experience. In Rainer Maria Rilke's it's called 'heart-work'. It is interesting to compare it with the scene in *Lady Chatterley's Lover* where Connie and Mellors first make love. Their first sexual congress is soon over. The pleasure is all Mellors': 'The orgasm was his, all his' (*Lady Chatterley's Lover,* 121). As with Durrell's bathroom scene, it is the male who instigates the sexual contact. Mellors touches her flank with the ubiquitous, Lawrencean blind instinctive caress (120). He draws her into the hut, and is in a hurry 'to enter the peace on earth of her soft, quiescent body' (120). Like Constance, Connie Chatterley's body is a soft, pliable form during this first sexual encounter. Like Lawrence with Mellors, Durrell soon has Affad outlining the 'history of sex' and his cult of Oriental sex magic.

Orgasm is the engine and the foundation of Durrell's sex magic; it is the glue that unites opposites. This sex magic, though portentous at times, is undercut by humour (for ex, 'the taming of the screw' [Q, 164]). It is not particularly heroic or relentlessly 'serious', in the manner of Lawrence's Mellors. It is a life-affirming philosophy, based on sharing and communion, not on greed, self-love and hoarding, a Gnostic/ Taoist philosophy of sexual materialism or materialist sexuality that goes beyond Karl Marx, Sigmund Freud, Luther or John Calvin. The endpoint is the silence that follows the shared orgasm, the Taoist silence, where 'he who knows does not speak', a

---

5 Penelope Shuttle & Peter Redgrove: *The Wise Wound: Menstruation and Everywoman,* Paladin 1986; Peter Redgrove: "Greening the Orgasm", *Resurgence* (150), Jan/ Feb 1992, 30-3; *The Black Goddess and the Sixth Sense,* Bloomsbury 1987

zone of 'super-sense', as Akkad calls it (M, 144).

Affad's sex magic is a distillation of Gnostic and Tantric sex magic, with some Taoist love magic thrown in. The goal is '[t]he thrilling yoga of love's double bind!' so that love '[m]akes here and now a simple everywhere'.6 The Grail is not mere pleasure, but ecstasy, not the merely adequate, but the sublime (89). In Durrell's sex magic, every part of sex must be made more and more 'conscious',7 so that the lovers will be deeper and deeper in phase. Orgasm becomes a divine and immense amnesia which is taken to the point of meditation then allowed to slowly melt (Q, 13). It is a Spenglerian/ Reichian view of sexuality, where civilization depends upon good fucking. When cultures go into decline, Durrell's Affad suggests, 'the first victim is the quality of fucking' (C, 268).

For Durrell's lovers at this stage in the *Quintet*, fucking is essential, sexuality is compulsory. Chastity, non-involvement, celibacy is out. During the years of writing *The Avignon Quintet*, Durrell had met Jolan Chang, a writer on Taoist love mysticism. His meeting with Chang is described in *A Smile in the Mind's Eye* (the title refers to a Chinese ritual). Durrell is cited in the preface to Chang's book on Taoist love mysticism, *The Tao of Love and Sex* (11). Chang's Taoist book of love discusses topics such as sexual positions (on top, from behind, side by side) which are given colourful Chinese names (*Leaping Wild Horses, Mandarin Ducks Entwined, Dark Cicada Clings to a Branch*); the control of ejaculation; types of penile thrusts (six shallow, one deep); old age; impotence; erotic kissing, and so on.

Jolan Chang's book is part 'pillow book', part bedside sex manual, and part poetic evocation of Taoism. 'The true joy of loving is an ecstasy of two bodies and souls mingling and uniting in poetry', writes Chang (37-38), a thought which Durrell would wholly endorse. In amongst the discussions on male and female orgasm, continence, yin and yang and the instructions on sex positions ('[s]he can gyrate in slow motion while her belly and breasts are in close contact with him. Or she can shake in quick, short thrusting motions like a fish caught in a net', says Chang, describing the 'female superior position', with the woman lying flat on the man, [62]), the poetry of erotic Taoism is continually stressed:

Taoism advises one to cultivate better taste, healthy living, and to enjoy

6 Durrell, 'Constrained By History', CVG, xiii-xiv
7 '"We are making the orgasm more and more conscious"', says Akkad in *Monsieur* (142)

earthly or heavenly joys more fully. To the Taoist there are no dividing lines between earthly and heavenly joys: they unite in ecstasy, for in the enjoyment of things natural or artistic, the Taoist is in communion with the Universe (his term for God). (12-13)

Much of Chang's erotic Taoism can be seen in Affad's cult of sex. It's all about cultivating natural rhythms and values, exploiting the body to the full, and wasting nothing. Not a drop of love or sperm must be spilt. Affad has a theory about the importance of oxygen, how it is the 'genetic food of both sperm and ovum' (C, 288), so that good fucking and well-oxygenated sperm and ova make for a good genetic result in the child. The future as embodied in children, in Affad's view of sex magic, is in jeopardy if lovers are not making love fully and tenderly.

The right kind of breathing is important too, and Affad propounds the yoga of breathing, a key element in Oriental mysticism (the breath exercises of yoga also appear in the *Quartet* – in Clea's rebirth, for example). As Affad puts it, we live 'in the space between each breath', so that life is constructed out of a 'chain' of breaths, one breath then another, like one heartbeat then another (S, 88). The rhythm of breathing must be synchronized in sex, so that when an orgasm is shared it is 'reciprocally *breathed*' (S, 149). The aspects of biology, genes and temperament are intimately connected to the quality of lovemaking. Bathed in 'well-documented' sperm, the vagina hums happily, like a cat purring, Affad says. Sperm has to be spiritually rich, otherwise the woman feels starved (C, 302).

There is thus a genetic, physiological and biological foundation to Affad's love magic. The rhythms of the blood, of menstruation, of the body are central. Always wholeness is stressed, a way of loving (of fucking) that includes every part of lovemaking, from eye contact through kissing to caressing and penetration. The energies of sex and orgasm are harnessed and expanded, Affad states, making fucking more and more synchronized and conscious (S, 89). The Oriental form of lovemaking 'uses everything', says Constance (C, 287).

Affad's Oriental sex magic is full of many contradictions and problems. Feminists have shown that a philosophy based on biology becomes essentialist, and falls into the traps of the phallic and ovular theories of identity and gender.8 Constance is in the psychic middle ground between Affad's enthusiastic Oriental metaphysical sex and Schwarz's sceptical European psychoanalysis.

While Affad propounds ecstatic lovemaking, Schwarz keeps his distance, saying that the whole things 'smells of Vedanta!' (C, 290). While Constance enthuses about the new couple who fuck with delicate desire not the old style lust, Schwarz thinks 'here she was getting enthusiastic about contra-puntal fucking or about lying all night kissbound in a honeysuckle sweat' (C, 291). For Schwarz, it seems as if Constance is simply gloating about having some good sex. Durrell's lovers do tend to get like this when they're deep in love, deep in fuck: how smug Clea and Darley are, or Blanford and Constance in *Quinx* (Con and Blan are in 'sweet symbiosis'; they are first loves finally united [Q, 175, 151]). And they take themselves so seriously. '"I loathe high-minded people like ourselves"', says Constance. Affad agrees, replying that '"all this sort of self-caressing sort of talk ruins fucking"' (S, 151). Their critical faculties fade when they're lost in love. They're amazed at their power. Constance has to remind herself, in the midst of fucking Affad, that '[i]t was just beauty and pleasure' (C, 324).

Being smug and self-satisfied is a problem for Durrell's idealistic lovers. After all, Durrell is trying to write about people who are actually *happy*. Yes, that terrifying word, *happy*.9 The lovers enjoy a Tantric union of 'calm sensuality' (S, 153) which is difficult to portray convincingly. Durrell knows that writing about happiness is extremely difficult. Nearly always one sounds like an utter clod. So, he has Schwarz tempering Affad and Constance's love with European scepticism, and to counter Clea and Darley's new found love Balthazar offers a dose of Alexandrian irony.

When they're on their own, though, there is no ironic voice to counter the happiness of Durrell's lovers, and the evocation of loving tenderness is a precarious enterprise. In *Quinx* one hears of Blanford's new-found bliss of being in love: 'how had he not been more conscious of the felicity of loving, the thrilling beauty of sharing?' (Q, 157). But this kind of passionate exaltation of love is extremely difficult to pull off. The narrator of the love affair in *Clea*, who is and is not Darley, admits the inadequacy of metaphor

---

8 'Simply to invoke anatomy risks a return to the crude essentialism, the phallic and ovarian theories of art, that oppressed women in the past', wrote Elaine Showalter ("Feminist Criticism in the Wilderness", in Showalter, ed, 250).

9 'But was there any happiness which was the equal of this? To be blissed-out by the kisses of the correct partner, to make love and fade?' (S, 152)

and language to circumscribe the wonders of being in love. But then he goes to do precisely that: to try and describe the bliss of being in love. The usual metaphors are used: it is Summer, cotton dresses, picnics, swimming, beaches, the island whose 'beauty was spell-binding' (Cl, 195).

The Clea-Darley Summer is a bliss-time of religious intensity, which the narrator compares to the rhythm of tides and water (197). In grappling for comparative metaphors the narrator continually admits to the inarticulacy of language, yet beyond/ above the narrator of *The Alexandria Quartet*, there is Durrell, who knows well that, though inarticulacy is the norm, the writer must write. However much a narrator states that 'words can never compass' the quiet rhythms of blood, sea, sky and sex, they have to, in a book. The metaphors strain, and the word 'heraldic' is forced to carry much of the meaning. Metaphors of clear water, clear mirrors, minds like mirrors, in *Clea*, reinforce the Taoist quietude towards which the *Quartet* has been steadily moving.

The other half of *A Smile in the Mind's Eye* concerns Lawrence Durrell's meetings with the enigmatic and beautiful Martine. They go to the lake in Italy where Nietzsche had his affair with Lou Andreas-Salomé. This quint-essentially European concoction – Nietzsche + Italy + Lou Andreas-Salomé + love + romantic liaisons beside the lake – form the Western counterpoint to the Eastern philosophy outlined by Jolan Chang. These two strands of thought – the Western and the Eastern – form the basis of *A Smile in the Mind's Eye* and *The Avignon Quintet*. In a letter of September, 1971, Durrell writes of going to Como and the Borromean Isles

> to meet a blonde dakini from Périgord who is walled into an ice block in Geneva, and who is coming down tomorrow to meet me by train. The small Wagnerian overtone is appropriate it was *here* at Orta that Nietzsche first told Lou about his plans for Zarathustra – this girl is partly coming for me, partly for the Sacro Monte where this huge momentous intellectual love story took place. (DML, 452)

Affad becomes a thinly-veiled authorial mouthpiece, much as Mellors, like Birkin in *Women in Love*, is the mouthpiece of Lawrence's philo-sophizing. Yet most of the characters in *Lady Chatterley's Lover* speak like Lorenzo: Connie, Clifford, Mrs Bolton, Hilda – all of them spout Lawrencean metaphysics, just as in Durrell's fiction each character in *Lady C* is a splinter of The One, D., the Devil himself – Durrell. The dialogues, as in Durrell's fiction, are often impossible to believe. No one comes out with such stuff, with no pauses and no scripts!

Lady Chatterley's Lover is a passionate plea for love between souls honest enough to open up to each other. 'It is a nice and tender phallic novel', said D.H. Lawrence, 'the last word, in all its meanings! - but very truly moral.'[10] Affad's philosophy of sex is also soft and tender, always emphasizing the mutuality of love, the need for the couple to be in tune with each other. Mellors calls his philosophy 'cunt-awareness', 'cunt-tenderness' (LCL, 256, 290). It is pure sensual contact, the utter touch of love. Connie is asked what it all is by Mellors: "'It's the courage of your own tenderness, that's what it is'" (290). This is a religious, Oriental stance.[11] As with Affad's cult of Oriental sex, Buddha is invoked. Mellors desires 'warm-hearted fucking', while Sutcliffe speaks of 'mercy-fucking'.

Lawrence's language is for many critics the problem with *Lady Chatterley's Lover*. Lawrence's vocabulary is deliberate: to get to the root of the problem, to reclaim the basic words for the body and its ecstatic functions. So there is *cock, cunt* and *fucking*. Lawrence explains it thus:

> ...I want, with *Lady C*, to make an adjustment in consciousness to the basic physical realities. I realize that one of the reasons why common people often keep - or kept - the natural glow of life, just warm life, longer than educated people, was because it was still possible for them to say fuck! or shit without either a shudder or a sensation. If a man had been able to say to you when you were young and in love: an' if tha shits, an' if tha pisses, I' glad, I shouldna want a woman who couldna shit nor piss - surely it would have been a liberation to you, and it would have helped to keep your heart warm.[12]

The revolution Lawrence was aiming for in *Lady Chatterley* is indeed centred around language, and the perception and function of language. Sometimes the attempt comes across as affectation, as when Mellors tries to impress Hilda by mentioning 'cunt an' tenderness' (256), or when Sir Malcolm talks about a 'good bit of fucking' to Mellors in the club, much as Toby and Sutcliffe discuss sex.

The end of *Clea* mirrors the end of *Lady Chatterley's Lover*. In both novels, the old world breaks up, and the protagonists split up, promising to

---

10 H. Moore, 1033, 1046.
11 Durrell, Vincent Gille said, went beyond 'the most legitimate despair' in order to 'set off on a quest for a vaster tenderness'. Richard Aldington bids us value Durrell's tenderness and sense of humanity. (Aldington: "A Note on Lawrence Durrell", W, 7)
12 letter, 28 December 1928, to Lady Ottoline Morrell, Moore, 1111

meet at a later date. In both novels, letters are passed to and fro, crystallizing the new states of mind. Darley leaves for France and a new future,
while the last line Clea says in the *Quartet*, is Lawrencean (and
embarrassingly bad): 'I wait, quite serene and happy, a real human being,
an artist at last' (C, 245). At the end of *Lady C*, Connie achieves fulfilment
and becomes... 'a woman'; in the Durrellian schema, art is necessary to
make life truly fulfilled, so at the end of *Clea*, Clea becomes more than 'a
woman', she becomes... 'an artist at last'. The *Quartet* is about this more
than anything else: the rebirth of two artists, Darley and Clea.[13]

Durrell used to smuggle copies of *Lady Chatterley's Lover* into England,
it was clearly an important book for him. The other two members of
Durrell's Parisian 1930s trinity, Henry Miller and Anaïs Nin, also valued
Lorenzo very highly. Miller wrote one of the better books on Lawrence,
The World of Lawrence: A Passionate Appreciation. Miller tackles the
'great' Lawrencean themes, of love, the universe and the sacred body.
Typically, Miller discusses the role of Friedrich Nietzsche and the
Übermensch in Lawrence's mythology, concerns which were very much
Miller's own. Miller met Frieda Lawrence in California and she told him:
'"[i]f only Lawrence had known you when alive! You would have been the
very friend he was looking for!"' (DML, 192).

Durrell's retort was to place Miller's philosophy above Lawrence's: 'you
would have done Lawrence a world of good: but do you think he would
have been able to know his own master – for after all your work pulverises
Lawrence's philosophy like an eggshell' (DML, 196). Anaïs Nin's book is
humbly entitled *D.H. Lawrence: An Unprofessional Study*. Nin rightly
emphasized the breakthrough Lawrence made in the realm of language and
expression. For Nin, Lawrence was the first writer to really describe how
women feel during love and lovemaking. Nin's own erotica and the
sensuality of her novels, such as *Cities of the Interior, House of Incest* and
Collages, derives from Lawrence's example.

D.H. Lawrence knew that '[f]or England, it is a very shocking novel:
shocking!' (Moore, 1047). He was not bothered by sexual language, he
claims: 'it isn't the names of things that bother me; nor even ideas about
them.' (Huxley, 55) Interestingly, the word *fuck* is introduced not by
Mellors, but by the group of intellectuals that surround Clifford towards
the beginning of *Lady Chatterley's Lover* (35-39). The intellectual

---

13 'The whole business of the four books, apart from other things, shows
the way an artist grows up,' Durrell said (in Young, 62)

conversations of Blanford and Sutcliffe make free with the all-time most censored word, *fuck*. The 'Anglo-Saxon words', as critics used to call *Lady Chatterley's Lover*'s censorable content, are words of power. They are very much the province of masculine power. It is the men that use these words. It is significant, for instance, that in *The Avignon Quintet*, Constance does not use the word. Sabine does use the word ('"We must fuck"' she says to Sutcliffe, as if talking to a child [Q, 82]).

The American anti-pornography feminist Andrea Dworkin was critical of Lawrence's use of four-letter or 'dirty' words. She wrote:

> D.H. Lawrence tried to reinvent the use of so-called obscene words; he believed that the use of sexual euphemism created the dirty connotation of the more direct language… The *phallic reality* he intended was ecstatic, not dirty, a sacrament of fucking, human worship of a pure masculinity and a pure femininity embodied in, respectively, the penis and the cunt (another word favoured by Lawrence). (*Intercourse*, 201-2)

Dworkin's view is that these words can never be redeemed from pornography:

> Dirty words stay dirty because they express a hate for women as inferiors, that hate inextricably, it seems, part of sex – a hate for women's genitals, a hate for women's bodies, a hate for the insides of women in fucking…. Lawrence's *phallic reality* meant *power over*, and his "ordinary, vulgar people" had the same religion. Women stayed dirty because women stayed inferior. (*Intercourse*, 202)

I don't agree anymore with Dworkin's feminist view of language and particular words within language, but Durrell is certainly part the modernist tradition of writers like Lawrence. And you can see something of this power relation in *Constance* and *Lady Chatterley's Lover*, where Mellors wields the 'obscene words' to gain 'power over' Connie. She is subdued by his words, his penis, his aggression, his sexuality. Constance, though, gives Affad back as much as he gives her. She is much more of a feminist than Connie Chatterley. While Connie has no career or profession or preoccupation, she just listlessly waits for love to come, Constance is driven by her interests in psychoanalysis and her social altruism. Constance gives – to her patients, to her friends – she is a do-gooder. She hands out bread to the people emprisoned on one of the trains and gets beaten by the soldiers guarding the train.

In the Affad-Constance erotic encounters, a battle takes place between the two lovers, as they pit their desires against each other. She goes for pleasure, he holds back until their breathing is synchronized, until they are working in unison in accordance with his Eastern yogic views:

> ...she was dying to feel, to prosper and harvest his orgasm, but he hung back, as if reluctant – in fact to sharpen her desire for him. They lay in an agony of impatience with thoughts of loving obedience pouring out between them like some vast waterfall. "Now!" she said. "Wait!" he replied, engrossed mentally in trying to accord their breathing, their very pulse-beat. Already he could sense the rich void of repletion they would enjoy afterwards, lying like drunks in each other's arms, driven to sleep like sheep, into a pen. He turned her lightly towards him and loosed the sails, feeling them draw breath, feeling their craft heel and strain and then gather weight with a shared ecstasy guiding it. She realised that she had never known what love was, what it could be. (C, 269)

Here we find the oceanic metaphors of Lawrence again – sex like a waterfall, sex like a ship. In *Kangaroo* is one of Lawrence's most famous chapters, where marriage is compared to a ship (and an unusual metaphor – lovemaking like sailing!).

The Affad-Constance lovemaking is altogether softer than the 'searing' experiences of Connie in *Lady Chatterley's Lover*.[14] Typical of the Affad-Constance lovemaking is the ship metaphor, the idea of sex as floating, of water, of sex as inducing a dream-state, the post-coital bliss of Tantric sex magic:

> So again that night the bed floated them both out to sea like some precious catafalque. Reality and dream again became coeval, time and space commingled. When sleep came it was deep as death might be. (C, 278)

Constance feels loved all-over, '"from top to toe, not an inch of you free from the honey"' (S, 151). For Constance, the new love she enjoys with Affad is a complete awakening, as with Connie in *Lady Chatterley's Lover*. It does not take a 'night of searing passion' and anal penetration to achieve the transformation, though. Constance's sexual transformation is much gentler than Lawrence's sexual depictions – the dark, fæcal sensuality of Will and Anna in *The Rainbow*, the anal sex of Ursula and Birkin in *Women in Love*, or the clawing, clitoral beak-like sex of Kate and Cipriano in *The Plumed Serpent*. The Constance-Affad lovemaking is more like that

---

14 For some critics, Durrell attained a statement of a cosmic, ecstatic vision of sexuality which Lawrence did not achieve.

envisaged by Rainer Maria Rilke in one of his 'letters to a young poet':

> ...perhaps the sexes are more akin than we suppose, and the great renewal of the world will perhaps consist in this, that man and maiden, freed from all false feelings and perversions, will seek each other not as opposites but as brother and sister, as neighbours, and will unite as human beings to bear in common, simply, seriously and patiently, the heavy sex that has been laid upon them.[15]

Here Rilke voices again the dream of an alchemical unity, the royal union of brother and sister, symbolized in alchemy by the conjunction of sun and moon, silver and gold, King and Queen, etc. In Durrell's mythopoeia, there are references to the holy love between Isis and Osiris (which became the basis of the incestuous relationships of the Ptolemies, Arsinoes and Cleopatras), to Lord Byron and his sister (echoed in Pursewarden and Liza – Pursewarden says he went to Egypt because of 'an interior poetic link with Osiris and Isis, with Ptolemy and Arisinoë', Cl, 167), etc. But it must be a gentle union, he stresses, and also it must occur at the right time. If Constance had met Affad at the beginning of *Livia*, she perhaps would not have been ready for him. Ditto Blanford and Constance, after Affad's death. In a letter to Lou Andreas-Salomé, Rilke writes:

> It is not enough for two people to recognize each other, it is enormously important for them to find each other at the right time and celebrate together deep and quiet festivals in which they can grow together in their desires.[16]

This is precisely, to the letter, Lawrence Durrell's conception of love. His lovers, when the recognition occurs, always hide away: Blanford and Constance go to the Carmargue in secret, Darley and Clea hide themselves, as do Felix and Benedicta.

So often Lawrence Durrell's thought chimes exactly with that of Rilke. As when, for instance, Rilke writes in a letter of April, 1903: 'artistic experience lies so incredibly near to sexual experience, to its pain and its delight, that both phenomena are really only different forms of one and the same yearning and joy'.[17] This is Durrell's main province also, this melding

---

15 Rilke: *Letters to a Young Poet*, tr. Reginald Snell, Sidgwick & Jackson 1945, 23
16 Rilke: *Briefe 1892-1904*, Insel Verlag, Leipzig 1939, 35
17 Rilke: letter to Franz Xaver Kappus, quoted in Eudo Mason: *Rilke*, Oliver & Boyd, 37

of love and art, of people who make art and make love. It is this interface between art and love that Durrell explores, in all his fiction.

For Constance, her 'full femininity' is achieved in the new Affad-inspired love (C, 273). Constance feels glorious because in Affad's yogic system the woman is queen, as in the Goddess worship and Muse poetry of Robert Graves, Peter Redgrove, William Shakespeare, Francesco Petrarch, Dante Alighieri, Edmund Spenser, Robert Herrick, etc. Constance realizes herself as a Goddess figure, though she does not use that language. Her realization, though, is on a cosmic scale. 'To be female was the principle of renewal and repair in the cosmic sense, it was she who made things happen, made things grow.' (C, 273) She becomes the Muse, midwife to the birth of Blanford as an artist, and his long-cherished project, the book

Here Durrell espouses Goddess-orientated philosophy, where women are glorified and positioned centrally in the cosmic scheme of things. The aim is nothing less than the rejuvenation of the universe through the power of love! It's the ultimate in romantic idealism. Of course, Durrell does not state it in those bare terms, but he is not alone in his worshipful view of women. Novalis, for instance, orbited wholly around his beloved Sophia, who died young and is the force that lies behind the magical darkness of Novalis' *Hymns to the Night*.

Rainer Maria Rilke, too, was much involved with women all his life, including the wondrous Lou Andreas-Salomé, who makes an appearance in *The Avignon Quintet*. Francesco Petrarch lived wholly for his beloved Laura, endlessly and exquisitely apostrophized in the *Rime Sparse* (in fact Petrarch has unsubtle misogynist views, expressed outside of the *Canzoniere*). For Dante, the *Rosa Mystica* and the holy of holies, the Godhead, were bound up with Beatrice Portinari.

By the end of *The Avignon Quintet*, the reader is convinced that Durrell's philosophy is inextricably linked to women and women's power. 'Alone the man could no nothing' – the two, man and woman, need each other to achieve fulfilment (C, 268). There is no solitary transcendence in the *Quintet*, but a metaphysics firmly based on the sexual couple. '"Alchemically speaking"', says Affad portentously, '"nothing can be achieved without the woman"' (C, 270).

In one sense, and despite the stereotypes and sexism, *The Avignon Quintet* can be seen as a novel of women's empowerment, where Constance achieves fulfilment. Constance is much less stressed up than the so-called 'New Woman' of the late Victorian novel, for instance. She does not torture herself like Thomas Hardy's Sue Bridehead or D.H. Lawrence's Ursula, Kate or Gudrun. She is, rather, the 'postmodern woman' becoming herself, if there were such a thing as a 'postmodern' person. In "Women of the Mediterranean", Durrell offers his idea of women's empowerment, which he sees as distinctly revolving around notions of sexuality:

> Her struggle, it seems to me, has always been the same one: to break through the pattern of sexual greed and self-indulgence in order to discover herself, to find a magical identification with the earth-rhythms whose slow pulses beat in her blood. (SP, 371)

This is pure Lawrencean philosophizing, and, like Lawrence, Durrell depicts women as Earth Mother, a figure in tune with the Earth. Durrell's reading of 'woman' is the usual one of patriarchy, setting culture against nature, activity against passivity, etc. (For example, he speaks of the 'slow pulses' of blood, a too common portrayal of 'femininity').

The fantastic and cosmically fulfilling sexual love that Constance and Affad and Darley and Clea feel can seem smug, too. At times, it seems as if Lawrence Durrell's lovers are grinning wanly at each other and sighing *'aren't we wonderful?!'* Few things are as vomit-inducing as utterly-in-love lovers, who swoon all over each other at every opportunity. When Darley returns to Alexandria after spending years apart from Clea, within a day or so he's making love with her. There is little courtship: Darley meets Clea in the café in the little square Bab El Fedan and they go on a homecoming tour of Alexandria: Clea take him to see Scobie's shrine, they ride in a gharry, they go to the Auberge and witness Semira making her first public appearance.

This magical day with Clea is written in Durrell's soppiest, most sentimental style. On this day (pages 66 to 86, Part V of *Clea*), everything goes swimmingly well, nothing mars the time the new lovers spend together. It's all too good to be true. And then, at the end of the day, after they've sipped champagne by candlelight in Clea's apartment, of course they fuck. But not it's not brutish or ordinary fucking, oh no, it's sweet, mystical lovemaking, accompanied by rain. The air raid interrupts their coitus, but only to add the glamour of instantaneous death to their orgasms.

How smug and self-satisfied Durrell's lovers can be.[18] Their smugness is justified a little by the horror of the world war around them. As Constance says, speaking of another happy love blossoming amidst the war-torn world (between her and Affad) '"[w]ith so much death in the world surely we have a right to a little love?"' (C, 347). In *Clea*, it all happens too easily. Darley hasn't seen Clea for years, yet they have sex within hours of meeting for the first time. It's not impossible, it's just so easy and unproblematic, in terms of the narrative. No problems with the body, no self-disgust, no worries about contraception, money, other people, etc. They just go at it.

The pontifications on sexuality in the *Quartet* are of the usual post-D.H. Lawrencean type: Darley, Clea, Pursewarden, Justine, and Balthazar all speak in a Lawrencean fashion of sex. If only Durrell's characters hadn't sounded so self-satisfied when they prated of sex, like Clea prattling on about the poetic, noetic, spiritual *rapport* of the 'sex act', talking about the exchange of odours and body-inflected data in sexual communion (Cl, 95-96). Darley pompously pontificates about the trinity of concepts in *Clea*: 'Arnauti, Pursewarden, Darley – like Past, Present and Future tense!' (why the exclamation mark? what is so important about Darley's sentence: 'like Past, Present and Future tense!' that is should have an exclamation mark?) He also speaks of the trio of women who express the mood of 'great verb, Love', Melissa, Justine and Clea (154).

The conceited stance of the lovers in *Clea* continues up until the end of *The Alexandria Quartet*.[19] Only hours after Clea has nearly drowned and had her hand hacked off in the spectacular underwater rebirth sequence, she is pontificating in that stuck-up way of Durrell's lovers. She says, and this is hard to take: 'Yes, Amaril turned me into a woman' (Cl, 222). What *abysmal* dialogue, worse than D.H. Lawrence (the obvious reference point here) at his bathetic worst. But, yes, Clea really does say 'Amaril turned me into a woman', and she means it. She's serious. Yikes. And don't forget the last line of Clea's letter: 'I wait, quite serene and happy, a real human being, an artist at last' (Cl, 245).

---

18 It is odd that Clea calls Darley by his surname, even when they are established as lovers. But this may be part of Durrell's penchant for boarding school/ public school/ board-room etiquette, where pupils/ companions are addressed as 'Philips', or 'Barrett Minor', and teachers are always 'Sir', while co-workers are 'old boy' or 'old chum'.
19 'If there is to be only one right view of love and life, Clea's may well be the most profound, most meaningful, and perhaps closest to that of Durrell himself', remarked Alan Friedman (1970, 73)

Sometimes I think that it's Clea who spouts out the more risible dialogue in *The Alexandria Quartet*, not Pursewarden, Balthazar or Justine. It's Darley who starts off this idiotic strain of dialogue. He comes to the hospital, to visit the woman who's nearly died in a traumatic event, and the first thing he says is, 'It is Amaril you're in love with' (ib.) How pathetic! His concern for her well-being, his delight at seeing her still alive, etc, is nil. He just hacks into the old chestnut of love and adultery. Poor Darley.

Clea muses about the 'New Man', the 'feminized' man, the kind women can identify with: it is Darley, of course, who fulfils Clea's criterion of the 'female' man. The smug, self-satisfied aura of Clea and Darley is expressed also in the quick and too-easy way that Darley becomes a 'real man'. While at the beginning of *Clea* Justine has a minor stroke, stinks of perfume and barks like a hag and Nessim is a lowly ambulance man with a lost eye and finger, Darley is described as no longer having a stoop or wearing spectacles (C, 67). In a flash, Darley is transformed from shy, retiring, academic English wimp to bronzed, relaxed Man of the Earth and superstud. Darley starts to be portrayed as a Mellors figure, self-confident, not caring about social finesse and vanity, a physical man who is in contact with nature. It's all just a little unbelievable.

The novel *Clea* loses some of the bite and passion of the rest of the tetralogy due to the relatively relaxed nature of the self-assured lovers, Clea and Darley. They are characters who could be extraordinary, as Justine could be. With strong personalities such as Narouz, Scobie and Pursewarden dead, *Clea* loses much. It's no surprise that these characters, in particular Scobie and Pursewarden, are continually revived by the surviving characters. The narrator has obviously not finished with them. He continues to squeeze comic anecdotes out of Scobie, and learned sophisms out of Pursewarden.

But with the Cleopatra figure (Justine) out of the way for much of *Clea*, the novel becomes diffuse and low-power. With Justine sidelined, there will be no agony, tragedy, or miracle. Darley, after all, is a tedious and grey character, the archetypal English bespectacled wimp. He is too flabby to produce any sparks. As a mediator between text and reader of the strangeness of Egypt and the glitterati of Alexandria in *Justine* and *Balthazar*, Darley was a suitably awed narrator. As a main character in *Clea*, he is tiresome. Darley's inactivity is quite different from the studied lassitude of Albert Camus' or André Gide's protagonists in *The Outsider* or *The Immoralist*. Darley simply does nothing, really.

When Clea kicks him out of the apartment when she wants some space, all Darley does is go for a walk across Alexandria, where it always seems to be gorgeously sunny, or thrilling in some way or other. Darley's ineffectuality makes his rebirth as a writer at the end of *The Alexandria Quartet* even more unbelievable. This leap into creativity would suggest that all the previous years have been artistic incubation of one form or another, but it isn't convincing. Durrell reveals that he's losing the plot of the second half of *Clea* because he injects some life into it by having those moments of sudden drama and violence, as when Fosca is shot in the harbour, or when Clea's hand is pinioned to the wreck. Henry Miller reckoned *Clea* was too compressed – it was 500 page book, he said, not a 200 page one. The opposite is true, I think: Durrell ran out of things to say; the excitement of writing faded; and he didn't want to 'round off' all the plot strands too obviously. This is not to say there aren't many good elements to *Clea*. There are. Somehow, though, Durrell had done it all by halfway through *Balthazar*.

The two letters plus Balthazar's musings at the end of *Clea* wrap up the plot lines of *The Alexandria Quartet* all too simply. Clea's news to Darley on his island draws to a close the multiple stories of the *Quartet* in crude fashion. All the characters look towards Europe: both Darley and Clea go to France; Mountolive lands a job in Paris; Balthazar visits Venice; Amaril goes to America; Justine and Nessim have secret 'international' operations, to be based in Switzerland. Both Darley and Clea quote Pursewarden, their joint guru, to justify their decisions. Clea in her letter quotes Pursewarden's views on the significance of France/ Paris for the growth of the artist, a view which may come from Friedrich Nietzsche, while Darley recalls Pursewarden's evocation of the 'chthonian world', clearly a version of D.H. Lawrence's 'dark gods' (Darley even mentions that 'the old dark gods are there' [Cl, 239]).

Balthazar is of course the last person that Darley sees in Alexandria, for he is the detached, ironic Cavafy/ Pan/ Tiresias-figure, commenting upon the follies of sex and death in the city of excess. He is the double of Justine in Durrell's notion of the 'bisexual psyche': both Justine and Balthazar remain ardent, desirous but also ironic, self-reflexive questers. It is Balthazar, during that last set-piece, the *mulid* of El Scob (where the old pirate is (ironically) fêted with fireworks by the very sailors who beat him to death), who tells Darley of the last gasps of Alexandria's many love-in-deaths. These final revelations of Balthazar's hinge around letters: Leila getting the fateful letter from Mountolive, and Pursewarden from Liza (Cl, 231). Verily 'the letter killeth'.

Much of the emotional life in Lawrence Durrell's fiction is lived in a state of potential. In Durrell's art, for instance, there are many permutations of sexual relationships possible – and the mature people do not limit themselves to one view of sexual possibility. Constance knows, for example, that women consider a number of 'sexual possibilities, several choices which circumstances might put her way' (C, 82).

At the beginning of Durrell's last novel, *Quinx*, Durrell's lovers enter a new, self-satisfied, visionary phase. They enjoy one of those mini-Paradises that occur throughout literature, a brief time together away from the mob, in the 'little' house in the Camargue. Durrell always uses the word 'little' when things are going well. In *A Smile in the Mind's Eye* he drives in his 'little' car to Switzerland, stays in 'little' hotels, eats in 'little' restaurants.

In their new bliss of love, Blanford and Constance take up the sex magic of Affad and launch it into the future. Blanford's usual sense of irony and English reserve deserts him as he spouts metaphysical gobbledegook: 'The orgasm if shared in this admits you to the realm between death and rebirth... Deal seriously *at last* with human love which is a yogic thought-form, the rudder of the human ship of fools...' (Q, 16) Thus Blanford rants. After popping the rhetorical bubbles of philosophers throughout the *Quincunx*, it's a turnaround to hear Blanford spouting similar hogwash. How fine is the line between great prose and mere mouthing, as Durrell well knows! Occasionally, as he outlines his post-Nietzschean view of the superhuman, transcendent lovers, Blanford pulls himself up short. '"Am I talking rubbish? It's euphoria, then!"' (Q, 16)

Again, the lovers realize that they are just the sort of people they really hate. But this knowledge does not prevent them from going for the Grail, sex-wise and speech-wise. Constance, for example, states that orgasm is a dress rehearsal for death, which is back to the old Sadeian/ Bataillean view of sex and death.[20] Constance, it seems, hasn't got that far beyond Sigmund Freud, although she says she parts company with the psychoanalysts (Otto Rank *et al*) in their notion of birth as a trauma.

Both Blanford and Constance are convinced that reality is 'bliss side up', that humans are 'born into bliss', that, as Sutcliffe puts it, 'Happiness, nay, *Bliss* is innate!' (Q, 153): guilt, sin and fear are invented by other humans

20 In *Tunc* Felix describes sex with Benedicta as 'the whole deathscapade of lovemaking' (137).

and ruin life (Q, 17). On the Fall and sin, Lawrence Durrell says that 'I am a pre-atonement, pre-redemption, and pre-original sin man'.[21] But in their Taoist philosophy love itself is an aberration, something created because of a wrong angle of inclination to the universe. Blanford remains amazed at the woman's power to reawaken him through sex.

21 Durrell, in *Encounter*, December 1959

Postscript

Lawrence Durrell remains a major writer in every respect, although he still hasn't been granted the same status as the major modernists, such as T.S. Eliot, Thomas Mann, James Joyce or D.H. Lawrence. I'd say he's every bit as significant, culturally, as any of the Western modernist writers, and much more inspiring and enriching than some of them.

Bibliography

All books are published in London, England, unless otherwise stated.

Abbreviations appear after each entry

Lawrence Durrell

Justine, Faber 1963 [J]
Balthazar, Faber 1963 [B]
Mountolive, Faber 1963 [Mt]
Clea, Faber 1961 [Cl]
The Alexandria Quartet, Faber 1968/ 83
The Dark Labyrinth, Faber 1964 [DL]
The Black Book, Olympia Press, Paris 1959 [BB]
Monsieur, or The Prince of Darkness, Faber 1974 [M]
Livia, or Buried Alive, Faber 1978 [L]
Constance, or Solitary Practices, Faber 1982 [C]
Sebastian, or Ruling Passions, Faber 1983 [S]
Quinx, or The Ripper's Tale, Faber 1985 [Q]
Tunc, Faber 1968 [T]
Nunquam, Faber 1970 [N]
A Smile in the Mind's Eye, Wildwood House, 1980 [SME]
Spirit of Place, Faber 1971 [SP]
Blue Thirst, Capra Press, California 1975 [BT]
Collected Poems 1931-1974, ed. James A. Brigham, Faber 1980 [CP]
The Ikons, Dutton, New York 1967
Selected Poems, Faber 1956
Selected Poems 1935-1963, Faber 1964/ 72
The Red Limbo Lingo: A Poetry Notebook, Faber 1971
Cities, Plains, People, Faber 1946
A Private Country, Faber 1943
On Seeming to Presume, Faber 1948
A Landmark Gone, Reuben Pearson, Los Angeles 1949
The Tree of Idleness, Faber 1955
Prospero's Cell, Faber 1962 [Cell]

Reflections on a Marine Venus, Faber 1960 [RMV]
Bitter Lemons, Faber 1963 [BL]
The Greek Islands, Faber 1978 [GI]
Sicilian Carousel, Faber 1974 [SC]
Caesar's Vast Ghost: Aspects of Provence, Faber 1990 [CVG]
Sappho: A play in verse, Faber 1967
An Irish Faustus, Faber 1963
Acte, Faber 1965
Pope Joan, tr. Durrell, Faber 1971 [PJ]
Antrobus Complete, Faber 1985 [AC]
White Eagles Over Serbia, Faber, 1957
Pied Piper of Lovers, Cassell 1935
Panic Spring, Faber 1937
Key to Modern Poetry, Peter Nevill 1952 [K]
"The Paintings of Henry Miller", Foreword to Henry Miller's *Paint As You Like and Die Happy*
The Big Supposer, ed. Marc Alyn, Grove Press, New York 1974 [BS]
& Robin Fedden, eds: *Personal Landscape: An Anthology of Exile*, Editions Poetry, 1945
"From a Writer's Journal", *The Windmill*, 11, 1947 [FWJ]
"From the Elephant's Back", *Poetry London/ Apple Magazine*, no. 2, 1982 [FEB]
"No Clue to Living", *Times Literary Supplement*, 27 May 1960
interview in Malcolm Cowley, ed: *Writers At Work: The 'Paris Review' Interviews*, 2nd series, Secker & Warburg 1963
"Lawrence Durrell Answers a Few Questions", *Two Cities*, 1959 [TC]
"The Kneller Tape", in *The World of Lawrence Durrell* [KT]
"Les Vies Singulières de Lawrence Durrell", *Les nouvelles Littéraires*, no. 269, April 1978
interview, in "Three Famous Writers Comment of the Anxieties of Our Time: François Mauriac, Jean Giono, and Lawrence Durrell", *Realities*, 120, 1960
interview, in Huw Wheldon, ed: *Monitor: An Anthology*, Macdonald 1962 [Mon]
"Entretien avec Lawrence Durrell", *Construire*, no. 4, January 1985
interview with Piero Sanavio, *La Stampa*, and in *World Press Review*, November 1983
"The Poetic Obsession of Dublin", *Travel and Leisure*, Autumn 1972
"From a Winter Journal", *Penguin New Writing*, no. 32, ed. J. Lehmann, Penguin 1947
Foreword to Jacques Lacarrière, *The Gnostics*
Paul Hogarth: *The Mediterranean Shore: Travels in Lawrence Durrell Country*, introduction & commentary by Durrell, Pavilion/ Michael Joseph 1988 [Med]
Literary Lifelines: The Richard Aldington-Lawrence Durrell Correspondence, ed. Ian S. MacNiven & Harry T. Moore, Faber 1981 [Ald]
Letters to Jean Fanchette, 1958-1963, ed. Jean Fanchette, Editions Two Cities, Paris 1988 [LJF]
The Lawrence Durrell Papers at Southern Illinois University Carbon-

dale Exhibit and Catalog, Carbondale 1988
Durrell archive at Southern Illinois University, Carbondale [Ill]
Durrell archive at the Centre d'Etudes et de Recherches Lawrence Durrell
at Sommières [Som]

with Henry Miller:

Lawrence Durrell and Henry Miller: A Private Correspondence, ed.
George Wickes, Dutton, New York 1963 [PC]
The Durrell-Miller Letters 1935-80, ed. Ian MacNiven, Faber 1988 [DML]
Art and Outrage, Dutton, New York 1960
*Art and Outrage: A Correspondence About Henry Miller, Perlès and
Durrell*, Village Press 1973 [AO]

Others

Robert Martin Adams: *After Joyce*, Oxford University Press, New York 1977

John Alcorn: *The Nature Novel from Hardy to Lawrence*, Macmillan 1973

Richard Aldington: *Portrait of a Genius, But...*, Reader's Union/ Heinemann 1951

Alithersis: *Cavafy*, Alexandria 1934

Walter Allen: *Tradition and English and American Novel From the Romantics to Our Time*, Phoenix House 1964

William Amos: *The Originals: Who's Really Who in Fiction*, Cape 1985

Gene Andrewski & Julian Mitchell: "Lawrence Durrell: The Art of Fiction XXIII: An Interview with Lawrence Durrell", *Paris Review*, 22, Winter 1959-60, 32-61

Harry T. Antrim & Eugene Lyons: "An Interview with Lawrence Durrell", *Shenandoah*, 2, Winter 1971, 42-58

Isobel Armstrong, ed: *New Feminist Discourses: Critical Essays on Theories and Texts,* Routledge 1992

Alison Assister & Avedon Carol, eds: *Bad Girls and Dirty Pictures: The Challenge to Reclaim Feminism*, Pluto Press 1993:

John Atkins: *Sex in Literature: the erotic impulse in literature*, Panther 1972

Peter Balbert: "The Loving of Lady Chatterley: D.H. Lawrence and the Phallic Imagination", in Partlow & Moore, eds, 143-158

—. and Philip L.Marcus, eds: *D.H. Lawrence: A Centenary Consideration,* Cornell University Press, Ithaca, New York 1985

S. Barker, ed. *Signs of Change: Premodern - Modern - Postmodern*, State University of New York Press, Albany, NY, 1996

Willis Barnstone, ed: *Greek Lyric Poetry*, Schocken Books, New York 1972

—. & Aliki Barnstone, eds: *A Book of Women Poets: From Antiquity to Now*, Schocken Books, New York 1980

Georges Bataille: *Literature and Evil*, tr. Alistair Hamilton, Calder 1973

Annette Kar Baxter: *Henry Miller, Expatriate*, University of Pittsburgh Press 1961

Michael Begnal, ed: *On Miracle Ground: Essays on the Fiction of Lawrence Durrell,* Associated University Presses 1990

—. "Lawrence Durrell", *Dictionary of Literary Biography*, 15, Bruccoli, Clark, Detroit 1983, 87-97

Catherine Belsey: *Critical Practice*, Routledge 1980

Bernard Bergonzi: *Gemini*, 1, no.1, Spring 1957, 26-27

Leo Bersani: *A Future For Astynanax*, Marion Boyars 1978

Michael Black: *D.H. Lawrence: The Early Fiction*, Macmillan 1986

Haskell M. Bloch & Herman Salinger, eds. *The Creative Vision: Modern European Writers*, Grove Press, New York 1960

Frances Bonner *et al*, eds: *Imagining Women Cultural Representations and Gender*, Polity Press, Cambridge 1992

F. Botting. *Gothic*, Routledge, London, 1996

—. *Sex, Machines and Navels: Fiction, Fantasy and History in the*

Future Present, Manchester University Press, Manchester, 1999

Jan Bremmer, ed: *From Sappho to de Sade: Moments in the History of Sexuality*, Routledge 1989

Jennifer L. Brewer: "Character and Psychological Place: The Justine/ Sophia Relation", *Deus Loci*, 5, Autumn 1981

James Brigham & Ian MacNiven, eds: *Deus Loci*, 1977-81

Derek Britton: *Lady Chatterley: The Making of the Novel*, Unwin Hyman 1988

P. Brooker, ed. *Modernism/ Postmodernism*, Longman 1992

—. & W. Brooker. *Postmodern After Image*, Arnold, London, 1997

Alan Brown, ed: *Festival in World Religions*, Longman 1986

J.D. Brown: *Henry Miller,* Ungar, New York 1986

Keith Brown, ed.: *Rethinking Lawrence*, Open University Press, Milton Keynes 1990

—. "Up to the Pisgah-sign", *Times Literary Supplement*, 31 May 1985

—. "Lawrence Durrell", in Scott-Kilvert, 1987

Sharon Lee Brown: "*The Black Book*: A Search For Method", *Modern Fiction Studies*, 13, Autumn 1967, 319-28

Sir Thomas Browne: *Religio Medici and Other Writings*, Dent 1906

Martin Buber: *I and Thou*, tr. Walter Kaufmann, T & T Clark, Edinburgh 1971

B. Buford, ed: *Granta*, no. 37, Autumn 1991

Christopher Burns: "Durrell's Heraldic Universe", *Modern Fiction Studies*, 13, Autumn 1969, 375-88

Anthony Burgess: *The Novel Now: A Student's Guide to Contemporary Fiction*, Faber 1971

J. Butler. *Subjects of Desire: Hegelian Reflections in 20th Century France*, Columbia University Press, New York, NY, 1999

— . *Antigone's Claim: Kinship Between Life and Death*, Columbia University Press, New York, NY, 2002

Deborah Cameron, ed: *The Feminist Critique of Language: A Reader*, Routledge 1990

Joseph Campbell: *The Power of Myth, with Bill Moyers*, ed. Betty Sue Flowers, Doubleday, New York 1988

James Van Dyck Card: "'Tell Me, Tell Me': The Writer as Spellbinder in Lawrence Durrell's *The Alexandria Quartet*", *Modern British Literature*, 1, 1976, 74-83

James P. Carley: "Lawrence Durrell and the Gnostics", *Deus Loci*, 2, September 1978, 3-10

—. "Lawrence Durrell's Avignon Quincunx and Gnostic Heresy", *Deus Loci*, 5, Autumn 1981, 284-304

—. "An Interview with Lawrence Durrell on the Background to *Monsieur* and Its Sequels", *Malahat Review*, 51, 1979, 42-46

Michael Cartwright, ed: *On Miracle Ground: Proceedings From the First National Lawrence Durrell Conference/ Deus Loci: The Lawrence Durrell Newsletter,* vol. V, no.1, Autumn 1981

C.P. Cavafy: *Collected Poems*, tr. Edmund Keeley & Philip Sherrard, Princeton University Press, New Jersey 1983

—. *The Complete Poems*, tr. Rae Dalven, Hogarth Press 1968

Jolan Chang: *The Tao of Love and Sex: The Ancient Chinese Way to Ecstasy*, Wildwood House 1977

R.T. Chapman: "'Dead or Just Pretending?'": Reality in *The Alexandria Quartet*", *Centennial Review*, 4, Autumn 1972, 408-18

Maurice Charney: *Sexual Fiction*, Methuen 1981

Gail Chester & Julienne Dickey, ed: *Feminism and Censorship: The Current Debate*, Prism Press, Bridport, Dorset 1988

Laura Chester, ed: *Deep Down: New Sensual Writing By Women*, 1987

Peter Christensen: "An Over Enthusiastic Response: Lawrence Durrell's Interpretation of Georg Groddeck", unpublished paper, 1990 [Lawrence Durrell Conference]

Susan Vander Closter: *Joyce Cary and Lawrence Durrell: A Reference Guide*, G.K. Hall, Boston 1985

John Coleman: "Mr Durrell's Dimensions", *Spectator*, 19 February 1960, 256-7

Edward Conze: *Buddhist Scriptures*, Penguin 1959

J.C. Cooper: *Yin and Yang: The Taoist Harmony of Opposites*, Aquarian Press 1981

Shelley Cox: *The Lawrence Durrell Papers at Southern Illinois University at Carbondale*, Southern Illinois University at Carbondale 1988

Walter G. Creed: "'The Whole Pointless Joke?': Darley's Search for Truth in *The Alexandria Quartet*", *Etudes-Anglaises*, 27, June 1975, 165-73

Mary Daly: *Pure Lust: Elemental Feminist Philosophy*, Women's Press 1984

—. *Beyond God the Father*, Women's Press 1985

—. *Gyn/Ecology: The Metaethics of Radical Feminism*, Women's Press, 1979

H. Dare: "The Quest for Durrell's Scobie", *Modern Fiction Studies*, 10, Winter 1964-5, 379-83

Reed W. Dasenbrock: "Death and the Counterlife of Heresy in Wyndham Lewis and Lawrence Durrell", *Deus Loci*, 4, Sept 1980, 3-18

Donald Davie: *Thomas Hardy and British Poetry*, Routledge & Kegan Paul 1979

Roland Decanq: "What Lies Beyond? An Analysis of Darley's 'Quest' in Lawrence Durrell's *The Alexandria Quarte*", *Revue des Langues vivantes*, 34, 1968, 134-150

Gaeton Delaforge: *The Templar Tradition in the Age of Aquarius*, Threshold Books, Putney, Vermont 1987

Gregory Dickson: "Spengler's Theory of Architecture in Durrell's *Tunc* and *Nunquam*", *Deus Loci*, Autumn 1981, 272-84

Jonathan Dollimore & Alan Sinfield, eds: *Political Shakespeare*, Manchester University Press 1985

John Drakakis, ed; *Alternative Shakespeares*, Routledge 1988

Gerald Durrell: *My Family and Other Animals*, Penguin 1959

—. *The Garden of the Gods*, Collins 1978

Sappho Durrell: "Journals and Letters", in Buford

Andrea Dworkin: *Intercourse*, Arrow 1988

—. *Letters From a War Zone: Writings 1976-1987*, Secker & Warburg, 1988

—. *Pornography: Men Possessing Women,* Women's Press 1984

Allen Edwards: *The Jewel in the Lotus: A Historical Survey of the Sexual Culture in the East,* Tandem 1969

Mary Eagleton, ed: *Feminist Literary Criticism,* Longman 1991

—. ed: *Feminist Literary Theory: A Reader,* Blackwell 1986

Mircea Eliade: *Ordeal by Labyrinth,* University of Chicago Press 1984

—. *Autobiography: Volume I: 1907-1937, Journey East, Journey West, tr.* MacWinscott Ricketts, Harper & Row, San Francisco 1981

—. *A History of Religious Ideas,* I, Collins 1979

—. *Yoga: Immortality and Freedom,* tr. Trask, Princeton University Press, New Jersey 1969

R. Ellwood. *The Politics of Myth: A Study of C.G. Jung, Mircea Eliade and Joseph Campbell,* State University of New York Press, Albany, NY, 1999

D.J. Enright: *Conspirators and Poets,* Chatto & Windus 1966

Stanley Eskin: "Durrell's Themes in *The Alexandria Quartet*", *Texas Quarterly,* 5, Winter 1962, 43-60

Julius Evola: *The Metaphysics of Sex,* East-West Publications 1985

John Ferguson: *An Illustrated Encyclopaedia of Mysticism,* Thames & Hudson 1976

Robert Ferguson: *Henry Miller: A Life,* Hutchinson 1991

Noël Riley Fitch: *Anaïs: The Erotic Life of Anaïs Nin,* Little, Brown, New York 1993

John Fletcher & Andrew Benjamin, ed: *Abjection, Melancholia and Love: the Work of Julia Kristeva,* Routledge 1990

Boris Ford, ed. *The New Pelican Guide to English Literature,* Penguin, 1984

E.M. Forster: *Aspects of the Novel,* Penguin 1974

—. *Alexandria: A History and a Guide,* Michael Haag 1986

Michel Foucault: *The History of Sexuality,* Penguin 1981

—. *The Use of Pleasure: The History of Sexuality,* vol. 2, Penguin 1987

G.S. Fraser: *Lawrence Durrell: A Study,* Faber 1968/ 73

—. *Lawrence Durrell,* Longman/ British Council 1970

—. *The Modern Writer and His World,* Penguin 1964

Sigmund Freud: *Standard Edition of the Complete Psychological Works of Sigmund Freud,* 24 vols, ed. James Strachey, Hogarth Press 1953-74

—. *Five Lectures on Psychoanalysis, Leonardo da Vinci, and Other Works, ed.* James Strachey, Hogarth Press 1971

—. *The Interpretation of Dreams,* tr. James Strachey, Penguin

Alan Friedman: *The Turn of the Novel,* Oxford University Press 1966

—. *Lawrence Durrell and The Alexandria Quartet: Art For Love's Sake,* University of Oklahoma Press, Norman 1970

—. ed: *Critical Essays on Lawrence Durrell,* G.K. Hall & Co, Boston 1987

Jennifer Linton Fruin: "The Importance of Narouz in Durrell's Hermetic Paradigm", *Deus Loci,* 2, no. 6, June 1979

H.R. Gibb: *Mohammedism,* Oxford University Press 1953

Pamela Church Gibson & Roma Gibson, ed: *Dirty Looks: Women, Pornography, Power,* British Film Institute 1993

R. Giddings *et al. Screening the Novel: The Theory and Practice of Literary Dramatisation,* Macmillan, London, 1990

—. & E. Sheen, eds. *The Classic Novel From Page to Screen,* Manchester University Press, Manchester, 2000

André Gide: *The Immoralist,* tr. Dorothy Bussy, Penguin 1960

—. *Et nunc manet in te* and *Intimate Journal,* tr. Justin O'Brien, Secker & Warburg 1952

—. *Journals 1889-1949,* ed. & tr. Justin O'Brien, Penguin 1967

—. *The Counterfeiters,* tr. Dorothy Bussy, Penguin, 1966

—. *Logbook of The Coiners,* tr. Justin O'Brien, Cassell 1952

—. *Paludes,* Secker & Warburg 1953

William Godshalk: "Some Sources of Durrell's *The Alexandria Quartet*", *Modern Fiction Studies,* 13, Autumn 1967, 316-74

Jocelyn Godwin, ed: *Music, Mysticism and Magic: A Sourcebook,* Routledge 1987

Eugene Goodheart: *Desire and Its Discontents,* Columbia University Press, New York 1991

W.A. Gordon: *The Mind and Art of Henry Miller,* London 1968

Ann Gossman: "Love's Alchemy in *The Alexandria Quartet*", *Critique,* 13, 1971-2, 83-96

Joan Goulianos: "A Conversation with Lawrence Durrell About Art, Analysis, and Politics", *Modern Fiction Studies,* 17, Autumn 1971, 159-166

—. "Lawrence Durrell and Alexandria", *Virginia Quarterly Review,* 45, 1969

Robert Graves: *The White Goddess,* Faber 1961

—. *Mammon and the Black Goddess,* Cassell 1965

Georg Groddeck: *The Meaning of Illness,* tr. Mander, ed. Schacht, Hogarth Press 1977

—. *The Book of It,* Vision Press 1950

Michael Haag: *Egypt,* Cadogan 1993

—. *Alexandria: City of Durrell, Forster and Cavafy,* I.B. Tauris, 2000

John Hagopian: "The Resolution of *The Alexandria Quartet*", *Critique,* 7, 1961, 97-106

F.C. Happold, ed. *Mysticism,* Penguin 1970

L. Hart. *Fatal Women: Lesbian Sexuality and the Mark of Aggression,* Princeton University Press, Princeton, NJ, 1994

—. *Between the Body and the Flesh: Performing Sadomasochism,* Columbia University Press, New York, NY, 1998

Ihab Hassan: *The Literature of Silence: Henry Miller and Samuel Beckett,* Knopf, New York 1967

Tiger Tim Hawkins: *The Common Muse of Henry Miller and Lawrence Durrell,* Ahab Press, San Francisco 1963

Stephen Hazell, ed. *The English Novel,* Macmillan 1978

Carolyn Heilbrun: *Towards a Recognition of Androgyny,* Harper & Row, New York, NY, 1974

Werner Heisenberg: *Physics and Philosophy The Revolution in Modern Science,* Harper & Row, New York 1958

Christopher Heywood, ed: *D.H. Lawrence: New Studies,* Macmillan 1987

Sarah Lucia Hoagland & Julia Penelope, eds: *For Lesbians Only: A separatist anthology,* Onlywomen Press 1988

Eleanor N. Hutchens: "The Heraldic Universe in *The Alexandria Quartet*", *College English*, 24, 1962, 56-61

E.R. Hutchison: *'Tropic of Cancer' on Trial: A Case History of Censorship*, Grove, New York 1968

Luce Irigaray: *The Irigaray Reader, ed.* Margaret Whitford, Blackwell, Oxford 1991

—. *Je, tu, nous: Toward a Culture of Difference*, tr. Alison Martin, Routledge 1993

Hartwig Isernhagen: *Sensation, Vision, and Imagination: The Problems of Unity in Lawrence Durrell's Novels*, inaugural dissertation, Bamberger Fotodruck, Bamberg 1969

F. Jameson. *Signatures of the Visible*, Routledge, New York, NY, 1990

—. *Postmodernism, or the Cultural Logic of Late Capitalism*, Verso, London, 1991

—. & M. Miyoshi, eds. *Cultures of Globalization*, Duke University Press, Duham, NC, 1998

C.G. Jung: *Memories, Dreams, Reflections*, Collins 1967

—. *Mysterium Coniunctionis*, Routledge & Kegan Paul 1955

—. *Psychology and Religion: West and East*, tr. R. Hull, Routledge & Kegan Paul 1981

Charles H. Kahn: *The Art and Thought of Heraclitus*, Cambridge University Press, New York 1979

Frederick Karl: *A Reader's Guide to the Contemporary English Novel*, Thames & Hudson 1972

Walter Kaufmann: *Nietzsche: Philosopher, Psychologist, Antichrist*, Princeton University Press, New Jersey 1968

Alfred Kazin: "Lawrence Durrell's Rosy-finger'd Egypt", in *Contemporaries*, Little, Brown, Boston 1962

Edmund Keeley: "Lawrence Durrell and Modern Philhellenism", unpublished MS, Princeton University, New Jersey 1988

—. *Cavafy's Alexandria: Study of a Myth in Progress*, Hogarth Press, 1977

—. & Philip Sherrard, eds: *The Dark Crystal: An Anthology of Modern Greek Poetry by Cavafy, Sikelianos, Seferis, Elytis, Gatsos,* Denise Harvey & Co, Athens 1981

Steve Kellman: *The Self-Begetting Novel*, Columbia University Press, 1980

Frank Kersnowski, ed: *Into the Labyrinth: Essays on the Art of Lawrence Durrell*, UMI Research Press, University Microfilms Inc, Ann Arbor, Michigan 1989

—. "Paradox and Resolution in Durrell's *Tunc* and *Nunquam*:, *Deus Loci*, 7, September 1983, 1-13

M. Kinkead-Weekes. *D.H. Lawrence: Triumph to Exile, 1912-1922*, Cambridge University Press, Cambridge, 1996

Bettina L. Knapp: *Anaïs Nin,* Frederick Ungar Publishing, New York 1978

G.Wilson Knight: *Neglected Powers,* Routledge & Kegan Paul 1972

Kendra Kopelke, ed: *Passager*, Lawrence Durrell number, no. 5, Spring 1991

Cheris Kramarae & Paula A. Treichler, eds. *A Feminist Dictionary*, Pandora Press, 1987

Julia Kristeva: *The Kristeva Reader*, ed. Toril Moi, Blackwell 1986

—. *Desire in Language: A Semiotic Approach to Literature and Art*, ed. Leon Roudiez, tr. Thomas Gora, Alice Jardine & Leon Roudiez, Blackwell 1982

—. "Interview with Julia Kristeva", tr. Margaret Waller, *Partisan Review*, no. 51, Winter 1984

—. *Tales of Love*, tr. Leon S. Roudiez, Columbia University Press, New York 1987

—. *Powers of Horror: An Essay on Abjection*, tr. Leon S. Roudiez, Columbia University Press, New York 1982

Joseph E. Kruppa: "Durrell's *The Alexandria Quartet* and the 'Implosion of the Modern Consciousness", *Modern Fiction Studies*, 13, Autumn 1967, 401-16

Weston La Barre: *The Ghost Dance*, Allen & Unwin 1972

—. *Muelos*, Columbia University Press, New York 1985

Jacques Lacan and the Ecole Freudienne : *Feminine Sexuality*, ed. Juliet Mitchell and Jacqueline Rose, Macmillan 1988

Jacques Lacarrière: *The Gnostics*, City Lights, San Francisco 1989

D. H. Lawrence: *Phoenix: The Posthumous Papers,* ed. Edward Mac-donald, Heinemann 1956

—. *Phoenix II: Uncollected, Unpublished and Other Prose Works*, eds. Warren Roberts & Harry T. Moore, Heinemann 1968

—. *A Selection from Phoenix,* ed. A.A.H. Inglis, Penguin 1971

—. *Study of Thomas Hardy and Other Essays,* ed. Bruce Steele, Cambridge University Press 1985

—. *The Rainbow*, ed. John Worthen, Penguin 1981/6

—. *The Complete Short Novels*, ed. Keith Sagar & Melissa Partridge, Penguin 1982/7

—. *Lady Chatterley's Lover*, Penguin 1960

—. *Women in Love*, ed. Charles L. Ross, Penguin 1982/6

—. *The Complete Poems*, ed. Vivian de Sola Pinto & Warren Roberts, 2 vols, Heinemann 1972

—. *The Collected Letters of D.H. Lawrence*, ed. Harry T. Moore, 2 vols, Heinemann 1962

—. *The Letters of D.H. Lawrence*, ed. Aldous Huxley, Heinemann 1934

—. *Selected Essays*, Penguin 1950

—. *Fantasia of the Unconscious and Psychoanalysis of the Unconscious,* Heinemann 1961

Patrick Leigh-Fermour: "The Landmarks of Decline", *Times Literary Supplement*, October 1977

Carolyn Ruth Swift Lenz, Gayle Greene & Carol Thomas Neely, eds: *The Woman's Part: Feminist Criticism of Shakespeare*, University of Illinois Press, Urbana 1980

Morton P. Levitt: "Art and Correspondence: Durrell, Miller, and *The Alexandria Quarte*", *Modern Fiction Studies*, 13, Autumn 1969, 299-318

Robert Liddell: *Cavafy: a critical biography*, Duckworth 1974

—. *Conspirators and Poets*, Chatto & Windus 1966

David Lodge: *Language of Fiction*, Routledge & Kegan Paul 1966

Paul H. Lorenz: "Quantum Mechanics and the Shape of Fiction: "Non-

Locality" in *The Avignon Quintet*, unpublished paper, 1990 [Lawrence Durrell Conference]

Sheila Macleod: *Lawrence's Men and Women*, Heinemann 1985

Ian MacNiven & Carol Pierce, eds: *Twentieth Century Literature: Lawrence Durrell Issue, I & II*, vol. 33, nos. 3 & 4, Hofstra University, New York 1987

—. "The Quincunx Quiddified: Structure in Lawrence Durrell", in MacNiven & Gamache 1987, 215-38

—. ed: *Deus Loci: The Lawrence Durrell Journal*, 1992

—. & Lawrence B. Gamache, eds: *The Modernists*, Fairleigh Dickinson University Press, Rutherford, New Jersey 1987

—. *A Descriptive Catalogue of the Lawrence Durrell Collection at Southern Illinois University*, Carbondale 1975

Susan MacNiven, ed: *The Lawrence Durrell Society Herald,* State University of New York, various issues, 1984-94

Norman Mailer: *The Prisoner of Sex*, New American Library/ Signet 1971

—. *Genius and Lust: A Journey Through the Major Writings of Henry Miller*, Grove Press, New York 1976

Siegfried Mandel: "In Search of the Senses", *Saturday Review*, 40, 21 Sept 1957

C. Manlove. *The Fantasy Literature of England*, Macmillan, London, 1999

Herbert Marcuse: *Eros and Civilization*, Sphere 1969

Lawrence W. Markert: "Symbolic Geography: D.H. Lawrence and Lawrence Durrell", *Deus Loci*, 5, no.1, 1981, 90-101

—. & Carol Pierce, eds: *On Miracle Ground II: Second International Lawrence Durrell Conference Proceedings, Deus Loci, The Lawrence Durrell Quarterly*, vol. 7, no. 5, 1984

Elaine Marks & Isabelle de Courtivron, eds: *New French Feminisms: an Anthology*, Harvester Wheatsheaf 1981

Jay Martin: *Always Merry and Bright: The Life of Henry Miller*, Capra, Santa Barbara, Calif. 1978

John Matthews & Graham Barrasford, eds: *Labrys: Lawrence Durrell*, 5, 1979

Keith M. May: *Nietzsche and Modern Literature: Themes in Yeats, Rilke, Mann and Lawrence*, Macmillan 1988

L. McCaffery, ed. *Storming the Reality Studio: A Casebook of Cyberpunk and Postmodern Fiction*, Duke University Press, Durham, NC, 1991

U. Meinhof & J. Smith, eds. *Intertextuality and the Media*, Manchester University Press, Manchester, 2000

Patricia Merivale: *Pan the Goat-God: His Myth in Modern Times*, Harvard University Press, Mass., 1969

Jeffrey Meyers, ed: *The Legacy of D.H. Lawrence: New Essays*, Macmillan 1987

—. ed: *D.H. Lawrence and Tradition*, Athlone Press 1985

Henry Miller: *A Henry Miller Reader*, ed. John Calder, Picador 1985 [HMR]

—. *Tropic of Cancer*, Calder 1963

—. *Black Spring*, Panther/ Granada 1974

—. *Tropic of Capricorn*, Calder 1964

—. *Sexus*, Calder & Boyars 1969

—. *Nexus*, Granada 1966

—. *Plexus*, Granada 1965

—. *The Air-Conditioned Nightmare*, Panther 1965

—. *The Cosmological Eye*, New Directions, New York 1961

—. *The Time of the Assassins: A Study of Rimbaud*, New Directions, New York 1962 [TA]

—. *The Colossus of Marousi*, Penguin 1950

—. *The World of Lawrence: A Passionate Appreciation*, ed. Evelyn J. Hinz & John J.Teunissen, Calder 1985

—. *Max and the White Phagoytes*, Obelisk 1938

—. *Aller Retour New York,* Obelisk 1935

—. *Sunday After the War,* New Directions, 1944

—. *The Wisdom of the Heart,* New Directions, 1941

—. *Remember to Remember,* New Directions, 1947

—. *The Books in My Life*, Peter Owen 1952

—. *My Life and Times*, Pall Mall Press 1972 [LT]

—. *Big Sur and the Oranges of Hieronymous Bosch*, New Directions, 1959

—. *Stand Still Like the Hummingbird*, New Directions, 1962

—. *Henry Miller on Writing*, ed. H. Moore, New Directions, 1964

—. *Henry Miller's Book of Friends*, Capra, Santa Barbara 1976

—. *Paint As You Like and Die Happy: The Paintings of Henry Miller*, ed. Noel Young, Chronicle Books, San Francisco 1982 [PHM]

—. *Letters to Anaïs Nin*, I, 1931-40, ed. Gunther Stuhlman, Village Press 1965

—. *The Letters of Henry Miller and Wallace Fowlie 1943-72*, Grove Press, New York 1975

—. "A Boost for *The Black Book*", *Booster*, 2, no. 8

Kate Millett: *Sexual Politics*, Doubleday, Garden City 1970

Colin Milton: *Lawrence and Nietzsche: A Study in Influence,* Aberdeen University Press 1987

Edward Mitchell: *Henry Miller: Three Decades of Criticism*, New York University, 1971

Toril Moi: *Sexual/ Textual Politics: Feminist Literary Theory,* Routledge 1988

—. ed: *French Feminist Thought*, Blackwell 1988

Jean Montalbetti: "Entretien: Lawrence Durrell en Dix Mouvements", *Magazine Littéraire*, Sept 1984

Harry T. Moore, ed: *The World of Lawrence Durrell*, Southern Illinois University Press 1962

Robert K. Morris: *Continuance and Change: The Contemporary British Novel Sequence*, Southern Illinois University Press 1972

John Mortimer: "Comus, Durrell, Wain and Kavan", *Encounter*, 57, 1958

M. Mulvey-Roberts, ed. *The Handbook of Gothic Literature,* New York University Press, New York, NY, 1998

Sally Munt, ed: *New Lesbian Criticism: Literary and Cultural Readings*, Harvester Wheatsheaf 1992

Jane Nelson: *Form and Image in the Fiction of Henry Miller*, Detroit 1970

Erich Neumann: *The Great Mother,* Princeton University Press, New Jersey 1972

Shirley Nicholson, ed. *The Goddess Re-awakening,* Theosophical Publishing House, New York 1989

Friedrich Nietzsche: *Beyond Good and Evil,* tr. H. Zimmern, Allen & Unwin 1907/67

—. *A Nietzsche Reader,* ed. R.J. Hollingdale, Penguin 1977

Anaïs Nin: *The Novel of the Future,* Collier/ Macmillan, New York 1970

—. *D.H. Lawrence: An Unprofessional Study,* Black Spring 1985

—. *Journals,* volumes 1-6, Quartet 1974-9

—. *Journal,* volume 7, Peter Owen 1980

—. *In Favour of the Sensitive Man,* Star/ Allen 1981

—. *A Woman Speaks,* ed. E. Hinz, Star/ Allen 1978/ 82

—. *Cities of the Interior,* Peter Owen 1978

—. *Collages,* Quartet 1979

—. *Delta of Venus,* Star/ Allen 1978/ 81

—. *Henry and June,* ed. Rupert Pole, W.H. Allen 1987

—. *A Literature Passion: Letters of Anaïs Nin and Henry Miller* 1932-1953, Allison & Busby 1992

Carol Nixon: *Lawrence's Leadership Politics and the Turn Against Women,* University of California Press, Berkeley 1986

Wendy O'Flaherty: *Women, Androgynes, and Other Mythical Beasts,* University of Chicago Press, Chicago 1980

Joan O'Grady: *The Prince of Darkness: The Devil in History, Religion and the Human Psyche,* Element Books, Dorset 1989

C. Olson. *Zen and the Art of Postmodern Philosophy,* State University of New York Press, Albany, NY, 2001

Sylvia Paine: *Beckett, Nabokov, Nin: Motives and Modernism,* Kenniket Press, National University Publications, Port Washington, New York 1981

Papus: *The Qabalah,* Thorsons, Northants 1977

Alfred Perlès: *My Friend Henry Miller: An Intimate Biography,* Spearman 1955

Jane Lagoudis Pinchin: *Alexandria Still: Forster, Durrell and Cavafy,* Princeton University Press, 1977

—. "Durrell's Fatal Cleopatra", *Modern Fiction Studies,* 28, 1982, and in Cartwright, 1981, 24-39

Richard Pine: *The Dandy and the Herald: Manners, Mind and Moralds From Brummell to Durrell,* Macmillan 1988

—. *Lawrence Durrell: The Mindscape,* Macmillan 1994

Bern Porter, ed: *The Happy Rock: A Book About Henry Miller,* Packard, Berkeley, Calif. 1945

Robert A. Potter & Brooke Whiting: *Lawrence Durrell: A Checklist,* Library of the University of California, Los Angeles 1961

Donald Prater: *A Ringing Glass: The Life of Rainer Maria Rilke,* Clarendon Press 1994

John Press: *Rule and Energy: Trends in British Poetry Since the Second World War,* Oxford University Press 1963

Peter Preston & Peter Hoart, eds: *D.H. Lawrence in the Modern World,*

Macmillan 1989

V.S. Pritchett: "The sun and the sunless", *New Statesman*, 13 February 1960

J. Raper *et al*, eds. *Lawrence Durrell*, University of Missouri Press, Columbia, MI, 1995

Otto Rank. *Art and Artist*, Knopf, New York 1932

Phyllis Read: "The Illusion of Personality: Cyclical Time in Durrell's *The Alexandria Quartet*,", *Modern Fiction Studies*, 13, Autumn 1967, 389-99

Kenneth Rexroth: *Assays*, New Directions, 1961

Philip Rice & Patricia Waugh, eds: *Modern Literary Theory: A Reader*, Arnold 1992

Dan Richardson & Karen O'Brien: *Egypt: The Rough Guide*, Penguin 1993

Jeremy Robinson: *The Passion of D.H. Lawrence*, Crescent Moon 1992

—. *Love, Culture and Poetry: A Study of Lawrence Durrell*, Crescent Moon 1989, and in Frank Kersnowski, ed: *Into the Labyrinth*

Paul Rodaway: *Sensuous Geographies: body, sense and place*, Routledge 1994

Robin Rook: *Lawrence Durrell's Double Concerto: The Alexandria Quartet and The Avignon Quintet*, The Delos Press, Birmingham 1990

Denis de Rougemont: *Passion and Society*, Faber 1962

Bertrand Russell: *A History of Western Philosophy*, Allen & Unwin 1971

J. Schad. *Victorians in Theory From Derrida to Browning*, Manchester University Press, 1999

B. Schapiro. *D.H. Lawrence and the Paradoxes of Psychic Life*, State University of New York Press, 1999

Robert Scholes: *The Fabulators*, Oxford University Press 1967

Arthur Schopenhauer: *Essays and Aphorisms*, tr. R. Hollingdale, Penguin 1970

Lisa Schwerdt: "Coming of Age in Alexandria: The Narrator", *Deus Loci*, 5, Autumn 1981, 218-30

I. Scott-Kinvert: *British Writers. Supplement 1: Graham Greene to Tom Stoppard*, Scribner's, New York 1987

Eve Sedgwick: *Between Men: English Literature and Male Homosexual Desire*, Columbia University Press, New York 1985

Victor Selwyn, Erik de Mauny, Ian Fletcher, G.S. Fraser & John Waller: *Return to Oasis: War Poems and Recollections From the Middle East 1940-46*, Shepheard-Walwyn 1980

A. Serageldin & M. El-sadek, eds: *The Arab City: Its Character and Islamic Cultural Heritage*, Arab Urban Development Institute, New York 1982

Elaine Showalter, ed: *The New Feminist Criticism*, Virago 1986

—. ed: *Speaking of Gender*, Routledge 1989

—. *Sexual Anarchy: Gender and Culture at the* Fin de Siècle, Virago 1992

Penelope Shuttle & Peter Redgrove: *The Wise Wound,* Paladin/ Grafton 1978/ 86

Carol Siegel: *Lawrence Among the Women: Wavering Boundaries in Women's Literary Tradition*, University Press of Virginia, Charlottesville 1991

Hilary Simpson: *D.H. Lawrence and Feminism*, Croom Helm 1982

Robert Snyder: *This is Henry, Henry Miller From Brooklyn*, Los Angeles 1974

Oswald Spengler: *The Decline of the West*, tr. C.F. Atkinson, ed. H. Werner, A. Helps, Allen & Unwin 1961

Michael Squires & Dennis Jackson, ed: *D.H. Lawrence's Lady: A New Look at Lady Chatterley's Lover,* University of Georgia Press, Athens 1985

Derek Stanford: "Lawrence Durrell", *The Freedom of Poetry: Studies in Contemporary Verse*, Falcon Press 1947

Howard Stanheit: "Who wrote *Mountolive*?: An Investigation of the Relativity-Aesthetic of Lawrence Durrell's *The Alexandria Quartet*", in Friedman 1987, 127-8

Freya Stark: *Letters*, vol. 1, Michael Russell 1982

George Steiner: *Language and Silence*, Faber 1967

Stendhal: *De l'Amour*, tr. Sale, Penguin 1975

H. Stevens & C. Howlett, eds. *Modernist Sexualities,* Manchester University Press, 2000

G. Stewart. *Between Film and Screen: Modernism's Photo Synthesis*, University of Chicago Press, Chicago, IL, 1999

William Stoddart: *Sufism: The Mystical Doctrine and Methods of Islam*, Thorsons, Northants, 1976

Harry R. Stoneback: "*Et in Alexandria Ego*: Lawrence Durrell and the Spirit of Place", *Mid-Hudson Language Studies*, 5, 1982, 115-128

Richard Swigg: *Lawrence, Hardy and American Literature*, Oxford University Press 1972

J. Tabbi. *Postmodern Sublime*, Cornell University Press, Ithaca, NY, 1995

Tambimutu, ed: *Poetry London/ Apple Magazine*, no.2, 1982

Chet Taylor: "Dissonance and Digression: The Ill-Fitting Fusion of Philosophy and Form in Lawrence Durrell's *The Alexandria Quartet*", *Modern Fiction Studies*, 17, Summer 1971

Lawrence Thornton: "Narcissism and Selflessness in *The Alexandria Quartet*", *Deus Loci*, 1, no.4, June 1978

A.T. Tolley: *The Poetry of the Forties*, Manchester University Press, Manchester 1985

Lionel Trilling: *Beyond Culture: Essays on Literature and Learning*, Penguin 1967

John Unterecker: *Lawrence Durrell*, Columbia University Press, New York 1964

Marie-Christine Valdeman: "Narrative Technique in *Monsieur*", unpublished paper, 1990 [Lawrence Durrell Conference]

Maurice Valency: *In Praise of Love: An Introduction to the Love-Poetry of the Renaissance*, Macmillan, New York 1961

G. Vincendeau, ed. *Film/ Literature/ Heritage: A Sight & Sound Reader*, British Film Institute, London, 2001

Vladimir Volkoff: *Lawrence le magnifique: essai sur Lawrence Durrell et le roman relativiste*, Juillard, Paris 1984

Benjamin Walker: *Body Magic*, Paladin 1979

—. *Gnosticism: Its History and Influence*, Aquarian Press 1983

John Waller: "Lawrence Durrell: A Clever Magician", *The Poetry Review*,

June 1947

Valerie Wayne, ed: *The Matter of Difference: Materialist Feminist Criticism of Shakespeare*, Harvester Wheatsheaf 1991

A.K. Weatherhead: "Romantic Anachronism in *The Alexandria Quartet*", *Modern Fiction Studies*, 11, Summer 1964, 124-136

Warren Wedin: "The Artist as Narrator in *The Alexandria Quartet*", *Twentieth Century Literature*, 18, July 1972

John Weigel: *Lawrence Durrell*, Twayne Publishers, New York 1965

Huw Weldon: *Monitor: An Anthology*, Macdonald 1962

Paul West: *The Modern Novel*, 2 vols, Hutchinson University Library 1963/5

George Wickes: *Henry Miller: Down and Out in Paris*, Village Press 1969

—. ed: *Henry Miller and the Critics*, Southern Illinois University Press, Carbondale 1963

—. *Henry Miller*, University of Minnesota Press, Minneapolis 1966

—. *Americans in Paris*, Doubleday 1969

Kingsley Widmer: *Henry Miller*, Twayne 1963

Helen Wilcox *et al*, eds: *The Body and the Text: Hélène Cixous, Reading and Teaching*, Harvester Wheatsheaf 1990

L.R. Williams. *Critical Desire: Psychoanalysis and the Literary Subject*, Arnold, London, 1995a

—. *Sex in the Head: Visions of Femininity in D.H. Lawrence*, Harvester Wheatsheaf, 1995b

—. *D.H. Lawrence, Writers and Their Works,* Northcote House, 1997

Colin Wilson: *The Sexual Misfits: A Study of Sexual Outsiders*, Collins 1989

Kathryn Winslow: *Henry Miller: Full of Life: A Memoir*, Los Angeles 1986

T. Woods. *Beginning Postmodernism,* Manchester University Press, Manchester, 1999

William Wordsworth: *Poems*, ed. Lawrence Durrell, Penguin 1972

Kenneth Young: "A Dialogue with Durrell", *Encounter*, 13, no. 6, December 1959

Jack Zipes: *The Brothers Grimm: From Enchanted Forests to the Modern World*, Routledge 1989

S. Zizek. *Tarrying With the Negative: Kant, Hegel, and the Critique of Ideology*, Duke University Press, Durham, NC, 1993

—. *The Fright of Real Tears: The Uses and Misuses of Lacan in Film Theory*, British Film Institute, London, 1999

CRESCENT MOON PUBLISHING

ARTS, PAINTING, SCULPTURE

The Art of Andy Goldsworthy: Complete Works(Pbk)
The Art of Andy Goldsworthy: Complete Works (Hbk)
Andy Goldsworthy in Close-Up (Pbk)
Andy Goldsworthy in Close-Up (Hbk)
Land Art: A Complete Guide
Richard Long: The Art of Walking
The Art of Richard Long: Complete Works (Pbk)
The Art of Richard Long: Complete Works (Hbk)
Richard Long in Close-Up
Land Art In the UK
Land Art in Close-Up
Installation Art in Close-Up
Minimal Art and Artists In the 1960s and After
Colourfield Painting
Land Art DVD, TV documentary
Andy Goldsworthy DVD, TV documentary
The Erotic Object: Sexuality in Sculpture From Prehistory to the Present Day
Sex in Art: Pornography and Pleasure in Painting and Sculpture
Postwar Art
Sacred Gardens: The Garden in Myth, Religion and Art
Glorification: Religious Abstraction in Renaissance and 20th Century Art
Early Netherlandish Painting
Leonardo da Vinci
Piero della Francesca
Giovanni Bellini
Fra Angelico: Art and Religion in the Renaissance
Mark Rothko: The Art of Transcendence
Frank Stella: American Abstract Artist
Jasper Johns: Painting By Numbers
Brice Marden
Alison Wilding: The Embrace of Sculpture
Vincent van Gogh: Visionary Landscapes
Eric Gill: Nuptials of God
Constantin Brancusi: Sculpting the Essence of Things
Max Beckmann
Egon Schiele: Sex and Death In Purple Stockings
Delizioso Fotografico Fervore: Works In Process 1
Sacro Cuore: Works In Process 2
The Light Eternal: J.M.W. Turner
The Madonna Glorified: Karen Arthurs

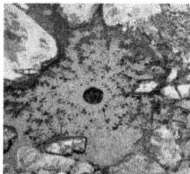

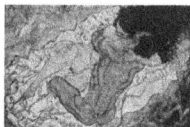

LITERATURE

J.R.R. Tolkien: The Books, The Films, The Whole Cultural Phenomenon
Harry Potter
Sexing Hardy: Thomas Hardy and Feminism
Thomas Hardy's *Tess of the d'Urbervilles*
Thomas Hardy's *Jude the Obscure*
Thomas Hardy: The Tragic Novels
Love and Tragedy: Thomas Hardy
The Poetry of Landscape in Hardy
Wessex Revisited: Thomas Hardy and John Cowper Powys
Wolfgang Iser: Essays
Petrarch, Dante and the Troubadours
Maurice Sendak and the Art of Children's Book Illustration
Andrea Dworkin
Cixous, Irigaray, Kristeva: The *Jouissance* of French Feminism
Julia Kristeva: Art, Love, Melancholy, Philosophy, Semiotics and Psychoanalysis
Hélène Cixous I Love You: The *Jouissance* of Writing
Luce Irigaray: Lips, Kissing, and the Politics of Sexual Difference
Peter Redgrove: Here Comes the Flood
Peter Redgrove: Sex-Magic-Poetry-Cornwall
Lawrence Durrell: Between Love and Death, East and West
Love, Culture & Poetry: Lawrence Durrell
Cavafy: Anatomy of a Soul
German Romantic Poetry: Goethe, Novalis, Heine, Hölderlin, Schlegel, Schiller
Feminism and Shakespeare
Shakespeare: Selected Sonnets
Shakespeare: Love, Poetry & Magic
The Passion of D.H. Lawrence
D.H. Lawrence: Symbolic Landscapes
D.H. Lawrence: Infinite Sensual Violence
Rimbaud: Arthur Rimbaud and the Magic of Poetry
The Ecstasies of John Cowper Powys
Sensualism and Mythology: The Wessex Novels of John Cowper Powys
Amorous Life: John Cowper Powys and the Manifestation of Affectivity (H.W. Fawkner)
Postmodern Powys: New Essays on John Cowper Powys (Joe Boulter)
Rethinking Powys: Critical Essays on John Cowper Powys
Paul Bowles & Bernardo Bertolucci
Rainer Maria Rilke
In the Dim Void: Samuel Beckett
Samuel Beckett Goes into the Silence
André Gide: Fiction and Fervour
Jackie Collins and the Blockbuster Novel
Blinded By Her Light: The Love-Poetry of Robert Graves
The Passion of Colours: Travels In Mediterranean Lands
Poetic Forms
The Dolphin-Boy

POETRY

The Best of Peter Redgrove's Poetry
Peter Redgrove: Here Comes The Flood
Peter Redgrove: Sex-Magic-Poetry-Cornwall
Ursula Le Guin: Walking In Cornwall
Dante: Selections From the Vita Nuova
Petrarch, Dante and the Troubadours
William Shakespeare: Selected Sonnets
Blinded By Her Light: The Love-Poetry of Robert Graves
Emily Dickinson: Selected Poems
Emily Brontë: Poems
Thomas Hardy: Selected Poems
Percy Bysshe Shelley: Poems
John Keats: Selected Poems
D.H. Lawrence: Selected Poems
Edmund Spenser: Poems
John Donne: Poems
Henry Vaughan: Poems
Sir Thomas Wyatt: Poems
Robert Herrick: Selected Poems
Rilke: Space, Essence and Angels in the Poetry of Rainer Maria Rilke
Rainer Maria Rilke: Selected Poems
Friedrich Hölderlin: Selected Poems
Arseny Tarkovsky: Selected Poems
Arthur Rimbaud: Selected Poems
Arthur Rimbaud: A Season in Hell
Arthur Rimbaud and the Magic of Poetry
D.J. Enright: By-Blows
Jeremy Reed: Brigitte's Blue Heart
Jeremy Reed: Claudia Schiffer's Red Shoes
Gorgeous Little Orpheus
Radiance: New Poems
Crescent Moon Book of Nature Poetry
Crescent Moon Book of Love Poetry
Crescent Moon Book of Mystical Poetry
Crescent Moon Book of Elizabethan Love Poetry
Crescent Moon Book of Metaphysical Poetry
Crescent Moon Book of Romantic Poetry
Pagan America: New American Poetry

MEDIA, CINEMA, FEMINISM and CULTURAL STUDIES

J.R.R. Tolkien: The Books, The Films, The Whole Cultural Phenomenon
Harry Potter
Cixous, Irigaray, Kristeva: The *Jouissance* of French Feminism
Julia Kristeva: Art, Love, Melancholy, Philosophy, Semiotics and Psychoanalysis
Luce Irigaray: Lips, Kissing, and the Politics of Sexual Difference
Hélène Cixous I Love You: The *Jouissance* of Writing
Andrea Dworkin
'Cosmo Woman': The World of Women's Magazines
Women in Pop Music
Discovering the Goddess (Geoffrey Ashe)
The Poetry of Cinema
The Sacred Cinema of Andrei Tarkovsky (Pbk and Hbk)
Paul Bowles & Bernardo Bertolucci
Media Hell: Radio, TV and the Press
An Open Letter to the BBC
Detonation Britain: Nuclear War in the UK
Feminism and Shakespeare
Wild Zones: Pornography, Art and Feminism
Sex in Art: Pornography and Pleasure in Painting and Sculpture
Sexing Hardy: Thomas Hardy and Feminism

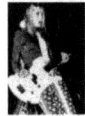

In my view *The Light Eternal* is among the very best of all the material I read on Turner. (Douglas Graham, director of the Turner Museum, Denver, Colorado)

The Light Eternal is a model monograph, an exemplary job. The subject matter of the book is beautifully organised and dead on beam. (Lawrence Durrell)

It is amazing for me to see my work treated with such passion and respect. (Andrea Dworkin)

Sex-Magic-Poetry-Cornwall is a very rich essay... It is like a brightly-lighted box. (Peter Redgrove)

CRESCENT MOON PUBLISHING
P.O. Box 393, Maidstone, Kent, ME14 5XU, United Kingdom.
01622-729593 (UK) 01144-1622-729593 (US) 0044-1622-729593 (other territories)
cresmopub@yahoo.co.uk   www.crescentmoon.org.uk

www.ingramcontent.com/pod-product-compliance
Lightning Source LLC
Chambersburg PA
CBHW062154080426
42734CB00010B/1683